BRAINS INSPIRING BUSINESSES

FOR LEADERS

Edited by:
Dr Paul Brown and Nandini Das Ghoshal

Contributors:
Caroline Brewin, Paul Brown,
Nandini Das Ghoshal, Leanne Drew-McCain, Khyati Kapai, Imogen Maresch,
Sue Paterson, Gerrit Pelzer, Emma Russell,
Rita Shah, Soraya Shaw, Emma Skitt,
Christin Tan, Sim Peng Thia

Publisher's Note

Every possible effort has been made to ensure that the information contained in this book is accurate at the time of going to press, and the publishers and authors cannot accept responsibility for any errors or omissions, however caused. No responsibility for loss or damage occasioned to any person acting, or refraining from action, as a result of the material in this publication can be accepted by the editor, the publisher, or the contributors.

First edition published in the United Kingdom in 2023 by ION Press, an operating division of ION Consulting Pte. Ltd., Singapore, in partnership with Ideas for Leaders Publishing, a business of IEDP Ideas for Leaders Ltd.

Apart from any fair dealing for the purposes of research or private study, or criticism or review, as permitted under the Copyright, Design and Patents Act 1988, this publication may only be reproduced, stored or transmitted, in any form or by any means, with the prior permission in writing of the publishers. Enquiries concerning reproduction should be sent to the publishers at the following address:

Ideas for Leaders Publishing
42 Moray Place
Edinburgh
EH3 6BT
www.ideasforleaders.com
info@ideasforleaders.com

ISBN
978-1-915529-09-1 – Paperback
978-1-915529-10-7 – Hardback
978-1-915529-21-3 – e-book

© ION Publishing, 2023
© Ideas for Leaders Publishing, 2023

Cover design: www.nickmortimer.co.uk
Typesetting: Sopho Tarkashvili

BRAINS INSPIRING BUSINESSES

Prologue: *Paul Brown* 9

CHAPTER 1: Brain Powered Confidence. /
Caroline Brewin 27

CHAPTER 2: Developing a Resilient, Engaged
Organization. / *Soraya Shaw* 69

CHAPTER 3: Neuroentrepreneurship and
Awakening the Entrepreneurial
Brain. / *Christin Tan* 89

CHAPTER 4: Transformative Executive Coaching:
Channelling the Chi 氣. /
Rita Shah 105

CHAPTER 5: Trust and Excitement at Work: making
a deliberate choice. / *Emma Skitt* 121

CHAPTER 6: Soft Skills through the Lens of Hard
Science: why leaders need to know about
the brain. / *Gerrit Pelzer* 153

CHAPTER 7: The Transience of Teams. /
Sim Peng Thia 181

CHAPTER 8: The Joy of Mindfulness. /
Nandini Das Ghoshal 197

CHAPTER 9: The Welcoming Organization:
being your true Self at work. /
Khyati Kapai 223

CHAPTER 10: **Thinking of Others. /**
Leanne Drew-McKain.............................261

CHAPTER 11: **Biology, Brains and Bias in Business. /**
Emma Russell 277

CHAPTER 12: **Play Your Way to Resilience. /**
Imogen Maresch 311

CHAPTER 13: **Getting to Know How the Brain Works: a historical review.** / Sue Paterson 341

PROLOGUE

Paul Brown

This is, we believe, the first book of its kind. It is certainly the first to come from ION Consulting's ION Press – a publishing venture in association with Ideas for Leaders. Its central purpose is to make using the new understandings about human behaviour in organizations that are coming not from psychology but from the modern brain sciences easily accessible to leaders. ION = International Organizational Neuroscience.

The fourteen contributors have all been dedicated to learning about how the brain works. Over the past ten years they have taken that knowledge out into their individual and corporate consulting practices. These chapters are their personal experiments at the coalface of consulting with what they have discovered whilst incorporating the value of knowing about the brain into their work.

In a slowly-dawning but intensely liberating realization, both intellectually and practically, we can now see that, after one hundred and twenty years of endeavour, psychology has not come up with any agreed basic definitions to such essential fundamentals as 'What is a Person?' or 'What is the Self?' As a Western academic discipline but taught worldwide, psychology seems to thrive on disputation. As the academic discipline it is, psychology turns out to be offering a set of *descriptions* about people rather than seeking valid *explanations* or agreed-among-all-psychologists understandings as to why they behave the way they do.

There is a major paradigm shift about understanding human behaviour going on in this 21st. century. We need to be conscious of it if we are to have the early advantage of its immense value. It is that the modern brain sciences are offering us a new, scientifically verified perspective on what we human beings are and how that manifests itself as complex human behaviour. Psychology's traditional claim to be 'the science of the human mind' or 'the science of human behaviour' overstates its assumed reliance on the essential replicable qualities of experiments that are fundamental to a true science. ION Consulting wants senior management and corporate consultants of many kinds to have the advantages of being able to use the new understandings of Brain and Behaviour in Organizations and Individuals for the benefits not only of profit but for creating of a sense of purpose, satisfaction, and enjoyment in achieving corporate operational and strategic goals that are the hallmarks of a sustainable organization. In such an organization human endeavour gets transformed into profit, without profit – important though it is - being the single target of performance.

ION Consulting is doing this by taking the published work of neuroscientists worldwide, in the knowledge that neuroscientists are not fundamentally interested in the complexities of real life human behaviour in organizations but, quite rightly, in the immense complexities of the brain, the whole of the central nervous system, and increasingly the relatively new knowledge about the way the gut influences the brain. We are of the view that the modern brain sciences are beginning to offer us the beginnings of an *explanation* about how we human beings are *who* and *what* we are – all essentially the same in the cellular sources that make each one of us; all completely different, because of life experience, in being 'Me'.

Psychologists have been widely interested in cognition – how the brain variously works through our thought processes. It has been an unquestioned assumption that we *think* our way through the world, that we are 'reasonable', and that it is our thoughts that control us. Descartes' famous 1637 dictum 'Cogito ergo sum' ('I think, therefore I am') powered, in part, the 17th century's European and, later, the American great expansion of shared knowledge called the Enlightenment. Arguably it led to the development of the sciences as we now know them, especially physics.

But the modern brain sciences are telling us that it is our *emotional* system that generates the myriad of feelings through which, by having them attached to experience, we can make sense of our world. Our thinking system is there to give us a *post hoc* understanding of what our brain has already decided.

The emotional and feeling system may be extremely well-developed or, alternatively, have been poorly stimulated at critical stages of early and then childhood development; so that what one individual takes for granted is quite beyond the range of another. Imagine a boy who has been brought up in a great house surrounded by fine pictures that are often looked at and discussed with his parents. His aesthetic system will have been naturally stimulated. As a late teenager he decides to go on developing his fascination with classical art by the art history degree he takes. As an adult, he becomes a world expert in recognizing apparently lost pictures from the eighteenth century that appear in auction catalogues from all over the world – pictures not properly attributed except as something like 'English gentleman, 18th century'. So he goes to the auction in question wherever it is in the world to validate his judgement by seeing the picture for real, buying very successfully.

Imagine on the contrary another boy brought up in an intellectually and emotionally impoverished environment, who has never been in a museum or gallery in his life, and has absolutely no appreciation in any conceivable way of the pictures the first person recognizes so readily. Then imagine this second person being asked, for some curious reason, to look at all the international sales catalogues received by the first person and choose which auctions the first person should attend. With no development of any kind of his aesthetic feelings, there could not be any basis except chance for any kind of choice.

As a side issue, but one of real social concern, the development of an individual's feeling system and its adult functioning is of increasing social importance now that legislation allows hurt or annoyance to be the basis of an accusation that might carry legal sanctions to the person accused without that person having any rights of reply. The accuser, or the accused, or both, may have emotional systems that are aggressive, defensive, accusatory or variably inappropriate in managing the give-and-take that facilitates normal social discourse. The courts are unable to explore such underlying mechanisms in any definable way: yet those feelings power the basis of legal proceedings. It is clear that parliamentarians pursuing this kind of socially enforceable legislation have no understanding at all of what brain and behaviour are now telling us about individual actions and responses.

• • •

The physical sciences started forming four hundred plus years ago via astronomy. Galileo (1564–1642), the Italian polymath astronomer, physicist and engineer, was clear from his own observations that the earth moved around the sun and was not the static centre of the universe that Catholic doctrine understood it to be. In 1616, he was shown the torture chambers that the Church would use on him if he maintained the heresy that the sun, not the earth was the centre of the universe. Under such threat he accepted the Church's position whilst maintaining his own private view during the following fifteen years of what was effectively house arrest. Galileo's experiences are a stark account of what might happen when a scientific system of accurate observation and experimental validation can come up against entrenched belief systems. *Darwin on Trial* (1991) by UC Berkeley law professor Phillip E. Johnson started the intelligent design movement in the States, which offers the proposition that the Bible's account of life was created by an 'intelligent designer': God. This polarizes opinion in the States regarding evolution and presumes that Darwinian evolutionary theory is simply wrong. Opponents of intelligent design insist that it is a pseudo-science because its claims cannot be tested by replicable experiment and it does not propose any new hypotheses. It is, in other words, another belief system, not scientifically based as Professor Johnson set out to show that it was.

It took twenty plus years for the early scientists to agree some essential working definitions of the subjects they had under consideration: but they were very clear that it was *only* replicable experimental justification that was the basis for such agreement. The Royal Society, the oldest still-existing scientific Society in the world, was founded in London in 1660 – the same year that Charles II was restored to the throne after Cromwell's attempt to create a permanent Commonwealth (1649-

1660) following the English Civil War (1642 - 1651). After the Restoration there was a great outpouring and release of emotional energy, manifesting itself in exaggerated dress, increasingly large wigs, exploratory sexual relationships and new buildings. The fear of not saying the things that Cromwell required for maintaining his Commonwealth and its Parliamentary practices evaporated. Newton's great work, *Principia Mathematica*, was published in 1687. From there the modern sciences, as we now recognize them, developed over the next two hundred and fifty years. The capacity of the earliest effective microscope in 1667 was 4x magnification. Improved hand polishing of lenses soon lifted that to 100x. Now, light microscopes can magnify 1500x. Telescopes appeared in 1608. The taxonomies of the worlds of the previously unseen and the infinity of space began to be open to systematic observation. Modern electron microscopes offer between one million and fifty million magnifications.

The paradigm shift of this twenty-first century is telling us that we each are, like the rest of the physical world, fundamentally an *energy* system not, primarily, as the Freudian twentieth century would have it, a psychological system. We now know that that energy is based on the unique e-motional (energy into action) patterning of each of our brains, which is what makes us the individuals that we each are. Created from individual life experience attached to our unique genetics, these patterns make the brain the central controller of our personal world. It is from this that each of us has been and is created as the person that we understand ourself to be. It is minute voltage electricity that powers the brain, our central controller, backed by sufficient food – our only source of energy – in the digested form of glucose. We also now know that our unique Self comes from the way our unique brain got itself organized through the first twenty-four years of each of our lives. We are driven, mostly non-consciously, by the 86 billion brain cells that our individual life experience has forged into these emotionally formed patterns, *not* by our thinking system.

As is now apparent, this paradigm shift is that each of us operating as our Self ('Me') and making sense of our personal world uses our thinking system as the way of finding out what the brain knows and has already decided, and that the key decisions as to what we do with our uniquely perceived world are much managed all the time below the threshold of consciousness. We could not, after all, have a thought without that thought already existing in its own neurochemical pattern. The brain got there before we knew it. It is the organ that is continuously tasked with ensuring we make the best adaptation that we can to any context at any point in time.

Unlike any other animal throughout the whole of evolution we humans are, so far as we know, the only species that has developed an adaptive language as we try to make sense of experience. That is one reason why the interpersonal culture of an organization is so profoundly important. Mediated by language, 'culture' is the power base of the company's capacity to focus the energy of its people upon the company's key strategic and operational goals. A strong shared culture focuses brains in the same direction – and ideally focuses on, and can read, the boss's brain. At best, 'culture' is the organization's belief system shared by all individuals as their own. ION Consulting's view is that the task of any leader is to release the energy of his or her people who, if they know they are really trusted, will gladly bend their energies towards corporate goals and derive a sense of purpose and meaning for their own lives in so doing. The true quality of working relationships is the key to this.

• • •

An unresolved question, though, is: 'What is energy?' There are four main sources of thought that underpin ION Consulting's current understanding.

Intending at high school to be a scientist, Margaret Wheatley became, through her own personal exploration. a student of systems theory and communications. Via Harvard and the field of organizational behaviour she became Professor of Management at Brigham Young University. There she started combining her understanding of quantum physics, self-organizing systems and chaos theory in formulating a scientifically derived understanding of the way the world works. In her 1992 book, *Leadership and the New Science*, she offers the view that information is the primal source of energy within a self-organizing universe.

At the time she was writing Wheatley could not have known that management practices were increasingly to focus through the next thirty years on performance, relentless business improvement and increasing profits. They became the only comparative test of organizational 'success'. But behind that there was no sense of 'Who really are the individuals who make those profits and how do they themselves function?' or 'What is an organization?' – questions, we believe, fundamental to a new HR. HR never has had any central reference points from which to either derive or discuss the individual and organizational framework in which it is operating. An excoriating piece about HR appeared worldwide in the UK's international newspaper, *the Telegraph,* in June 2022.[1] No other part of an organization attracts rolled eyeballs in the way that many conversations about HR do. Psychology, in claiming to be the science of behaviour or the science of the mind, has not served HR well, failing to give it any scientific basis for its professionalism. The same can be said for organizational theory. As far back as 1910, Yerkes[2] was asking why it was (in America) that the emerging new subject of psychology was largely populated by individuals

---

[1] https://www.telegraph.co.uk/news/2022/06/17/hr-monster-destroyed-workplace/ Last accessed 09.03.2023.

[2] Yerkes (together with his colleague Dodson) are the only individuals whose names have been attached to a Law in psychology that has stood the test of time – the Yerkes-Dodson Law. The best known behavioural psychologist of the 20th century – animal experimenters B.F. Skinner [1904 – 1990] and variously Professor at Harvard [1974–90] and elsewhere and, prior to Skinner, J.B. Watson 1878–1958, gave his name to various devices that he believed would improve learning: but, however good and truly scientific his experiments were, it is difficult to generalize from a pigeon that can reliably peck at a disk in a rocket in space to human behaviour (see https://www.google.com/search?q=When+did+the+social+sciences+develop? Last accessed 09.03.2023).

He brought up a daughter in part using a Skinner box, which lead to a great deal of social and erroneous misapprehension about what he was doing as a parent. J.B. Watson defined his own interest in his most famous statement: "Give me a dozen healthy infants, well-formed, and my own specified world to bring them up in and I'll guarantee to take anyone at random and train him to become any type of specialist I might select – doctor, lawyer, artist, merchant-chief, and, yes, even beggar-man and thief, regardless of his talents, penchants, tendencies, abilities, vocations, and race of his ancestors. I am going beyond my facts and I admit it, but so have the advocates of the contrary and they have been doing it for many thousands of years." – John B. Watson, *Behaviorism,* 1925. See also https://www.verywellmind.com/john-b-watson-biography-1878-1958-2795550 (last accessed 09.03.2023).

who had no formal background in scientific method. He wondered if psychology might generate a new kind of science. It did, becoming part of what in the late nineteenth century emerged as the social sciences. Wikipedia offers the view that:

> The first period [in the development of the social sciences] began with their emergence in the late nineteenth century and continued on through the first half of the twentieth. In this first period social scientists were intellectual commentators, and gadflies to the world and its problems.[3]

The second main contribution to our thinking has been the 2014 publication of Dr. Joe Dispenza's *You Are The Placebo*: making your mind matter. From both personal and professional points of view Dispenza explores how the power of the way we 'see' things from accumulated experience has a profound effect upon our behaviour and feelings. And though published more than a decade ago, neuroscientist Nessa Carey (2012) has a particularly readable book that will extend an understanding of why we each are the way we are.

That takes us into the still-developing field of epigenetics, to which there are two main strands. The first is molecular epigenetics – the extraordinary detail of what the neurochemicals of brain and body are up to, nanosecond by nanosecond, creating our behaviour. Molecular epigenetics is not our specific concern here though. It is the less well-defined field of what might be

---

[3] https://www.google.com/search?q=When+did+the+social+sciences+develop?Last accessed 09.03.2023.

called social or perceptual epigenetics that is our interest.

As our perception is entirely derived from our own individual life experience, and could not be any other, then we all come to any situation with a unique background. How then do people share common goals, organizationally or in any other circumstance? It is because they will agree with (not just intellectually but believe in) another's perception. How often, though, have you been in a meeting where people say 'yes' to some proposal but no real action follows? Internally they prefer their own view(s) of the situation.

At ION Consulting we now see that the leaders' fundamental task is to really know where they want to get to and communicate that in such a way that staff attach to the leader's goals. A leader cannot lead effectively unless s/he can get subordinates' brains to tune to hers or his. Trust is the main carrier signal for that, though shared excitement may start the process. As between designated leaders the skills in getting one's own way are immensely variable. Three Prime Ministers in the UK during the autumn of 2022 are public examples of the fact that being appointed as leader even at the highest level does not necessarily endow the necessary qualities. In September 2023 we await Rishi Sunak's capacity to grow into the role.

The third element of our own background thinking is Peter Hoffman's (2012) *Life's Ratchet: How molecular machines extract order from chaos*. 'What is life?' he asks. As a physicist seeing the potential power of integrating his science with biology, he has set out to find an answer. Although no single answer is forthcoming, the book is a crucial part of our reformulation of the individual as an energy system.

Daniel Goleman's *Emotional Intelligence* (1995) brought the word 'emotion' into the beginnings of corporate use in a manner that had never before been possible. It is perhaps regrettable that too soon and too energetically it became a matter of measurement. How much EI does s/he have? Such a question ignores context the whole time. Reformulating EI as Intelligent Emotions puts the emotions as the source of what gives meaning to experience when eventually attached to words. Romesin (2008) started reflecting on what the emotions were in the early 1980s: " ... we human beings [transcend the molecular dynamics] in the unity of body and mind through the integration of our emotions as we live our existence of loving language relational-reflective beings ... " (p. 7).

As already observed at the beginning of this Prologue, twentieth-century psychology (and psychiatry also) so completely failed to establish any agreed working understandings of major concepts about people like: 'What is a Person?' or 'What is the Self?' that one cannot now but be curious as to why professionally they were – and still are – accorded the institutional and popular responsibility for helping 'people' who need help.[4] Building on my work over the past fifteen years, it has been part of ION Consulting's continuing endeavour through its six-month *Science of the Art of Coaching* programme to propose a working definition of 'the emotions', so that psychology, psychiatry, leaders at all levels in organizations, even politicians, share a common, defined understanding of what they are

---

[4] Occupational psychology has, by and large, defined 'the person' through the use of psychometric instruments. But such instruments can change their working concepts: another factor analysis, another definition of 'the person'. Who now uses the 16 Personality Factor psychometric that was widely in vogue in the 1970s and 1980s?

talking about when they use the word 'emotions'; and, more importantly, might therefore have some sense of the modern understandings of their power in shaping our brains to make us the individuals that we are. That work is displayed in the emotional 2023 iteration fan in this book and that, sometimes in earlier versions, is variously referenced in contributors' chapters.[5]

Called (for want of a memorable reference) the *London Protocol of the Emotions*, it is we believe the only attempt in the literature to describe the emotions on the (fundamental to human relationships) avoidance / attachment dimension; and at the same time link that to survive / thrive, the basics of the sympathetic and parasympathetic nervous systems, the major neurochemicals involved[6], and the resulting 'f ' behaviours displayed – 'f' because of 'feelings'. 'Faith' is an f word that also carries with it profound belief, both in oneself and the other.

---

[5] The fan also makes it visually clear that the (alas very widespread) use of the terms 'negative' (= 'bad') and positive (= 'good') adjectives to define emotions, much encouraged by positive psychology (what is negative psychology?) is a major error. The basic emotions are a whole system, rather like the weather. A major storm may be very inconvenient if one has organised a garden party or an outdoor wedding and not acquired a great supply of umbrellas; but that rain is crucial to the earth's well-being, however much one might be wishing for the sun. If, however, the drainage system is not working and sewage flooding results, then the rain is not being properly managed in its context. The same is the case with emotions badly managed. It is highly appropriate, in context, to experience the escape / avoidance emotions and manage them appropriately too. It's where meaning comes from. That is what we mean by hyphenating this powerful word into *e-motions*. That is the basis of energy creating behaviour and the capacity to make sense of situations through the emotional and feeling system.

[6] There are over a hundred neurochemicals that are involved in brain and behaviour, and the interactions between them all are very poorly understood, though being extensively researched worldwide. At the current stage of knowledge, *The London Protocol* (which has itself developed in teaching and CPD sessions through others contributing ideas) uses the main known neurochemicals that the literature recognizes.

It will be seen that, except for Trust / Love, each segment of the fan has colour that grades downwards, attempting to show that there can be varied strengths of each emotion in any specific context. Trust and Love are, we posit, absolutes. Trusting 'a little' or loving 'a bit' are not either trust or love even if it is convenient to use such ideas as a way of expressing doubts of some kind about one's whole approach to the other person – or to oneself. This is why attempts in organizations to 'develop higher levels of trust' are bound to fail, because they take an incremental view of the emotion. The only way to increase trust in organizations is for the most senior leader to trust his or her reports absolutely. If s/he cannot, but believes any individual concerned has real value to the organization and skills that would be a loss if the individual were not in post, then that person needs thoughtful development of some absent capacity if s/he is really willing to do so in the recognition that the boss is on to something of value in that proposed development. If, however, a judgement is made that the individual concerned really does not have what is needed at the level at which s/he needs to be functioning, then why is s/he there at all?

These then are ION Consulting's editorial starting points in provoking and encouraging the contributors of these chapters into print. Caroline Brewin starts us off in Chapter 1 with irritated startle. For any reader wishing to have some wider theoretical base to the brain sciences, Dr Sue Paterson's final chapter is for that reader. Dr Gerrit Pelzer's Chapter 6 makes the case from his extensive experience of *why* leaders need to know about the brain.

For the Editors, the excitement of the emerging chapters as the book has developed is that we can see both the passion and the practices of the variety of ways in which this group of individuals use their knowledge about the brain in their individual and organizational consulting work.

• • •

Enough. Be surprised, we hope. Most of all, enjoy.

References

Carey, Nessa (2012) *The Epigentics Revolution: how modern biology is rewriting our understanding of genetics, disease and inheritance.* New York: Columbia University Press.

Dispenza, Joe (2014) *You are the Placebo: making your mind matter.* USA / UK: Hay House Inc.

Goleman, D. (1995) *Emotional Intelligence.* UK: Bloomsbury Publishing

Hoffman, Peter M. (2012) *Life's Ratchet: how molecular machines extract order from chaos.* USA: Basic Books / Hachette Pubishing Company.

Johnson, Phillip E. (1991 /2010 paperback). *Darwin on Trial.* Washington DC: Regnery Publishing / Salem Media Group.

Romesin, H.M. (2008) *The Origins of Humanness in the Biology of Love.* Exeter, UK: Imprint Academic.

Watson, J.B. (1925) *Behaviorism.* New York: W.W. Norton.

Wheatley, Margaret J. (2006) *Leadership and the New Science: discovering order in a chaotic world.* USA: Berrett-Koehler Publishing.

Biography

Dr Paul Brown is a Visiting Professor, Henley Business School, UK; a consulting clinical and organizational psychologist by background and more than fifty years of practice; previously a Visiting Professor at London South Bank University (the first professorial appointment in the world (2008–12) to use the title 'Organizational Neuroscience', we believe, created by Professor Tony Day in his then Department of Engineering, Science and Building Systems); the Nottingham Law School (2001–12) as Visiting Professor in Individual and Organizational Psychology); and Monarch Business School, Switzerland, as Visiting Professor in Organizational Neuroscience (2014–23). He is Chairman of ION Consulting International Pte Ltd, Singapore. ptbpsychol@gmail.com / paul.brown@ion-consulting.org

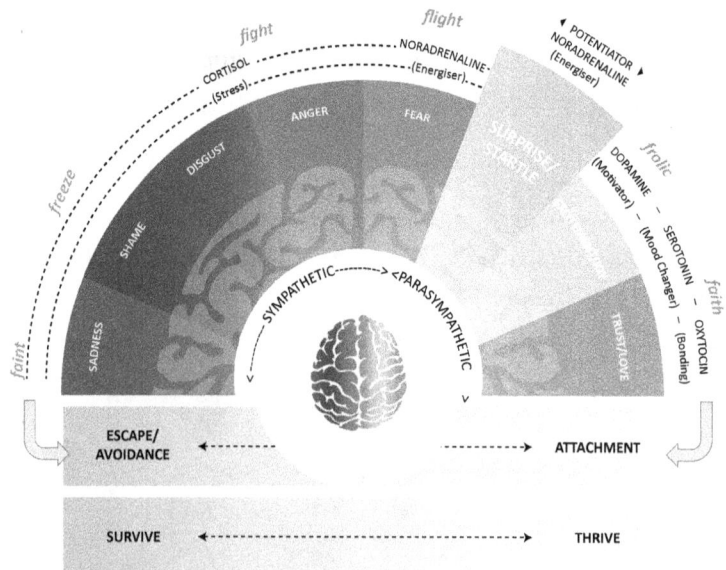

The London Protocol of the Emotions
ION Consulting International Pte Ltd 2023
see colour representation of this diagram on inside front and rear cover pages

CHAPTER 1

Brain-powered Confidence

Caroline Brewin

I couldn't believe it – I had done it again. Another stupid mistake, this one sent to all of the Global Senior Leadership Team. I had checked the email so many times as I knew I couldn't make yet another error. How on earth could I have missed it???

I was a few weeks into the biggest role of my life – Chief of Staff to the CEO of a 25,000 person organization. In all honesty, I was still trying to figure out what that actually meant, but I knew I had had to take it – it would have been the first job of which anyone outside of investment banking actually understood the title.

I had been in the investment banking industry since leaving university – rather more by mistake than by design. But over the years I had done well, mostly through pure determination, hard work and perhaps being a little different to many of the 'geeky finance people'. This opportunity had been offered after a gruelling (but ultimately rewarding) few years doing two jobs – standard for me – leading two global teams and fixing all sorts of broken people and processes. I was told the new role would be an 'adventure' – working with an extraordinary leader who I respected and could have fun working with. It was the right step to take.

However, since I had started, I knew I had been 'winging' it. There wasn't a job specification, so I was trying to construct the roles and responsibilities from speaking to others in vaguely similar roles. It was a jack-of-all-trades job in some ways, with a focus on people, strategy, communications and engagement. Oh, and making sure the CEO was up to speed for all meetings and issues that popped up (an enormous task disguised as a footnote). There was *so much to do*. I was working 15-hour days, trying to get through it, but was not even close to having my head above water. I felt six foot under.

And I was not getting any feedback on how it was going. My direct boss was a very high achiever – an incredibly bright man with the ability to process and recall information at a remarkable level. He loved the numbers and minutiae, as well as going at 1000 mph. Whilst I was used to a fast pace, this was something else; and because I was trying so hard to keep up my very high standards, my stress levels were rocketing. The only feedback on how I was doing were small eyebrow raises; or worse, silence on the mistakes that were growing and the increasing piles of work.

In the absence of the feedback that I needed, I assumed the worst.

My mind felt wound up in a tight, clenched fist; unable to think clearly and use the skills that I knew I had. I was picturing being sat down and told "it's not working out". The humiliation! My head was whirring; my stomach was sinking and I was hardly sleeping, worrying about it. It got to a point where I had to take action – do or die.

So I asked my boss for a meeting. I told him how I was doing my best, but I was struggling with the volume and pace of work. "I feel like you are a Japanese high-speed train and I'm clinging on to the side for dear life". The response was unexpected. "Caroline, you're doing an amazing job! We are so happy – keep it up" ... The relief was palpable and it was like a switch flicked in my mind.

From that point forward, I stopped making stupid mistakes. I could think clearly and creatively; problem solve with an attitude of 'give it a go'. My confidence was restored and I was off and running.

What had happened in that scenario is part of the reason I am here today. The power of understanding how my *brain* worked was what drove me to have that conversation. I suspected what was happening was a physical response, not the reality of the situation, and armed with that knowledge, I was able to take action and ultimately take control. This was a big part of the reason I wanted to focus on the neuroscience of confidence – because there is huge power to be had from knowledge in this area. So many people need it, both personally and professionally, but very few have the understanding of it, so suffer and underperform unnecessarily.

We will come back to the science of what was happening in my brain shortly. First, let's look at confidence itself.

What is confidence?

The *Oxford Dictionary* defines confidence as: "An appreciation of one's own abilities, qualities or judgement". This is what we would traditionally expect to think around confidence – knowing your skills and capabilities. The traditional human resources (HR) model for confidence is also focused on these inputs, with the associated competency models for developing skills and training.

The Confidence Code (Kay and Shipman, 2014) noted a slightly different definition by psychologist Richard Petty et al. (2002), which, with the knowledge of how the brain works, is much more astute: "Confidence is the stuff that turns thoughts into action." Knowing more about the brain than once we did, and that it is driven by our emotional system, with our thinking system there to give us an account of what the brain already knows, that definition might now be: "Confidence is the stuff that gets feelings into thoughts and into action."

The key to this is that it is 'action' based – the more you 'do' the better it gets and that is what gives you the confidence to try something else. It is belief in your ability to manage the unknown; when to say 'No'; or when to go out of the comfort zone and do hard things.

When you lack confidence, it is that powerful fear of failure that leads to inaction, *guaranteeing* failure. How many times a day does someone avoid trying something, due to being afraid of failure? How much innovation, talent, how many challenges and improvements are organizations missing out on, just because their employees are afraid of taking a step? How many organizations want confident people but create the conditions that limit them? Imaginative thoughts in self-limiting organizations result in no action except the suppressing of the thoughts.

Lack of confidence is not exclusive to women, but research shows it is more prevalent in women than men. There was a fascinating piece of research by Estes, University of Milan (2013), where they got men and women to take a 3D test; women got lower marks in the test as they did not even attempt the hard questions. When they were required to attempt all questions, they got the same marks.

Ian Robertson also speaks of this action element in his book *How Confidence Works* (2021):

> Confidence is made up of two parts. The first is the bet you make with yourself that you can do something. This is the 'can do' element. The second is the belief that if you do that thing, then the world will change a little. This is the 'can happen' part.

Combining that with the re-definition of Richard Petty's action concept "Confidence is the stuff that turns thoughts into action" (Petty, Briñol and Tormala, 2002), then the more evidence you have of taking a step and the world *not* ending, the more you have confidence to try again.

The issue is, if you fundamentally lack belief in yourself – at the level of the 'Self' – training at a surface level is not going to work. That is just addressing a small part of the puzzle, when the real need is to be looking much deeper.

In a discussion with my wonderful mindfulness teacher in 2020, Jane Grafton, she described confidence as "Grounding in your true self; integrating your internal and external authenticity. Letting go of effort." Of all the definitions of confidence, this is the one that really creates a mindset shift for me.

Why? From the many discussions, coaching sessions and incredible women I have interacted with, one of the biggest challenges they feel is that they do not want to compromise themselves to fit in – "It's just not me," they say.

Brendon Burchard (2017) puts it beautifully: "The more you lie to yourself by not being authentic, the less confidence you have."

In fact, you can end up with the 'backfire effect', where your brain actually can end up digging your mental heels in ever more, even if there is clear, factual contradictory evidence. Professor Brendan Nyhan of the University of Michigan (Nhyan and Reifler, 2010), whose work was originally focused on politics and the Iraq War, found that being given contradictory evidence can actually make us solidify our position even more. If we lie to ourselves about our confidence, without really feeling it deeply, we may well feel an even stronger pull internally of being a 'fraud'.

So, what is happening in our brains? This is one of the most important things that everyone should know and which happens to all of us under stressful situations.

Each of our brains runs off around 20–25 watts of energy at any point in time. It cannot 'power up' to 40 watts when required – it would fry like an egg. So, well below the threshold of conscious awareness, it manages its energy resources according to the perceived requirements of the immediate moment. When we are under stress, or 'threat' as the brain perceives it, this limited energy our brain can use gets funnelled to the part which needs it most – the snake brain – for survival. This is the part of the brain first developed in the foetus and is associated with breathing, heart rate, digestion and sleep. Under threat, it communicates to the sympathetic nervous system, acting as an accelerator to power the body up for fight, flight, freeze or faint.

This mechanism has kept us, and our ancestors, alive for many millions of years. In fact, the main survival components of the human brain are also found in the brain of the lamprey (it looks a bit like an eel) and which existed 500 million years ago, albeit with much fewer nerve cells in each part.

This ancient brain hardware has us primed and ready to survive; useful for dealing with woolly mammoths for our caveman ancestors, not so useful for trying to work effectively in an office. The outcome is that our pre-frontal cortex, the 'executive' functioning part of the brain, is deemed less necessary at the point in time when we get the 'rabbit in the headlights' effect. This can be experienced as not being able think clearly and limits our ability to come up with any clever responses at that point in time (but so often brilliant ones afterwards!).

What was happening to me, in my Chief of Staff role, was that the fear was growing and, in the absence of any feedback to the contrary, my brain was going into survival mode. This was why I was making the stupid mistakes, instead of being creatively adaptive as the job required of me.

Unchecked, this neurobiological response can completely erode confidence – shaking the foundations of years of experience, knowledge and talent, turning you into a nervous wreck. Running out of adaptive capacity, or having it blocked, is not fun.

The mere understanding of what is happening at this point in time is extremely helpful for people. It takes away the judgement of 'being emotional' and opens up the door for opportunities to see how to manage those situations more effectively. Now that we realize everything is powered by the emotions, whoever thinks or says: "S/he's being emotional" is themselves being emotional.

How does lack of confidence show up?

Who do you think about when you think of confidence? Richard Branson, Elon Musk, Jordan Belfort, the Wolf of Wall Street perhaps? Or is it more Christine Lagarde, with her effortless calm and understated wisdom?

One of the challenges we face is that many of those who are perceived to be modelling confidence and perhaps demonstrating control, charm, and decisiveness, often also show some elements of arrogance, bullying, brashness and perhaps even aggression. When we look up towards the top of organizations, many of the traits which are valued and rewarded are those of the traditional, hierarchical, white, middle-aged male. Sadly, often, the women who are sitting at the table with them have got there because they have had to shape themselves in a similar fashion – 'They may not look like us, but they *act* like us so they can join our club'. This misses out on the fundamental value of neurologically-based diversity and hence the opportunity which is there by having different, authentically confident brains around the table.

I saw this several years ago when I decided I wanted to help women within my finance organization with coaching. I was focused specifically on the Vice President (VP) level, with a view to try and fill the gap between VP and Director – the number of women at the more senior level was significantly less than it should (or could) have been.

So, I put together a plan. Applicants put forward their submissions and we selected those to take part. At the start as part of that process I sat down with each manager and applicant to get feedback on their key development areas: things that were holding them back from that next level.

The feedback came in different wrappers: she's not good at presenting; she doesn't speak up in meetings; she isn't 'seen' at that level; she lacks 'gravitas'; she's not ready; she's not ambitious or hungry; she lacks leadership qualities; she's not really focused on progression. But when I started coaching these women, there was one common thread that underpinned all of them: they lacked self-confidence. It was absolutely the one thing that sat bubbling under the surface and drove the behaviours or perceptions that were holding them back. When I focused in on that area, that was where we saw real, fundamental, long-lasting change.

What is the impact of lack of confidence?

When we zoom out, it is apparent that lack of confidence emerges and impacts in a wide variety of forms in real life – personally and professionally.

People who lack confidence struggle with setting boundaries; they say 'Yes' too much and find themselves overloaded with work and personal commitments. They fear saying 'no' will upset people, be thought selfish or rude, and so they get caught in a cycle of stress and exhaustion. At an extreme level this culminates in burnout, which has become an epidemic in itself, with over 49% of employees globally saying in a study (McKinsey et al., 2021) that they felt some level of burnout. Within the workplace, it means they take on too much and are then penalized in promotion panels for 'not being able to manage their workload'. In fact, often it is because they are frightened to say 'no', or do not know how to, that they end up being the recipient of all the work or action points.

Lack of confidence can mean staying in a toxic relationship because of fear of the unknown, which further damages confidence. It can mean not bringing-up *that* discussion that really needs to happen, even though it is scary. Strong relationships are built on a foundation of communication – both positive, and with the ability to pursue some of the harder messages. Without such communication, the core issues do not get dealt with and, one day, can cause a person to reach their breaking point.

Lack of confidence can also come in the form of procrastination ("If I don't start then I can't fail") and also leads to perfectionism, which means wasting precious time unnecessarily. Both of these result in not delivering, despite the capability to do so. At times, when I felt under huge pressure in terms of performing, the tendency to perfectionism (often sharpening up power point slides) was extreme and almost crippling. How would my time have been better spent? Taking a step back and figuring out what would have the most impact longer term – that's where you progress. I spoke to a great friend in a FTSE 100 company who was in a similar role to mine, though on a much larger scale. She was very clear: '80% of the work I do doesn't need to be perfect. But I know what 20% does, and that's what I focus on when I need to'. That attitude and self-confidence meant she was able to cover more, better, faster and focus on the strategic, high impact issues.

Within organizations, the broader impact of lack of confidence is a hugely under-valued issue. Quality organizations are spending a significant amount of time trying to achieve gender balance, but what happens if women do not have the confidence to speak up when they are there? Research noted in *The confidence code* found that women speak 75% less than men when in the minority. There are several outcomes of this.

Firstly, you may have a 50/50 split around the table, but unless you can bring the joint contributions of the brains to the table, you are not maximizing the cognitive capability of that group. Male and female brains work differently – Connor's work (2013) at the University of Pennsylvania using functional Magnetic Resonance Imaging (fMRI) showed some definitive evidence of this. Using nearly 1,000 brain scans of boys and girls, men and women from ages 8–24, they showed female brains having much greater activity between the brain's two hemispheres than did male brains, which operated more in one hemisphere or the other. It suggests that the male brain is an 'either/or' system while the female brain is 'both/and'.

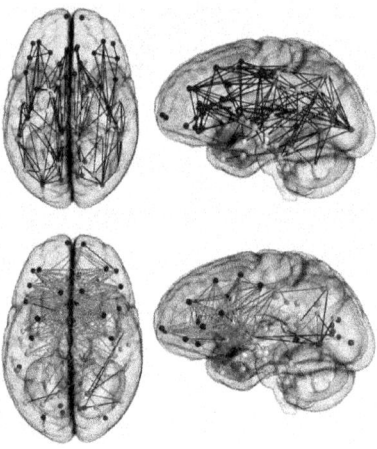

Figure 1.1 fMRI images of brain networks show increased connectivity from front to back and within one hemisphere in males (upper) and connectivity between the right and left hemispheres in females (lower). Reproduced with permission from Ingalhalikar et al. (2013) 'Sex differences in the structural connectome of the human brain', 'PNAS, 3(2), pp. 823–828. Available at https://doi.org/10.1073/pnas.1316909110 (Accessed: 15 April 2023).

This seems to imply and back up the experience of men making decisions quickly, looking at it from a more binary perspective 'this or that' (often interpreted as being more confident) vs. women, looking at things from a broader perspective 'both-and' so apparently being slower (seen as less confident). In fact, the research implies that the female brain is processing across more data points to come to decisions. Both modes of operating have their merits, but a team knowingly taking advantage of a combination of the two, will likely be much more powerful than one gender alone.

Research on the brains of children finds clear differences emerging early on in the brains of boys and girls. In utero, girls are wired for connection, lacking a surge of testosterone which otherwise for boys shrinks the brain's centres for communication, observation and processing of emotions (Brizendine, 2007). Girls typically quickly engage, look for visual cues of reassurance and connection – that was all part of the survival mechanism. In her wonderful book, *The Female Brain* (2007), Louann Brizendine, M.D. explains why this may be useful:

> If you can read faces and voices, you can tell what an infant needs. You can predict what a bigger, more aggressive male is going to do. And since you're smaller, you probably need to bond with other females to fend off attacks from a ticked off caveman – or cavemen.

As girls grow older, the language they use is collaborative; they make decisions together and avoid stress, conflict and displays of status: "Let's play together." It's about partnering in their interactions and building relationships; less about winning, more about the interaction in the game. This may be because females in a bonded social group are more likely to help each other in a time of threat. Boys, on the other hand, focus on the competition – they want to beat the other, with less focus or care on what they think of them (Brizendine, 2007).

First-hand experience has shown me time and time again that this plays through into adults and organizations. I would often see the men compete and argue, with the women able to broker a win-win solution. The point here is that there is a wonderful gift of having a *balance* of male and female brains creating the greatest value. This is also important for a balanced approach to risk, people matters, clients and the rest of the critical decisions an organization faces.

Much evidence is emerging of this power through the more equal representation of women on Boards. Studies from 350 FTSE companies, which have executive committees with at least 33% female representation, found they had 10 times the profit margin of those with less representation (Pipeline, 2019). McKinsey's research in 2019 also found Diverse Executive Teams were more likely to financially outperform by 25%.

The second impact of women's lack of confidence in organizations is the organization ending up with the 'broken rung' phenomenon, as coined by McKinsey et al. in their *Women in The Workplace* report (2021). This is where women are stuck at the lower levels of the corporate ladder – they do not even get a start at the junior management levels, hence cannot progress through the organization to the more senior levels. If they lack confidence in their capabilities to 'have a go' they do not even *apply* for the junior role. This means they are then not seen as management material, leading to a skewed corporate pyramid, with them trying to play catch-up throughout their careers and corporate levels.

Thirdly, from a regulatory perspective, this is a real concern. Regulators, particularly in the troubled finance industry following the financial crisis, have been hugely focused on the importance of organizations creating a 'speak-up' culture. People need to feel safe to challenge; to call out poor behaviour; to get something half-noticed up to the surface of attention if they sense something strange happening (which could be the first thread of a major fraud or a Nick Leeson / Barings-type incident). Regulators are reliant on confident people who challenge the status quo and, if needed, become whistle-blowers to avoid these major events occurring. Lack of confidence means they will back away from such a situation rather than take the personal risk based on their trust in themselves and their intuition to bring it up.

Coming back to the female vs male brain, it may well be that women have more of that sense of 'something not being right' as women's neural networks are attuned from a very young age to sense danger or something amiss. This could well have been a function of being the physically weaker species and so they and their young were more at risk from attack (Brizendine, 2006). Having those sharp senses could have been a matter literally of life and death. Nowadays, this could be leveraged as a great strength if only organizations were aware of differences in male and female perception.

Fourthly, we go back to the key point around the brain prioritizing survival. If you lack confidence, you are running in a state of fear to whatever level your brain is interpreting the situation. That means the potential creative, problem-solving capabilities of the brains around the table are being capped. What if the person who lacks confidence actually *has* the solution, has an entirely different way of looking at the issue, but is too frightened of raising their idea for fear of rejection, conflict or looking stupid? Confidence across a team means all sorts of ideas being raised, challenged, pivoted and sharpened in pursuit of getting the best possible outcome for the organization.

Your brain's bouncer

Have you ever noticed how, when you start searching for something on your phone – a new house, car, computer – you will find you get served up that item time and time again, whether on ads, searches, new articles or YouTube videos? This is the computer algorithm doubling down on what you want, like or see with a view to sell you more of it – metaphorically or physically. The more you like articles about hating Trump, the more of them you will see. The same happens with your brain.

Look around the room now and look for anything you see that is red (yes actually do it).

Now, write down all the blue things you saw (I bet you are looking back around the room!).

This is your brain's filter, the Reticular Activating System (RAS), cleverly helping you sieve through the millions of inputs it has at any point in time. Why does this happen? We are designed to filter these inputs to our brains, because there is no way we could consciously process all the stimuli and activity which are constantly happening. Imagine being aware of your heart beating, blood flowing, breathing, the person shouting at their children next door, blinking and your performance on a zoom call all at once – it really would be mind-blowing! The Reticular Activating System regulates wakefulness and is also like a bouncer on the door of your brain, deciding who gets to come in. The good news is that survival information gets straight through, unfiltered (very important for our ongoing species). Otherwise, it flags up only the 'essentials' that are deemed important to your conscious mind. This

is extremely important – as these essentials are defined by the following:
1. The thoughts we focus on (like our red or blue exercise).
2. Our beliefs.
3. What we identify with.

A great example of this is a dentist – they will see wonky teeth everywhere!

Bought a white car recently? You will notice white cars everywhere.

This works alongside a concept in psychology called 'confirmation bias'[1], which is defined by the *Cambridge Dictionary* as 'the fact that people are more likely to accept or notice information if it appears to support what they already believe or expect'. We subconsciously select to retain only the information that confirms what we already believe. Why does this matter with confidence? If you tell yourself you are bad at presenting you will look for evidence to *reinforce* that you are a terrible presenter.

The messages we tell ourselves are crucially important in how we see and operate in the world. They precipitate the actions that we take.

Another key contributor towards confidence is the default-mode network (DMN)[2]. This is defined by the American Psychological Association (APA) as 'a specific, anatomically defined brain system preferentially active when individuals are not focused on the external environment'. So, when we are not focused on a task, it hums away like a generator, thinking about the past or the future – often coming up with all sorts of stories or scenarios which did not or will not ever exist.

---

[1] See https://www.verywellmind.com/what-is-a-confirmation-bias-2795024
[2] See https://dictionary.apa.org/default-mode-network

You know when you are playing out a conversation in your mind that you are worried about: 'I would say this, then they would say that ... which would upset me, so I would respond with ...' (and so it goes on). There is little or no value in this process of rumination, but it can completely take over and cause actual physical anxiety in the body, even though it is completely fabricated. The APA goes on to say "ongoing unconstrained self-reflective thought might be the natural (default) state of the mind when individuals are not otherwise engaged." This is also evidenced by fMRI images of the brain showing the same areas activated when thinking about the past or future as when the DMN is active (*APA Dictionary of Psychology*).

Why does this impact confidence?

This impacts confidence because the mind's natural tendency is to focus on the emotions associated with 'escape' or 'survive' in keeping you safe. If we don't regulate them, this will be the default mode of thought. Over time it grinds down your confidence levels.

Evidence suggests that 60%–70% of the thoughts we have are those associated with 'escape' emotions (Raghunathan, 2013). Interestingly, the word 'emotion' can be hyphenated into 'e-motion' – energy results in action. Emotions exist to tell us what is happening in our environment, to assimilate that and take action. These escape emotions can be distilled into: fear, anger, disgust, shame and sadness. See front and back covers for the *London Protocol of the Emotions*.

This makes perfect sense as a species – the more quickly we notice threat, the faster we are able to react, and the safer we will be, so able to continue to live and reproduce. But the complication arising from this is that the vast majority of situations we experience nowadays do not actually threaten our physical safety. Office politics is a great example of this: how sick or angry do you feel when you feel like you are being undermined, stabbed in the back? Is it threatening your life? No. But your brain does not know that and instead leaps into action, preparing you to fight/flight/freeze/faint. It is our Self that feels threatened and may not be able to cope.

The 'attachment' emotions – excitement/joy and love/trust – whilst important for social and for parent-to-child connection, are secondary for continuation of the species at a biological level. So, it makes sense that our brains are more tuned to look for the things that may trigger escape emotions; hence one may consider the DMN working in this way.

It is also the escape/avoidance/survival emotions that sear more strongly into our awareness. People tend to remember the bad more vividly, process it more efficiently and pay more attention to it. Stereotypes and bad impressions form more quickly and the escape emotions produce longer-lasting effects – which makes sense, given that they are the ones protecting us.

When we overlay this with the concept of prioritization of energy in the brain, then it is also possible to start to work through behaviours and how they contribute towards confidence.

Let us look at a scenario that many of us have faced: It's your performance review, your manager talks at length about the many areas you've exceeded expectations, and then it comes – the dreaded 'development area'. It's one small thing – 'try and speak up more in meetings'; or, 'that mistake you made six months ago'; but the red mist ensues as you feel yourself getting angry, upset, with a hot face and perhaps even hot tears. What do you then think about for the next two weeks? There's little reference to the 55 minutes of praise, but only turning the *development area* (bah!) around like a Rubik's cube in your mind. *How could they? Why me? It's so unfair! I'm rubbish at my job. I should resign now before they sack me.*

Mindset and limiting beliefs

Mindset is defined by the *Cambridge Dictionary* as "a person's way of thinking and their opinions". The quality and content of our mindset is a key driver of the belief that we have around our capabilities; the outcome of taking actions and how grounded we feel in our own sense of self. If the way we are thinking and our opinions of these things are based on fear, our mindset will limit how we step into the world with confidence.

How then we shape, control and manage our mindset is a fundamental part of how confident we are. This is where the inner critic and its cousin, *Imposter Syndrome*, come into the confidence story.

The inner critic, sometimes called 'the saboteur', is that little (sometimes big) voice which judges, threatens, commands and monitors weaknesses or mistakes. It says things like "you look like a cow in that outfit" or "you should stop acting like an idiot" or "you messed this up again" or "if you don't work hard enough, you'll get sacked". This negative self-talk is often the echo of a parent, sibling, teacher or other childhood experience, that has formed a strong neural pathway carrying through to adulthood. Everyone's developmental experiences are different; and influences in upbringing make them louder or quieter, but without question they can be very nasty and so very damaging on confidence levels.

Reflecting though on the functioning of the brain, this likely exists to keep us safe – whether from taking risks; avoiding rejection or failure, loss of security or change (even if it does not really feel like that at the time).

The result of the inner critic firing up with a litany of comments can itself create a very real physical stress response: the sympathetic nervous system is activated, with cortisol and adrenaline pumping, causing sweaty palms, heart racing, shortness of breath and the other fight/flight survival responses. Then a kind of self-fulfilling prophecy can occur as the stress responses reduce the effectiveness of performance and the critic can say "See – I knew you would mess it up." When this continues at a low, constant level, the outcome can be a persistent background of anxiety that has the potential to become chronic stress and eventually burnout.

Imposter Syndrome can be seen as the cousin of the Inner Critic. It was a term introduced in an article published in 1978, entitled *'The Impostor Phenomenon in High Achieving Women: dynamics and therapeutic intervention'* by Pauline R. Clance and Suzanne A. Imes (1978). They defined it as "a psychological pattern in which an individual doubts their skills, talents, or accomplishments and has a persistent, internalized fear of being exposed as a 'fraud'". The key point about the syndrome is that there is external evidence that person *has* the skills, but they believe they have got there with luck and do not deserve to be where they are.

There are three important features to note about Imposter Syndrome:

Firstly, it is different to Self-Doubt, though they can both be present. Self-Doubt is about what you can *do* (the skills you have), whereas Imposter Syndrome is at an

Identity level – about who you think you *are* (Josa, 2019). Importantly, *you have the skills* but you still tell yourself the story you can't do it. The kind of thought patterns that you hear are: "I'll get found out", "I'm a fraud."

Secondly, those experiencing Imposter Syndrome discount their achievements, attributing them to luck or coincidence, rather than their own abilities or intelligence. This was something I would do all the time in my investment banking career. I would look up to a role, then whenever I got promoted and ended up in that role, I would think: "Oh they just couldn't find anyone else."

Thirdly, it is context dependant, so may only come up when someone has changed role and stepped out of their comfort zone, thinking 'they will find me out'. This is why it is often experienced by high performers – they may be comfortable in one role but then if asked, for example, to join a board, they feel they should not be there.

The outcomes of Imposter Syndrome can show up in different ways – anxiety, fear of failure, perfectionism (fight), people pleasing, procrastination (freeze) as well as continuously activating your sympathetic nervous system and causing those dreadfully familiar stress responses.

Clare Josa talks in her book, *Ditching Imposter Syndrome* (2019), about the Imposter Syndrome Iceberg – a useful concept in thinking about the causes and behaviours of Imposter Syndrome. Below the water's surface is the inner voice, driven by values, deeply subconscious level beliefs and identity ("*I am* a fraud"). Above the surface of the water, where you see the tip of the iceberg, are the *actions* which are outcomes of these beliefs – they are the symptoms of what is below. Traditional development training tends to treat the top of the Iceberg – the symptoms of lack of confidence: bad presentation skills or poor communication.

What that misses is the true underlying driver: 'I'm not good enough' or 'I'm a fraud'. Only when you can address these can you make long-lasting changes to someone's belief of themselves and therefore their confidence levels. From a neurobiological perspective, the rewiring of neurons (neuroplasticity) will only take place if there is repetitive change or such a strong change at a point in time that it forges a new pathway and so new behaviour. This may indicate why these thought patterns and habits are so hard to change. We need to make the 'push' factor so strong that the brain prioritizes that change permanently – not dance around on the tip of the iceberg.

Change and lack of control

The brain does not like change. The lack of familiarity, lack of control of any situation, equates to danger (I haven't been down this path before therefore it may not be safe). This depends on the person and their level of comfort with change – to some it may be very scary, to others it may be more exciting. But once you have a pathway laid down, it is hard to shift from that behaviour or thought pattern.

The impact of this on confidence levels is important.

If someone is feeling threatened by their circumstances being out of their control, this can elicit that same survival response in their brain and body, further driving them down a spiral of lack of confidence. Covid-19 was a very interesting example of this, where we saw an almost primal response from people, particularly at the start when people were dying and we did not have a vaccine to protect us. We saw people hoarding, fighting, showing aggression and being fearful – trying to control whatever could be controlled but, paradoxically, showing behaviours of being out of control driven by fear. In these kinds of high stress situations, brain scans show that activity in the areas for compassion in the brain can be impaired – people tend to focus more inwards, protecting themselves and those closest to them (Siegel, 2019).

But once we were able to get to grips with what was within, or outside of our control, the situation calmed. People could get masks, stay at home, wash their hands and sanitize – this was a choice and level of control they had, to reduce the stress of the situation and so grow in confidence.

Organizational change is another excellent example of this. When there is tremendous change going on in a company, with potential layoffs looming (but who knows where) and an unclear future, the confidence across the troops cracks and creativity grinds to a halt. Everyone is worried about their job, role and future – "Yes, but what about *me?*".

Working in banking, where there was so much change, regulatory pressure, cost and headcount pressure, I would see this time and time again. Each time a new management team was created (which was often) there would be a freeze, like musical chairs, then a rush of political manoeuvring and closed-door conversations, hoping not to be the one standing chair-less at the end. The fear would be palpable, and only when people knew they were 'safe' could normal business resume.

Looking at *The London Protocol of the Emotions*, people were focused inwards on survival with the escape-avoidance emotions. The organizational problem was that in pressing this trigger so often people became chronically scared, never knowing when the axe might fall, the result being a constant state of underlying anxiety and stress – and management wondering why performance was not what it should be. Imagine if all that energy (e-motion) was used instead in a creative approach to solutions, the greater wellbeing of the team and others, rather than each individual focused on themselves.

The Kübler-Ross Change Curve (see Figure 1.2) was derived from the 'grief curve' by Dr Elisabeth Kübler-Ross and David Kessler in their book, *On Grief and Grieving: finding the meaning of grief through the five stages of loss'* (2005). It is a useful tool to understand how this can have an impact on people – whatever the change is.

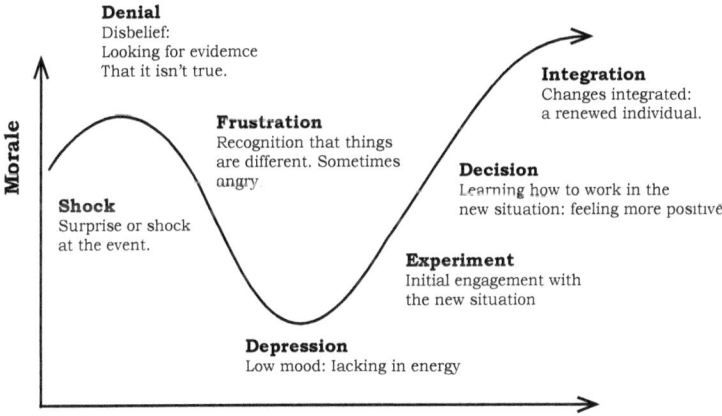

Figure 1.2 Kübler-Ross and Kessler (2005) On grief and grieving: Finding the meaning of grief through the five stages of loss. New York: Simon & Schuster. Source: The Kübler-Ross Change Curve® www.ekrfoundation.org

When people understand this and the emotions they may well feel during change, that in itself can allow them to 'be' and let the parasympathetic system calm the sympathetic nervous system response.

The cognitive bandwidth that people use up trying to control things outside of their control, is often huge. They are snatching at feathers, never grasping them, despite furious effort. The outcome? Confidence is reduced, because they are not getting the results they feel they 'should' do: "I'm a failure." They judge themselves on targets and expectations which are completely unrealistic, leading to further negative thoughts and rumination. The RAS will be conditioned to be looking for (perceived) failure, with the default mode network steaming away on what should have been, not what actually is.

Tribal behaviour and confidence

Most people remember that terrible feeling when the teacher says "Okay. Let's pick teams" and the brutal selection process begins. The dread ensues as one by one people around you move smiling to their gang ... "Oh goodness, no ... please don't let me be last."

The fear of exclusion does not disappear as we grow up. It echoes through our personal and professional life too. Research from Eisenberger et al. (2006) showed that social and physical pain produce similar brain responses. Whether caused by social rejection or physical pain, the brain scans showed the same areas associated with distress.

We are built and motivated chemically for connection. Oxytocin is a neurotransmitter released in the brain that generates social bonding, reproduction, childbirth and ongoing child rearing. This is what wires us for connection – whether with a parent, as a parent, partner, loved one or even colleague. Oxytocin gained the nickname as the 'trust', 'cuddle' or 'love hormone'. Paul J. Zak's research

(2017) shows that high levels of oxytocin cause people to work harder to help the group achieve its goals.

Why is this so important? Because social connection is a crucial part of our existence and ability to stay safe. Human offspring are not born able to fend for themselves like reptiles; we need care and support for many years before we are able to cope in the world. Likewise, when homo sapiens first roamed the Earth, we needed our tribe to protect us from the perils of the times – whether it be the woolly mammoth, sabre-toothed tiger or hazardous environment. So, acceptance into a group is crucial for our brains to feel safe – being part of our tribe is, to our brain, a matter of life and death.

So we are wired for social interaction. When we have a strong network of support this paves the way for us to act with confidence and take risks. If there is a perceived threat of exclusion from our tribe, our confidence can be shattered and our stress levels go sky high. Existence of core human values (integrity, honesty, kindness) builds a social safety net which leads to better sleep, less stress and better health (Slavich, 2020). Research from Waldinger et al. (2015) shows the level of social connection you have is the best predictor of wellbeing and longevity.

This is often discussed today in the context of psychological safety, defined by Amy Edmondson (1999), as 'a belief that one will not be punished or humiliated for speaking up with ideas, questions, concerns or mistakes.' Underpinning this is the freedom to be 'myself' – the foundation of confidence.

Creating a confident self

Letting go is, without question, one of the strongest mechanisms I have seen for creating confidence:

- Letting go of bravado, pretence, trying too hard and showing off.
- Letting go of trying to be everything to everyone; instead, knowing where your real strengths are and sitting comfortably in that space.
- Letting go of the desperate grip on an unattainable goal of trying to be someone else.
- Letting go of a perception of who I 'should' be and anchoring in the knowledge of 'who I am'.

It is about waking up every day with integrity – knowing you have not compromised yourself or what is important to you for the sake of winning or progression. One should understand the politics but not succumb to the Machiavellian games, releasing the essential me from the requirement to be glossy; the filtered version (which we women are socially conditioned to see ourselves striving to be at every turn).

From that place of knowledge, no one can challenge you, because without question, you know better than anyone else how to be you.

And when that realization happens, you can feel the huge collective sigh of relief. "Confidence is about being me? I can do that!" The release, with that permission, is palpable. Scary too, because there is vulnerability associated with taking off the façade; but so liberating. No longer do you have to waste the extraordinary extra cognitive energy involved in not being yourself; being scared of what people will see underneath and that this would not fit into the mould.

How does this start? By deeply understanding who you are and where you have come from. When you know yourself you can trust yourself. What challenges have shaped you, built your particular resilience levels and created the person today? When one can reflect on those darkest moments and can see there is another chapter, full of light and growth on the other side, this creates incredible personal power. It is always there but so easy to skip over with the pace of life and often the focus on the negative.

Part of that knowledge of who you are comes from your values. Many people go through their lives with no conscious clue as to these key building blocks which define how you see and experience the world. But, once conscious, they enable you to make the best possible decisions, understand your reactions and live a more aligned life to what really resonates with your purpose.

A wonderful example of this was a client doing my confidence course. She had been in the same job for years and had not felt she was good enough to try for the next level. Once she understood more about her values, her life journey and her resilience, she grew in confidence and decided to apply. She did not get it, but was delighted all the same. "I had my best interview ever!!" She was 100% herself; she performed the best she had ever done in an interview – calm and articulate, because she was not trying to be someone else. She let go and trusted that what she could control was how she turned up – what she could not control was the other people and considerations in the interview process. That gave her tremendous personal power. She may not have got that promotion this time, but with her new confidence, it is certainly 'not yet' rather than 'never'.

Knowing deeply who we are is also core to us being able to conquer effectively the power of the inner critic and our limiting beliefs. To manage our confidence, we need to manage the messages we give ourselves, which are shaping the way we see ourselves operating in the world.

The first key step with this is the simplest – noticing it. When you start to tune into the mind chatter and what kind of messages it is giving you, the level of negativity on repeat can be a bit of a shock. It is incredible how harsh and judgemental you can be to yourself, in a way that you would never dream of being to anyone else. Reshaping those thoughts in a way that you would speak to others can start to shift the continuous messaging to build, rather than destroy confidence.

Mindfulness and meditation are both wonderful ways for managing high stress, as well as for preventing it and having it as an emergency tool for moments when the mind is racing down a path of negative thinking. Making this part of your armoury will create further anchors for confidence, with your ability to manage stress and anxiety.

Significant research shows those who meditate regularly are more positive and less stressed (Economides, Martman and Bell, 2018). Neuroimaging studies show that after eight weeks of meditation, meditators actually have increased grey matter density in their brain. The activity in their amygdala is lower, which means less susceptibility to stress and anxiety. There is also more activity in the part of the brain associated with memory and learning, the hippocampus.

Meditation also increases your capacity for compassion and has been shown to decrease racial bias and impulsive behaviour. Two recent studies with oncology and paediatric nurses (Morrison Wylde et al., 2017; Kriakous et al., 2020) indicated that nurses who had a mindfulness-based stress reduction (MBSR) practice reported significant decreases in compassion fatigue, burnout, stress, and experiential avoidance as well as increases in life satisfaction, mindfulness and self-compassion (Duarte and Pinto-Gouveia, 2016).

A practical example of using this was when I was accused by a particularly aggressive and toxic individual of lying to audit. This is a sackable offence, so not to be taken lightly at all, but was totally untrue and entirely uncalled for. During the follow-up meeting to the offending email, I used my mindfulness training to reduce the anxiety and avoid being clouded by the red mist of an amygdala hijack.

I tuned into the feeling of my feet on the floor, my breath in and out of my nostrils, and pictured breathing in as cool blue, breathing out as fiery orange. It really worked and enabled me to manage the situation to the best of my ability, rather than being clouded by anger and fear. That provides another brick in the confidence path for the next challenge.

A very interesting piece of research by Alison Wood Brooks (2013) at Harvard looked at managing anxiety from a different perspective. She found that rather than trying to calm down when in stressful situations like going to present on stage, in fact tapping into the mindset of arousal was a more useful approach.

The principle was that the parts of the brain associated with anxiety are also associated with excitement. So having subjects reframe their anxiety as excitement, by saying "I am excited" before they went on stage, led them to adopt an 'opportunity mindset' rather than 'threat mindset'. Effectively you are not trying to bring arousal down, but leveraging it in a different way, which Alison Wood Brooks called 'arousal congruence'. This is a very useful tool for improving confidence, particularly given that so many people feel that sense of deep fear around public speaking or similar situations.

"God, grant me the serenity to accept the things I cannot change, the courage to change the things I can, and the wisdom to know the difference."

~ *Serenity Prayer*

In his book, *The 7 Habits of Highly Effective People* (1989), Stephen Covey articulates the Serenity Prayer beautifully by distinguishing between our Circle of Concern (things we care about but cannot control) and the Circle of Influence (things we care about and can impact). This was developed to include the Circle of Control – things which are directly in our control to change.

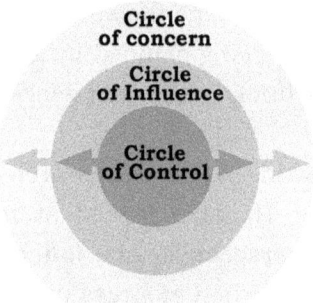

Figure 1.3 from Stephen Covey (1989), The 7 habits of highly effective people. New York: Simon & Schuster. Source:https://tinyurl.com/3mmafyzr

Albert Einstein once said: "Failure is success in progress."

This thought process was helpful for a pitch I performed recently to a potentially hugely significant client for my business. This had required thorough preparation, support of amazing mentors and deep knowledge of my subject. I was grilled by the client, but managed the questions and walked away from it knowing I could not have done better. Did I get the client? No, they didn't feel it was the right fit for them. But did it knock my confidence – absolutely not, because I had controlled everything within my power that I could. I had taken a step, tried it and performed at my best. I could not control what they saw as 'a good fit for the organization', but I could control how I showed up to that discussion, with all the preparation and hard work behind it. Focusing on what I could control was the key.

Creating an optimised environment with the balance of male and female brains

"Twelve promotions. One woman. TWELVE. So, you are telling me that we had 11 men better than all the other women up for Managing Director?" I was on the warpath. My manager was looking uncomfortable as I drew a pie chart of the result, just to ensure the message was getting across. "They just weren't ready, Caroline – they weren't good enough." I replied, "But *what does good look like*? It looks like white middle-aged male!"

This conversation has echoed in my mind for years, and I believe this is a big part of the foundation for the ongoing struggles for gender equality at a senior level.

The lens through which the decisions are being made is one that defines that 'success looks like the character and behaviours of seniority of hundreds of years in the past'. Sadly, this is even true for the women too – they do not see that they match up to those standards and hence *believe* the message that they are not ready either. Unless this perception of what good looks like changes, the environment is unlikely to change enough to support the incredible power of the *combination* of male and female brains.

Where do you start in the organization?

There is no doubt that the most senior women will already have considerable confidence to have reached where they are – they will have the battle scars to prove it. Are there areas they doubt themselves? Absolutely, as there will be with the men too. Is there value in them acquiring more self-awareness, self-confidence; boosting their existing talents even further? Definitely.

McKinsey's research from early 2021 sighted how critical investment in "immersive and engaging development programmes" is for senior leadership, to increase their adaptability to facilitate an environment based on psychological safety. Psychological safety is defined as "a shared belief held by members of a team that the team is safe for interpersonal risk taking." (Edmondson, 1999) and is crucial for the brains of the organization to operate to their maximum potential.

Confidence starts with this self-awareness, whatever gender you are:

> It's critical that learning programs prompt leaders to engage with and shift their underlying beliefs, assumptions, and emotions to bring about lasting mindset changes (McKinsey et al., 2021).

A big 'bang for your buck' also exists in investing in the upcoming female leaders. This is the talent not yet at the Board, but the emerging mid-level leaders. This is often the group who are weighing up their priorities of family and work – they want to progress but if they do not feel the compromise is really worth it, then why bother?

If they can truly grow into their potential and see it is worth the effort – they are not minimized, taken for granted or their skills undervalued – they will continue to invest their precious time and talent towards the more senior roles. They will have the confidence to apply for new opportunities and stretch roles; areas that they would have otherwise seen outside of their capabilities. This is the talent pipeline to feed the precious upper echelons of leadership and inspire those below.

To be clear, this is not about 'fixing the women'. That is a misconception masking the problem at hand (whilst I focus here on confidence for women, not all men are confident and plenty of senior men lack confidence in different areas). This is not addressing a weakness, but doubling down on and releasing their strengths. Enabling confidence here is about bringing out the deepest level of potential from the female brains in the organization. It is about lifting the lid on your company's performance. It is about giving them permission to be themselves and to flourish in that form, not squashed and moulded into an alternative which limits its contribution.

When you give women the confidence to be themselves, with all their power, logic, calmness and wisdom, you harness a current, a deep ocean of talent that can both bring people together and enhance how they can rise up collectively. Women naturally look for opportunities to collaborate, not compete; to put aside the 'best solution for me' and find the 'right solution for us'. Once you give them the permission to be authentically themselves, to see that high performance can be quiet and unassuming, not just brash and loud, you will see contributions you never saw before.

Finally

Ultimately, confidence is driven by both the Self and the environment in which that Self exists. The Self needs to accept and believe in who 'I am': unfiltered, with knowledge of its strengths and capabilities and, with that knowledge, the ability to take action and try new things. Then the integration of who the Self feels it is and who s/he needs to be is complete.

However, if the environment in which that Self operates creates fear, our brains will be focused on that threat and adapt our behaviour accordingly. Over time, even the most confident person can lose this self-belief through incessant minimization and grinding down of their convictions. The interplay of both the Self and the interpersonal environment are therefore crucial to maximize the capitalization of people's capability.

If forward-thinking organizations, led by exceptional leaders, recognize this and are able to nurture each person to feel integrated and valued as themselves, then those that are able will rise above the rest.

Confidence is their rocket fuel for success.

References

Brizendine, L. (2006) *The female brain*. London: Bantam Press.

Brooks, A.W. (2013) 'Get excited: Reframing performance anxiety as excitement', *Journal of Experimental Psychology*, 1–15. Available at: https://www.hbs.edu/ris/Publication%20Files/xge-a0035325%20(2)_0287835d-9e25-4f92-9661-c5b54dbbcb39.pdf (Accessed: 11 March 2023).

Brown, P. (2022) 'The London Protocol of the Emotions: Refining the solution to an emotional muddle', in Lanz, K. and Brown, P. (2020) *All the brains in the business: The engendered brain in the 21st century organization*, pp. 132–142. Switzerland: Palgrave Macmillan.

Burchard, B. (2017) *High performance habits: how extraordinary people become that way*. Australia: Hay House, Pty. Ltd.

Clance, P.R. and Imes, S.A. (1978) 'The imposter phenomenon in high achieving women: Dynamics and therapeutic intervention', *Psychotherapy: Theory, Research & Practice*, 15(3), 241–247.

Connor, S. (2013). 'The hardwired difference between male and female brains could explain why men are "better at map-reading"'. *The Independent*, 3 December. Available at: https://independent.co.uk/life-style/the-hardwired-difference-between-male-and-female-brains-could-explain-why-men-are-better-at-map-reading-8978248.html (Accessed: 11 March 2023).
Covey, S. (1989) *The 7 habits of highly effective people*. New York: Simon & Schuster.

Duarte, J. and Pinto-Gouveia, J. (2016) 'Effectiveness of a mindfulness-based intervention on oncology nurses' burnout and compassion fatigue symptoms: A non-randomized study'. Available at: https://pubmed.ncbi.nlm.nih.gov/27744228/ (Accessed: 11 March 2023).

Economides, M., Martman, J. and Bell, M.J. (2018) 'Improvements in stress, affect, and irritability following brief use of a mindfulness-based smartphone app: A randomized controlled trial'. Available at: https://link.springer.com/article/10.1007/s12671-018-0905-4 (Accessed: 11 March 2023).

Edmondson, A. (1999) 'Psychological safety and learning behavior in work teams', *Administrative Science Quarterly*, 44(2), 350–383. Available at: www.jstor.org/stable/2666999 (Accessed: 11 March 2023).

Eisenberger, N.I., Jarcho, J.M., Lieberman, M. and Naliboff, B.D. (2006) 'An experimental study of shared sensitivity to physical pain and social rejection'. Available at: https://www.scn.ucla.edu/pdf/Eisenberger,Jarcho,Lieberman,Naliboff(2006).pdf (Accessed: 11 March 2023).

Estes, Z. (2013) 'Attributive and relational processes in nominal combination', *Journal of Memory and Language*, 48(2), 304–319.

Josa, C. (2019) *Ditching Imposter Syndrome: How to finally feel good enough and become the leader you were born to be*. UK: Beyond Alchemy Publishing.

Kay, K. and Shipman, C. (2014) The confidence code: The science and art of self-assurance – What women should know. New York: Harper Business.

Kriakous, S.A., Elliott K.A., Lamers, C. and Owen R. (2020) 'The effectiveness of mindfulness-based stress reduction on the psychological functioning of healthcare professionals: A systematic review'. Available at: https://pubmed.ncbi.nlm.nih.gov/32989406/ (Accessed: 11 March 2023).

Kübler-Ross, E. (1969). On death and dying. New York: Scribner/ Simon & Schuster.

Kübler-Ross, E. and Kessler, D. (2005) On grief and grieving: Finding the meaning of grief through the five stages of loss. New York: Simon & Schuster.

Lanz, K. and Brown, P. (2020) All the brains in the business: The engendered brain in the 21st century organization. Switzerland: Palgrave Macmillan.

McKinsey & Company and LeanIn.Org (2019) *Women in the workplace 2019*. Available at: https://www.mckinsey.com/~/media/McKinsey/Featured%20Insights/Gender%20Equality/Women%20in%20the%20Workplace%202019/Women-in-the-workplace-2019.ashx (Accessed: 11 March 2023).

McKinsey & Company & Leanin.Org (2021) Women in the Workplace 2021. Available at: https://www.mckinsey.com/~/media/mckinsey/featured%20insights/diversity%20and%20inclusion/women%20in%20the%20workplace%202021/women-in-the-workplace-2021.pdf (Accessed: 17 April 2023).

Morrison Wylde C., Mahrer N.E., Meyer R.M.L. and Gold J.I. (2017) 'Mindfulness for Novice Pediatric Nurses: smartphone application versus traditional intervention'. Available at: https://pubmed.ncbi.nlm.nih.gov/28888505/ (Accessed: 11 March 2023).

Nyhan, B. and Reifler, J. (2010) 'When corrections fail: The persistence of political misperceptions', *Political Behavior*, 32, 303–330. Available at: https://doi.org/10.1007/s11109-010-9112-2 (Accessed: 11 March 2023).

Petty, R., Briñol, P. and Tormala, Z. (2002) 'Thought confidence as a determinant of persuasion: The self-validation hypothesis', *Journal of Personality and Social Psychology* 82, 722–741. Available at: doi:10.1037//0022-3514.82.5.722 (Accessed: 23 April 2023).

Pipeline (2019) 'Women count 2019: Role, value, and number of female executives in the FTSE 350'. Available at: https://execpipeline.com/wp-content/uploads/2020/12/The-Pipeline-Women-Count-2019.pdf (Accessed: 11 March 2023).

Raghunathan, R. (2013) 'How negative is your "mental chatter"?' Available at: https://www.psychologytoday.com/gb/blog/sapient-nature/201310/how-negative-is-your-mental-chatter (Accessed: 11 March 2023).

Robertson, I. (2021) *How confidence works: The new science of self-belief.* London: Bantam Press.

Siegel, D.J. (2019), 'The mind in psychotherapy: An interpersonal neurobiology framework for understanding and cultivating mental health'. *Psychology and Psychotherapy: Theory Research and Practice*, 92, 224–237. Available at: https://doi.org/10.1111/papt.12228 (Accessed: 11 March 2023).

Slavich G.M. (2020) 'Social safety theory: A biologically based evolutionary perspective on life stress, health, and behavior', *Annual*

Review of Clinical Psychology, 16, 265–295. Available at: https://doi.org/10.1146/annurev-clinpsy-032816-045159 (Accessed: 11 March 2023).

Waldinger, R.J., Cohen, S., Schulz, M.S. and Crowell, J.A. (2015) 'Security of attachment to spouses in late life: concurrent and prospective links with cognitive and emotional well-being', *Clinical Psychological Science*, 3(4), 516–529. Available at: https://www.ncbi.nlm.nih.gov/pmc/articles/PMC4579537/ (Accessed: 11 March 2023).

Zak, P.J. (2017) *Trust factor: The science of creating high-performance companies.* New York: AMACOM.

Biography

Caroline Brewin is the founder of Brain Powered Coaching, which uses an innovative, neuroscience-based approach to empowered Leadership and Confidence. With this foundation, she focuses on the development of high-performing individuals and their delivery of exceptional business outcomes. Caroline has over eighteen years of Global Investment Banking experience and eight years as a professionally trained Executive Coach.

From Chief of Staff to DEI and complex Regional / Global roles, she's seen it first-hand: the long-term success and profitability of organizations are inextricably linked to the trust, motivation and diversity of their people. Through her Executive Coaching, Corporate Partnerships and unique Confidence programmes, she is committed to empowering individuals and Corporates to achieve their personal and professional potential.

CHAPTER 2

Developing a Resilient, Engaged Organization

Soraya Shaw

Introduction

Our team wellness scores and our overall team happiness, engagement and belief in our values and purpose have continued to climb throughout the pandemic – in fact they now sit at record highs. All this at a time when they could understandably be expected to bottom out.

The insight that the entire team got from the brain-based resilience training was extremely powerful. It helped them not only to cope with an entirely new set of emotions but to excel in a very hostile business environment.

In turn, this learning then helped us each build greater resilience and equipped us with the necessary tools to allow every team member to support each other in their own personal growth.

Founder Travel Company specializing in the UK to Asia

Any business or people leader wants the best minds for their business: agile brains that are innovative, can handle disruption, and can make connections to solve complex problems and find solutions; minds that are emotionally intelligent and collaborative, making others feel confident; brains and minds that are healthy, honest, inspired and inspiring to drive business into the future, and that have a purpose and a belief in what they are doing. The result of all this is a culture and environment that all organizations strive for.

However, in this increasingly complex and demanding world, exhaustion, lack of motivation, burnout and ill-health can easily have a negative impact on the resilience and well-being of individuals and teams, no matter their status or experience. This can then create a downturn in the business with all the unwanted knock-on effects – a bit like a falling deck of dominoes.

For anyone reading this, have you either experienced overwhelming stress or known someone close to you who has? And the way depletion of resilience didn't happen overnight but slowly crept up?

But what is resilience? And what is stress? And what has the brain got to do with it?

First, let's define what resilience means.

In 2013, the psychologists David Fletcher and Mustafa Sarkar conceptualized resilience based on overcoming adversity through positive adaptation. In other words: "The role of mental processes and behaviours in promoting personal assets and protecting an individual from the potential negative effects of stress."

Neuroscience tells us that resilience sits at the core of how we view and handle potentially extremely difficult situations in our lives. Many studies, including my own, have shown that how cognitively and emotionally resilient we are influences how we approach worry and anxiety, seeing them as either something negative and to be avoided or something positive to be embraced and responded to as a healthy challenge.

For many differing reasons, the pandemic that began in 2019 exacerbated stress levels resulting globally in mental ill-health, reduced resilience and burnout. A 2019 study by Gary Britton and colleagues suggests that, on average, approximately 77% of a population worry daily about three things, with 2% of the population being found to have excessive and uncontrollable worrying to the extent that it harms their health. Also, it has been suggested that 85% of anticipatory fear is based on imagination, which is why building resilience within work teams, leaders and the general population is important (Wilkinson, 2020).

Because of the speed of change, resilient organizations can no longer fall back on past set plans or strategies when there are problems because events are moving so fast that, by the time implementation is in place, these have become out of date. Therefore, not only does a resilient organization need to become comfortable with ongoing improvising and adapting while trying to make sense of the changing situations: it also needs the expensive talent and brains it employs to be functioning well to be able to do this.

It is obvious that this ability to be flexible and to respond with confidence and certainty when making decisions relies on leaders and their teams being at their best and enjoying a high degree of well-being. This way, their mental agility is not impaired by the blocking effects of stress to both face uncertainty and to be flexible and nimble in problem solving and assessing future needs.

A wealth of statistical data continues to be compiled exploring the impact of the pandemic aftermath socially, economically and mentally. A report from McKinsey & Company in 2021 estimated that the annual impact of poor mental health on global productivity was $1 trillion. In the same year, the consultancy practice, Deloitte, noted in their *Global Human Capital Trends Report* that the impact of COVID-19 had meant that organizations around the world had had to look at new ways of working and operating – ways in which human needs must come first to ensure that people move from uncertainty to prosperity.

All this is also set against an accelerating drive of new technology moving industry from the fourth industrial revolution called the Age of Information (4IR) to the blurring of boundaries between the physical, digital and biological worlds of a fifth Industrial Revolution (5IR) that fosters a new balanced, collaborative working relationship between smart technologies and humans, allowing greater opportunity for humans to use their creative flair and solution-seeking abilities.

However, during the past few years, the global phenomenon of 'always switched on' has seen an increase in human stress and worry, exacerbated by the swift development and increase in the use of digital and agile technologies, plus human–robotic integration. The 2021 World Economic Forum report, *Digital Transformation Initiative*, estimates that technological growth will add $100 trillion to the global economy over the next ten years, but, in doing so, could cost millions of job losses across many sectors as 5IR becomes established.

The human imperative

As scientific research accelerates, both because of investment and from rapidly developing non-invasive technology such as nanotechnology, we are continuously benefitting from our understanding and knowledge of how we, as humans, operate as an integrated energy system.

How the human system is managed and nurtured in organizations, communities and government is central to how populations will continue to thrive, and avoid decline and distress, thereby having an impact on how societies and global economies will move forward against a changing work and life backdrop.

Ongoing advances in neuroscience are giving us a deeper understanding of how our brains are the 'integrator' of all that we feel, think, experience and do. Without sounding dramatic, this knowledge and application will determine the health and wealth of nations. We already know from studies that the exposure and reactivity to daily stressors can have a long-term impact on the risk of chronic physical health conditions, depending on how individuals respond to stressors (Piazza et al., 2013).

For a leader, understanding the fundamental importance and impact of good mental well-being and health within and as part of the organization is an imperative for the organization's cultural DNA, demonstrating what we are calling 'neuro-safety'.

Furthermore, as a leader with an understanding of the way the brain works, role modelling your values and purpose builds resilience in yourself and your staff because all the brains in your organization have a shared direction and clear goal, thereby maximizing the use of expensive human energy. By creating a thriving environment and encouraging a mindset where curiosity exists, mistakes provoke learning and all the available diversity of thought and ideas are used, and the results are shown in responsibility being shared and self-organized, not devolved to and circumscribed by specific departments.

As we design and build a sustainable future, the increase in collaboration and relational skills within the framework of 5IR heralds the era of being human within the workplace and the shared pleasure of excelling.

Neuroscience principles of stress

We have looked at the background to resilience and its importance in our futures, but how is stress manifested within us as individuals?

Stress experienced as distress is defined as the product of an imbalance between the appraisal of environmental demands ('stressors') and an individual's resources ('stress response'). Its triggers include everyday work and life stressors, as well as significant events such as bereavement, unexpected uncertainty, loss of status and income, divorce and war conflicts (Lazarus and Folkman, 1984).

In addition, the excessive work pressures of 21st-century life, the exacerbated emotions caused by the danger and uncertainty of the pandemic, and the consequent re-imagining of the role of work, have resulted in many people's mindsets associating stress as being unhealthy, having an impact on their mental health, and therefore dangerous and to be avoided.

While short-lived stress is a proper response to a wide variety of circumstances, it is the *persistence* of unrelieved stress from which the physical and emotional pathology of stress comes.

The brain is commonly seen as the main organ that identifies and mediates stress responses throughout the body (Osório et al., 2016). In our daily lives, low-level anxiety towards perceived pressures and stresses is a normal response and can be seen as our brain's evolutionary survival scanner monitoring for danger and evaluating the threat so that we can react before the danger is upon us (Burnett, 2021).

This threat detection system is made up of dedicated networks and processes involving emotional and physiological responses from within the nervous system, mediated by neurochemicals.

Cortisol is commonly seen as the stress neurochemical, released by the hypothalamic-pituitary-adrenal system that has a central role in regulating the response of homeostatic systems in the body such as cardiovascular and immune functions (Davidson and McEwan, 2012).

When our brains experience uncertainty, this has an impact on the thalamocortical network resulting in arousal chemicals flooding our brains. These, in turn, activate the protective behaviours associated with fight or flight and the physiological responses that influence the immune and cardiovascular systems as well as our individual emotional and cognitive responses.

This cascade inhibits the effective functioning of the prefrontal cortex (PFC) – a key component of the thalamocortical network that is particularly vulnerable to stress, shutting it down to limit the use of precious energy resources and so impairing top-down cognitive control. What this means is that our ability to reach higher-order decisions is severely compromised.

Reserving energy has significance because our brains do not have vast revenues of daily energy, being limited to 20% of our metabolic energy. Therefore, most people feel exhausted when their brains are emotionally aroused due to the triggering of their survival instincts and the depletion of this precious energy.

With the PFC offline and the limbic system, informally referred to as the 'mammalian brain', switching into more primeval survival control, our ability to be able to formulate abstract thought, focus, access our working memory, engage goal-directed behaviours and make strategic decisions becomes difficult, if nigh impossible.

Crucially, if chronic cortisol persists, it can lead to withdrawal from supportive relationships. Also, its toxic effect on the body and brain includes neural degeneration in the hippocampus responsible for memory consolidation and the imbalance of the body's natural homeostasis, which in turn can lead to poor physical and mental health, cardiovascular problems and a variety of other unwelcome physiological responses.

From these processes, we know that how a person thinks about stress may alter their biochemistry and how they respond to the stressors (McGonigal, 2015). The autonomic nervous system (ANS) is a central component of emotional response. Evidence suggests that, when the parasympathetic nervous system is activated, a host of beneficial neurotransmitters are released, transforming our stress response to an enhancing experience, thereby benefiting the general function and homeostasis of our bodies. Conversely, when we remain in a negative mindset, our brain and body believe that we are still in danger and the sympathetic nervous system is activated, increasing the release of stress-related overactive neurotransmitters, especially cortisol that, if left activated, can have a negative impact on our physical and brain health.

Strategies to build a resilient environment

But how to create and build a culture and work environment where resilience and well-being are part of the fabric, encouraging everyone to want to bring all their brains and the best of themselves to work and within their lives?

What follows is an up-to-date understanding of the modern neuroscience (the brain and nervous system) learnings that can inform preventative techniques to address anxiety and improve resilience that will benefit organizations and their leaders; and whose success or not has a knock-on effect to wider society and communities.

While role design, agile practices, reskilling, innovation and the like have an important part in organizational resilience, these performance markers will be harder to achieve if organizations don't have a collective spirit of energy, trust, shared purpose and a resilient mindset.

Those organizations that invest in developing a culture informed through the application of neuroscience, and so understand the role our brains have in shaping a humancentric company, will enjoy the benefits and rewards of engaged, motivated staff.

The meaning of this takes on a new importance if we consider that recent research suggests that it is not uncommon for people at work to only focus with 70% of their brains, leaving 30% of their brains disengaged and distracted (Lanz and Brown, 2019). If businesses are losing a third of the latent brain power available to them, and that is capacity associated with innovation, creativity and sound decisions that come from a focused and healthy brain, they are losing a great deal.

During the COVID-19 pandemic, a new term, 'doom-scrolling', entered our language. It describes the habit of scrolling through social media for bad news. Research suggests that, as individuals, our brains prefer either good or bad news dependent on our neuronal rewards network (Crum et al., 2013), which could explain why some people seem to thrive on bad news, and hence why reassessing one's mindset is so important.

Role of applied neuroscience and the brain's stress response

It is important to remember that our brains are all mapped differently, supporting different personalities, with mindsets shaped by the way our DNA expresses itself as a result of accumulated beliefs, cultures, environment, experiences and memories.

In their 2013 paper, 'Rethinking stress: The role of mindsets to determine the stress response', Alia Crum and her colleagues define mindsets as a "mental frame or lens that selectively organizes and encodes information, orientating an individual toward a unique way of understanding the experience and the corresponding actions and responses they take." Simply put, we predict situations through the lens unique to our individual brains and the mindsets we have established and through which we view the world.

My own study in 2019 (unpublished MSc thesis), based on the studies by Crum and McGonigal already cited, have also provided evidence that adopting a more optimistic mindset to stress by taking a 'stress-is-enhancing' approach can result in improved performance leading to greater attention, satisfaction, better health outcomes and, consequently, potentially healthier lives.

Furthermore, individuals who perceive that they can cope with stressors, seeing the situation as a positive challenge or opportunity, experience positive mood states that activate the parasympathetic nervous system, thereby increasing cardiac efficiency and vasodilation that increases blood flow. It also signals an approach orientation towards others and individuals interacting more with their environment, thereby increasing opportunities for cognitive, social and physical resources (Eagleman, 2015). Developing positive emotional states has also been shown to broaden thoughts and actions, building personal resources and increasing insights (Blackwell et al., 2015).

Conversely, the neurological circuit that governs the physical and chemical responses to stress activates the sympathetic nervous system associated with flight or fright, increasing the risk of mental ill-health and negative long-term effects.

As noted earlier, studies also suggest that chronic cortisol elevation – the stress hormone – results in the narrowing of attention and thinking, poor working memory and emotional processing, and negative re-evaluations, potentially leading to withdrawal from supportive relationships. If cortisol remains chronically elevated because of ongoing stress, this can also have a toxic effect on the body and brain, including neural degeneration in the hippocampus responsible for memory consolidation, which in turn results in poor decision making and memory recall.

The way mindsets modify stress

So how can we introduce the neuroscience of stress in a way that supports the modification of mindsets toward stress and not as always being something dangerous and to be avoided?

There is now enough evidence to show that how anyone perceives stress and its associated challenges positively or negatively can have a significant impact on healthy cognitive, emotional and physical resources, and that these in turn have a profound effect on relationships, life satisfaction and longevity. An individual's stress response is therefore substantially determined by their mindset and the perception and meaning given to the stressor or event that causes the stress.

Of significance to anyone's evolving perceptions of stressors and the stress response is the fact that neuroscience has demonstrated that the brain has significant plasticity (neuroplasticity) in structure and function (Keller et al., 2012). This implies that mindsets are malleable, and that, through new learnings or experiences, an individual's perceptions of a situation can adapt (Yeager and Dweck, 2020).

The study conducted by Keller and colleagues in 2012 tracked 30,000 adults in the US over an eight-year period. It asked participants to what extent stress affected their health. Those who perceived that stress affected their health and reported a large amount of stress over the past year had a 43% increased risk of premature death. This suggests that the "perception that stress negatively affects one's health is a proxy for negative expectations and that those with this perception will report their health as poor and potentially be neglecting their health care" (p. 683).

The 2021 studies from Carol Dweck and David Yeager also looked at resilience and mindset in relation to honing a more growth versus fixed mindset. While neither mindset is set, because either one can be adopted dependent on the task, these studies broadly suggest that those who have a more growth-orientated mindset are more likely to have higher psychological well-being and resilience through providing a protective barrier toward negative life events such as competitive and stressful situations, particularly when faced with setbacks as they strive to learn from the experience. This then implies that one's mindset perspective can be a catalyst either for impairing or improving mental health.

Conclusions

By taking an applied neuroscience approach, organizations can create cultures that promote and value the neurodiversity of thinking from each individual. Further, by establishing environments and practices that promote positive performance and mitigate against negative stress, they will relish the advantages that growth mindsets bring.

We hope that, by adopting applied neuroscience and brain-based principles, organizations and professional practitioners can support the re-evaluation of individuals' perceptions toward stress to see it as an adaptive, learning and therefore positive experience.

In July 2021, research from the North Carolina State University (Flynn et al., 2021) found that resilience was not a stable attribute but rather a dynamic process that fluctuated as individuals responded to a variety of circumstances and therefore stressors over time. They found that, when employees' experiences within their organization increased emotional exhaustion over time, this decreased commitment. However, those who scored high on emotional stability were better able to maintain higher levels of commitment. These are important findings for companies because resilience influences employee retention and, consequently, performance that itself will systematically have an impact on the bottom line for better or worse. What it suggests is that ongoing check-ins with employees are important, as are processes to foster resilience such as training, job design, work re-imagining and active well-being structures.

Some thoughts for future trends in the world of work

- As work becomes more automated with robots, artificial intelligence and growth in digital technology heralding the 5IR, change is going to exacerbate worries regarding job losses, lack of autonomy and control while, for others, it will be viewed as challenging and offering new opportunities. As a leader of change, how can you harness the insights from applied neuroscience to limit the activation of what could potentially be debilitating for those you manage?
- Organizations will need to be able to depressurize and de-stress staff using, among other interventions, honest conversations to avoid activating the stress pathways in the brain. Upskilling, retraining and role design are important components for both physical

and mental health, confidence and an individual's mindset toward their capabilities. These will need to be coupled with integrating resilience mindsets.
- Flexible, hybrid working arrangements and technology could have an impact on isolation for staff not engaged with others. This is detrimental to an individual's well-being and sense of worth, but also to their ability to learn, ideate, reach decisions and feel part of the organization's culture. Creating a balance will be one way of ensuring that people can benefit from relationships.
- Developing leadership that values human contact and concern will embed mental well-being into the fabric of organizations, thereby ensuring innovative and collaborative high performance and healthy challenges, especially with generational changes and more inclusive diversity.
- In 2017, the author of this chapter conducted neuroscience-informed research with professionals in the communications industries, introducing a brain-based perspective towards awareness of the stress response and how to use this understanding to develop a working model of how individuals can build resilience. Resilience practices had been used with at-risk individuals such as within the army, police and public sector, but this was the first research with a professional industry group. It used an existing resilience programme but with the introduction of a neuroscience intervention. The results suggested that introducing the context of stress and prevention from a neuroscience perspective gave participants the knowledge and tools to reassess their responses and view stress more positively, seeing it as within

their control rather than something imposed on them. The four domains that participants identified and believed gave them control over the impact of stress and their own perceived mindsets towards it are shown in Figure 2.1 below.

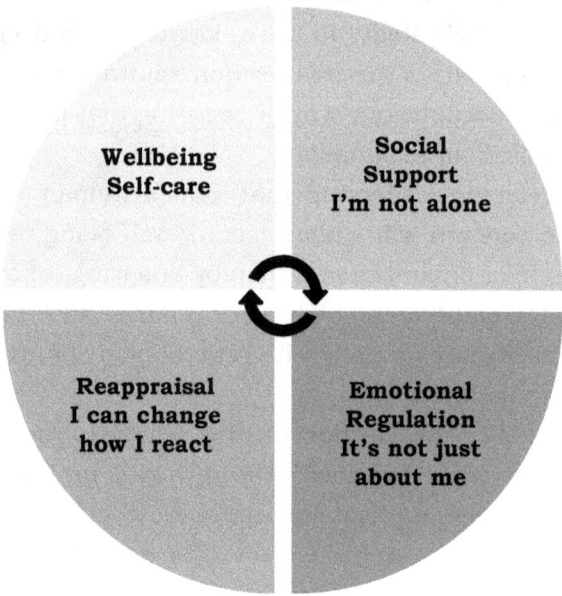

Figure 2.1 The Shaw Resilience Model: 2017©

References

Blackwell, L., Rodriguez, S. and Guerra-Carrillo, B. (2015) 'Intelligence as a malleable construct', in Goldstein, S., Princiotta, D. and Naglieri, J. (eds) *Handbook of intelligence: Evolutionary theory, historical perspective and current concepts.* doi: 10.1007/978-1-4939-1562-0_18. New York: Springer Science+Business Media, pp. 263–279.

Britton, G.I., Neale, S.E. and Davey, G.C. (2019) 'The effect of worrying on intolerance of uncertainty and positive and negative beliefs about worry', *Journal of Behavior Therapy and Experimental Psychiatry*, 62, pp. 65–71.

Burnett, D. (2021) *Psycho-logical. Why mental health goes wrong – and how to make sense of it.* London: Guardian Faber.

Crum, A., Salovey, P. and Achor, S. (2013) 'Rethinking stress: The role of mindsets to determine the stress response', *Journal of Personality and Social Psychology*, 104(4), pp. 716–733.

Davidson, R. and McEwan, B. (2012) 'Social influences on neuroplasticity: Stress and interventions to promote well-being', *Nature Neuroscience*, 15 April, 15(5), pp. 689–695. doi: 10.1038/nn.3093.

Deloitte (2021) *Global Human Capital Trends Report.* Available at: www2.deloitte.com/us/en/insights/focus/human-capital-trends.html (Accessed 3 October 2022).

Dweck, C. and Yeager, D. (2021) 'Global mindset initiative introduction: Envisioning the future of growth mindset research in education', 25 August. Available at SSRN: https://ssrn.com/abstract=3911564 (Accessed 3 October 2022).

Eagleman, D. (2015) *The brain: The story of you.* Cannongate, Edinburgh: BBC TV Series. pp. 29–31.

Fletcher, D. and Sarkar, M. (2013). 'Psychological resilience: A review and critique of definitions, concepts, and theory', *European Psychologist*, April p.14.

Flynn, P., Bliese. P., Korsgaard, M.A. et al. (2021). 'Tracking the process of resilience: How Emotional Stability and Experience Influence Exhaustion and Commitment Trajectories', *Group &*

Organization Management, 46(4), 692–736. Available at: https://doi.org/10.1177/10596011211027676 (Accessed 3 October 2022).

Fredrickson, B. (1998). 'What good are positive emotions?', *Review of General Psychology*, 2(3), pp. 300–319.

Keller, A., Litzelman, K., Wisk, L.E. et al. (2012). 'Does the perception that stress affects health matter? The association of health and mortality', *Health Psychology*, 31(5), pp. 677–684.

Lanz. K. and Brown. P. (2019) *All the brains in the business. The engendered brain in the 21st century organization.* Switzerland: Palgrave Macmillan.

Lazarus, R. and Folkman, S. (1984) *Stress, appraisal and coping.* New York: Springer.

Liu, J., Vickers, K., Reed, M. et al. (2017) 'Reconceptualising stress: Shifting views on the consequences of stress and its effects on stress reactivity', *PLoS One*, 12(3): e0173188.

McGonigal, K. (2015) *The upside of stress.* UK: Penguin Random House.

McKinsey & Company (2021) 'What employers are saying about the future of remote work'. Available at: https://www.mckinsey.com/business-functions/people-and-organizational-performance/our-insights/what-employees-are-saying-about-the-future-of-remote-work (Accessed 3 October 2022).

Osório, C., Probert, T., Jones, E. et al. (2016). 'Adapting to stress: Understanding the neurobiology of resilience', *Behavioural Medicine*, 43(4), pp. 307–322.

Piazza, J, et al. (2013) 'Affective reactivity of daily stressors and long-term risk of reporting a chronic physical health condition', Annals of Behavioral Medicine, 45(1), pp. 110–120.

Shaw. S. (2019) 'Shifting stress mindsets in a group of advertising professionals'. Unpublished MSc thesis: PDF 4860, Middlesex University.

Wilkinson, D. (2020). Emotional Regulation Course, Resilience Study, *The Oxford Review*.

World Economic Forum (2021). Digital Transformation Initiative.https://reports.weforum.org/digital-transformation/introducing-the-digital-transformation-initiative/

Yeager, D.S. and Dweck, C.S. (2020). 'What can be, learned from growth mindset controversies', *American Psychologist* 75(9), pp. 1269–1284.

Biography

Soraya Shaw is an applied organizational neuroscientist having achieved her MSc under the Professorship of Dr Paul Brown in 2019. With a background in global creative and strategic communications, Soraya consults with C-suite leaders and their teams to embed evidence-based neuroscience best practice, knowledge and insights into their organizations to empower everyone to bring all their brains to work. With a new world of work, life, learning and wisdom evolving, Soraya believes that by creating agile-led healthy cultures where divergent thinking, strategic and innovative collaborations, open communications and well-being are valued is the future of being human.

CHAPTER 3

Neuroentrepreneurship and Awakening the Entrepreneurial Brain

Christin Tan

We started

What comes to mind when you think of entrepreneurs? Action-oriented, business-minded, creative (ABC)? Yes, for those of us whose first language is English, we almost always start with our ABCs. Entrepreneurship is no exception. We often think of entrepreneurs as people starting a business – yet, truth be told, it is much more than that. The essence of being entrepreneurial suggests that we start something new. That makes all of us entrepreneurs to begin with. As a baby when we make our first cry, when we take our first step, when we grow to eat solid food – nobody teaches us how to cry, walk or eat: they happen naturally the more we engage in trial and error.

Entrepreneurship is like that. There is no entrepreneur who gets it right the first time. As with anything in life, nobody wakes and starts doing everything right. But everyone who wakes can start doing something new and different today. This includes the awakening of our entrepreneurial brain.

I started

I started this journey to search out the entrepreneurial brain with questions:
- What is an entrepreneurial brain?
- How do we know it is an entrepreneurial brain?
- What does an entrepreneurial brain do that is different from a non-entrepreneurial brain?
- What is the function or purpose of an entrepreneurial brain?
- What is natural to the entrepreneurial brain?
- What is not intrinsic to an entrepreneurial brain?

There is nothing wrong with these questions. In fact, they are good research questions and I plan to stick by them (or perhaps come up with new ones) in my pursuit of a doctoral degree. However, I do want to reiterate from the onset the importance of asking questions, seeking answers and accepting the fact that we may not always have the answers we need, or that it takes time to discover (and rediscover) them – as with anything in life.

The same applies to the entrepreneurial brain. It is not something we acquire from the outside. It comes from within, something we are given from the start. We all have a brain and that brain is entrepreneurial. While we may learn new knowledge and acquire new skills along the way (and we need to), the greatest starting point is to acknowledge within ourselves that we have it within us to be entrepreneurial. It is everybody's calling to start something new, do something different, or do things differently – although for what purpose, and to what end, differs between individuals.

I changed my mind

My own purpose in raising awareness about the entrepreneurial brain was so that I could change people's lives for the better. We know that entrepreneurship, as a catalyst for innovation and job creation, has significance for prosperity and well-being at the individual, family, community, societal and national levels. There is a wealth of research on entrepreneurship in business, management, economics and sociology but neuropsychology's contribution is yet to be fully exploited, demanding a more scientific, systematic approach to the study (Frese, 2009; Hisrich et al., 2007).

What started as a noble cause to change the world has resulted, I must confess, in my changing my mind. Not everybody is called to start a business, but everyone is called to be entrepreneurial – that is, to start something new, do something different, or do things differently that will meet a need, solve a problem, or simply because you enjoy doing it (great if you can get paid doing it, but that can come later.)

We change our mind

It is true. Before we can help others, we need to help ourselves – as we are told to do when aircraft safety masks come down. We need to put on the mask first before we can help our child (someone whom we deeply care about and feel responsible for) with their mask. The same goes with entrepreneurship. Before we can put together something that would benefit others, we need to experience the benefits ourselves. We cannot start a baking class or a bakery without first liking to bake or experience baking. Neither can we sell something online without first trying the product ourselves (technically we can, although the probability of it being a long-term venture is questionable).

This brings me to an essential point: there is no entrepreneurship without the entrepreneur – entrepreneurship is an expression of the entrepreneur. It can be an expression of how the entrepreneur sees the world, through art pieces that are created, pictures taken, images put together. It can be an expression of personal stories through words, books or articles put together in writing. It can also be an expression of the entrepreneur's imagination, expressing itself through graphics, videos and movies.

As with life, entrepreneurship is neither a static nor a linear process. Some get better at it by doing the same thing over and over again. Practice does make perfect. But that is only true when you think that what you are doing is already perfect, you just need to get better at it, only to be proven wrong with time because life is hardly perfect nor is anything a constant.

Most of us who understand that change is the only constant, and who want to thrive above the changes, need to start by changing our mind. It is like how we almost always see the same side of the moon because of synchronous rotation but from different angles (did you know that?). We can rise above our situation and any life circumstances when we change the way we think. That is the beginning of unlocking the power of our entrepreneurial brain. If we want to make that thought very up to date, that is 'neuroentrepreneurship'.

Why neuroentrepreneurship or the study of an entrepreneurial brain (purpose and function)?

There is a fascinating modern-day myth that people are either left-brained or right-brained. If we are more analytical and methodical in our thinking, we are believed to be left-brained. If we are more creative, emotional and intuitive, we are believed to be right-brained. While it may be true that the brain does indeed have two hemispheres, one left and one right, there is no research evidence to prove that the dominance of one side of the brain is the reason behind someone's personality traits (Shmerling, 2019).

We can of course study different parts of the brain and their functions. For example, there are three brain systems (reptilian, limbic, neocortex) and four lobes of the brain (occipital, parietal, temporal, frontal); and technological advances in neuroscience may be able to help us better understand the nervous system, including how the brain is structured, how it works, how it develops, how it malfunctions and how it can be changed.

But for those of us who are interested to learn more about neuroentrepreneurship or the entrepreneurial brain, we are most interested in how entrepreneurs think and feel. Specifically:

- how they integrate their thought processes to create whatever it is they understand;
- how entrepreneurship works from a brain-based perspective;
- how entrepreneurial abilities may be enhanced or developed both intrinsically and extrinsically;
- what can inhibit such development or cause the entrepreneurial brain to not function at its optimum; and
- how the entrepreneur's mind may be changed for a different (better) entrepreneurial approach and outcome.

What is neuroentrepreneurship?

Neuroentrepreneurship focuses on a brain that involves different types of thinking and the development of cognitive abilities to influence behaviour and improve entrepreneurial outcome. It is perhaps noteworthy at this juncture to draw a distinction between entrepreneurial brain and entrepreneurial mind. While the two terms are often used interchangeably, brain is a physical organ within the entrepreneur that does the thinking, whereas mind relates to the mental or cognitive process of thinking.

The essence of the entrepreneurial brain is that it likes to start something new, do something different or do things differently. It takes pleasure in novelty, challenging its limits (if any) and making new discoveries about itself and the world – be they real or imagined. An entrepreneurial brain experiences great joy when it is able to make something imagined come to life. In a way, it is a life giver. It has the ability to create something that is yet to be by giving it form and existence.

Take cooking or baking, for example. Ingredients can be common or similar, but the final dish that is served is an expression of the person making the dish. This person may be experimenting for the first time by following a recipe. From the first experience, they are likely to tweak subsequent experiences to try a different recipe, make the same dish differently, or create a dish or recipe that is uniquely their own. They get better and better at doing what they do, and the time taken to do the same things gets reduced as they become more efficient and effective.

An entrepreneurial brain recognizes that inherent in itself is the ability to evolve throughout its lifespan in response to new experiences. What that means for an entrepreneur is the ability to change your mind towards life goals (function), and how you organize your resources to achieve them (structure) with new experiences. While we may not know exactly how that happens (or how our brain actually changes neurochemically), we know when we change our mind about life goals and how to get there.

It is like travelling. We are planning for a vacation. Our initial idea of a holiday may look very different from the eventual destination and the journey we take to get there. If we are planning a trip for the first time, we may spend a longer time researching where to go, how to get there and what to do. However, with experience, the entrepreneurial brain is able to form connections with similar experiences that it registered previously, and thereby shorten the process of doing it or do it better.

This is why neuroplasticity, or the capacity for our brain cells to change in response to our experience is enhanced when we expose our brain to different experiences over time (Call, 2019; O'Reilly, n.d.). Exposing our entrepreneurial brain to multisensory stimulants is akin to feeding our body with different vitamins. If we eat only certain types of food, the nutrients we are getting from a limited range of food may not be as wholesome or holistic as those from a wider range (assuming all are healthy options).

Likewise, if we are able to stimulate different parts of our brain by engaging in a variety of sensory activities, involving sight, hearing, smell, taste and feel, this will help ensure that our brain faculties remain active and fit, as does the body when different muscles are exercised.

How is an entrepreneurial brain structured, or how does it work? (Brain functions come together to serve a purpose)

An entrepreneurial brain is inquisitive and fancies asking questions. It likes to ask not just 'why' questions but also 'why not?' There is joy at starting something new or looking at things tangentially. With the latter question comes the challenge and the figuring out of 'how' to make things work. How far can we go with the new idea, what new value can it bring to the marketplace, and how can it be made (more) profitable or purposeful?

Tan and Jellis (2012, 2013) in their study of entrepreneurs, identified 'hope' as having two dimensions: willpower and pathways. Willpower refers to the motivation and expectancy individuals have for achieving a valued goal, whereas pathways complement this willpower by providing psychological resources that help find multiple alternative pathways to the goal. This pathway thinking helps entrepreneurs achieve goals despite the presence of obstacles.

What is natural to the entrepreneurial brain?

An entrepreneurial brain is highly adaptive. It has the ability to process widely varied information faster than the blink of an eye, store complex experiences, and adapt to changes within and outside our body (Sincero, n.d.). An entrepreneurial brain is also highly resourceful. It has the ability to draw what is needed from multiple sources (sensory memory, short-term memory, long-term memory, working memory) and make the best with what is available to come up with an optimal solution.

An entrepreneurial brain is constantly scanning for opportunities. In a world where there is information and sensory overload, now more than ever before because we are living in the digital age, an entrepreneurial mind is not easily distracted but rather constantly on a lookout for opportunities or alternative pathways to achieve goals (highly opportunistic). It pauses when it perceives a seemingly compelling proposition (that is, when the opportunity has caught its attention) and it can, in a split second, based on complex experiences stored in memory, decide whether the opportunity is worth pursuing.

What we commonly term 'intuition' or 'gut feel' may well be based on previously analytical processes that have become automatic. Suffice to say, we all have a brain that is far more intelligent than we know or can imagine. And this is especially true of the entrepreneurial brain (highly intuitive).

Last but not least, our entrepreneurial brain is highly resilient. It has the ability to bounce back from adverse or stressful situations, not so much to return to the previous level of functioning but rather to achieve a new level of functioning that would otherwise have been impossible had it not been for the setback (Tan and Jellis, 2012, 2013).

What is less intrinsic for an entrepreneurial brain (but can be developed)?

Reflective thinking is what an entrepreneurial brain does to help ensure that this new level of functioning is bringing the entrepreneur closer to achieving their goals. Reflective thinking is an active, meaning-making process that leads to a deeper understanding of the experience and a deliberate consideration of learning before applying new knowledge to other situations. Asking questions like, "What did I learn from the experience?" and "How would I do it differently?" help to facilitate reflective thinking.

Self-efficacy is the positive belief or confidence in one's ability to perform specific tasks in different contexts (Tan and Jellis, 2012, 2013). It is an increasing, positive and realistic view about self that is self-reinforcing, which can only come with experience and reflecting on those experiences. Like any new sport or skill, we may not know how to play from day one. But with learning (starting something new), practice (doing something different), reflection and adaptation (doing things differently), pressing on and not giving up (being resilient), shifting gears or recalibrating when needed (being resourceful and opportunistic), trusting the process and going with the flow (being intuitive), we get better each day in unlocking our fullest potential by awakening our entrepreneurial brain.

What difference can an entrepreneurial brain create?

An entrepreneurial brain creates possibilities. It has the power to create something that did not previously exist. It is designed and intended to form connections – new connections – that give expression to visions, new ideas, new impulses and energy to want to experiment and try something new, or simply new ways of allowing the entrepreneur to express their entrepreneurial self. In doing so, it is able to gain mastery – a special quality of the entrepreneurial brain.

What can cause our entrepreneurial brain to function at its optimum?

While an entrepreneurial brain does not easily succumb to limitations, it can malfunction or not function as optimally as it should. The bidirectional connection between the brain and gut has come to the forefront of the medical research community in recent years. A troubled gut can send signals to the brain, just as a troubled brain can send signals to the gut. This is because the brain and the gastrointestinal system are intimately connected (Clapp et al., 2017).

What this means for the entrepreneur is an awareness that physiological distress, such as intestinal discomfort or irritable bowel syndrome, may be the cause or product of a troubled brain. While it is more commonly known that stress can cause irritable bowel syndrome, an unhealthy gut can affect entrepreneurial brain functioning and energy level. It is therefore important to take care of your gut health by eating healthily, drinking water or keeping hydrated, and sleeping adequately, just as these daily activities do good to physical and mental health as well.

Similarly, as we stimulate different parts of our entrepreneurial brain by exposing it to new experiences, questions, problems and challenges, this can help ensure that our brain faculties remain active and fit, as exercise does to the body when different muscles are used. Which types of thinking or cognitive abilities would you like to start developing first? Pursue new pathways and seek new learnings as the process itself helps to awaken our entrepreneurial brain.

Let's start: today

Like a toddler taking their first steps, learning how to walk despite falling again and again, so is the journey of our rising to our calling to start something new, do something different, or do things differently. Do you remember asking questions like, "What if I fall down? If only someone can teach me how to walk?" No! I certainly don't remember asking myself that as a kid – we just do! And walk we did. So don't take it personally if you fall down trying. It is not about you. Nobody wakes and starts doing everything right. But everyone who wakes can start doing something new and different today.

As we start the day anew, as long as it is 'today', we have another chance to try again – another opportunity to do better. Entrepreneurship is defined by both the functioning of the entrepreneurial brain and the action of the entrepreneur, and should not be narrowly defined by a specific outcome or end result, like a start-up company (Frese, 2009). Take action today, to be the best that you can be, in discovering your entrepreneurial brain.

In conclusion

Allow me to summarize by leaving with you a favourite quote:

Life did not promise us a bed of roses, and we only live once.

We owe it to ourselves to experience life to its fullest and, by awakening our entrepreneurial brain (or changing our mind) to start something new, do something different, or do things differently, we can choose to make life wholly worthwhile.

References

Call, M. (2019) 'Neuroplasticity: How to use your brain's malleability to improve your well-being'. Available at: https://accelerate.uofuhealth.utah.edu/resilience/neuroplasticity-how-to-use-your-brain-s-malleability-to-improve-your-well-being (Accessed: 28 September 2022).

Clapp, M., Aurora, N., Herrera, L. et al. (2017) 'Gut microbiota's effect on mental health: The gut-brain axis', Clinics and practice, 7, 131–136. Available at: https://www.ncbi.nlm.nih.gov/pmc/articles/PMC5641835 (Accessed: 28 September 2022).

Frese, M. (2009) 'Towards a psychology of entrepreneurship: An action theory perspective', Foundation and Trends in Entrepreneurship, 5, 437–496. Available at: https://www.researchgate.net/publication/261636907_Towards_a_psychology_of_entrepreneurship_-_An_action_theory_perspective_Foundation_and_Trends_in_Entrepreneurship_56_437-496 (Accessed: 28 September 2022).

Hisrich, R., Langan-Fox, J. and Grant, S. (2007) 'Entrepreneurship research and practice: A call to action for psychology', American Psychologist, 62, 575–589.

O'Reilly, N. (n.d.) 'Neuroplasticity'. Available at: https://www.physio-pedia.com/ Neuroplasticity (Accessed: 28 September 2022).

Shmerling, R.H. (2019) 'Right brain/left brain, right?' Available at: https://www.health.harvard.edu/blog/right-brainleft-brain-right-2017082512222 (Accessed: 28 September 2022).

Sincero, S.M. (n.d.) 'Neuroplasticity'. Available at: https://explorable.com/neuroplasticity (Accessed: 28 September 2022).

Tan, C. and Jellis, M. (2012) 'The use of an entrepreneurial personality measure to develop a sustainable human competitive advantage', Assessment and Development Matters, 4, 13–16.

Tan, C. and Jellis, M. (2013) Entrepreneurial personality for a sustainable competitive advantage. Germany: Lap Lambert Academic Publishing.

Biography

Christin Tan is a practitioner psychologist in organizational and coaching psychology by day, and a serial student and entrepreneur by night. She started her first business in her early twenties, and subsequently founded what is known to be 2wardsustainability or the 2WS Group of companies today. Graduated with an MBA (Entrepreneurial Management), MSc (Occupational Psychology), and book co-author of *Entrepreneurial Personality For A Sustainable Competitive Advantage*, Christin is pursuing her PhD in entrepreneurship psychology and applied organizational neuroscience. In her free time, she enjoys volunteering and mentoring entrepreneurs in social technopreneurship – that is, entrepreneurship through technology serving a social cause.

CHAPTER 4

Transformative Executive Coaching: Channelling the Chi 氣

Rita Shah

It was a busy Friday afternoon several years ago when I received an incoming query email from a company I had not heard of before. The company representative stated that they were looking for a professional executive coach for a leadership coaching assignment.

No information about the person to be coached was offered – just the general, please send us your profile and 'how much?'.

I was curious about this company – what was the nature of its business, how large was it, where was it headquartered – and I googled to find out more. It turned out that it was a leading global design and branding company with a clear pledge for sustainable and responsible business. There was an internal global environmental action group, sitting at the highest level of the parent company, and this gave the impression that the company was serious about its commitment to sustainability.

My interest in the subliminal effect of design on the brain, combined with the company's front and centre environmental responsibility statement, made it an easy decision: I wanted to start a conversation with them.

Fast-forward two months, after a series of interviews and contract negotiations, I was appointed executive coach to the Managing Director (MD), Tony. Little did I know it then but this assignment turned out to be one of the most rewarding and fulfilling executive coaching engagements I've ever had and we remain firm friends to this day.

> TONY: I was given a few profiles of a variety of coaches. After narrowing it down to three coaches, I spoke to all and immediately felt at ease with Rita Shah from The Success Lab. It was an easy decision. Over the following months, I realized it was one of the best decisions I have made in my career.

Tony walked into my office three weeks later for our first executive coaching session. We had agreed that getting out of his office environment was critical for him to focus on this highly personalized leadership journey, something he had never experienced before. I sought and got his commitment to be fully present during our sessions, which meant turning off all devices that enabled him to work remotely. Although an unthinkable prospect for most leaders, Tony was willing to trust me on this. In fact, he later remarked that he loved that he was out of the office and able to turn everything off throughout our coaching sessions.

This was a start to adapting his everyday behaviour. With my knowledge of the applied neurosciences, I understood that gaining Tony's trust even before we met for our first session was vital. I was aware that his brain might be ringing alarm bells because how we would be working together would be a completely new and different experience for him. And, as is natural, his primal instinct would kick in, questioning the validity of a previously unexplored way of working. In an environment of high trust, however, our brains signal safety, openness to new experiences and letting others in.

When I say 'my office', I should explain that it is not a typical office but a space that subliminally primes exploration, creativity and risk-taking. The neutral colour palette and minimalism evoke a sense of calm and expansiveness. The lack of clutter enables focus. The transparent, writeable walls give a sense of endless possibilities and foster imagination. All design elements were deliberate for the purpose I intended for my office. I was lucky to have an architect who understood the significance of my purpose and, with his expertise, brought it to life. Great design has a wonderful impact on how we feel, on our well-being.

So Tony and I started on the journey together having an internal environment of trust and an external environment conducive to realizing his aspirations. Our inner and outer selves – our relationship within ourselves and our relationship with the external world – were being mobilized in pursuit of the coaching goals.

Tony and I come from very different backgrounds and experiences. That was evident from the beginning. He is a British male who entered the workforce in his teens in 1980s' northern England. I, on the other hand, followed the typical path of a middle-class Asian woman, reading law at university abroad and embarking on a professional career. On paper, it looked unlikely that we would have what is known in the industry as 'coaching chemistry'.

Corporate organizations tend to want to match their leaders with executive coaches who have previously worked in a similar industry, and with a similar background, in order to understand the systems around the leader and to have a shorthand. One thing that they may not realize is that someone from the same industry might have some inbuilt biases. Such a coach is more likely to unconsciously steer the leader in the direction of the coach's own previous experiences. Arguably, the value of having an executive coach without those natural biases provides a higher likelihood of transformative work.

So how did we have chemistry? Tony described it as my ability to put him at ease immediately. All his worries about the process and his self-doubt vanished. He had never been one to speak openly to strangers on personal matters or to self-analyze. He had carried with him a feeling that he was not educated enough to analyze himself or come up with good enough ideas, especially to a highly educated professional coach whom he assumed was able to read every thought and posture. But, when actually speaking with me, he forgot about all the assumptions he held and was just himself.

When Tony came in for our first coaching session, it was the first time we had met in person. As we live in different cities, it had been convenient to have preliminary discussions by telephone and video calls. But, because we had already begun to develop trust, there was little first-meeting awkwardness. Our brains were tuning in to each other – anticipating signals, gauging boundaries.

One of our initial topics of discussion was the overall purpose of the coaching. What did Tony really want from this personal and professional growth journey that we were about to embark on together? We identified the big picture – that coaching would help him transition from his comfort zone of leading operationally to becoming a well-rounded MD. Throughout his career, he had been in operational roles and excelled in them. As MD, he had to learn to lead differently: to focus more on the long-term vision than the day-to-day running of the business. We then explored the areas he felt he needed to focus on during coaching that would be key to the transition – all this in the context of a non-stop, high-pressure and results-driven environment, with a high risk of financial loss if he and his team were not on top of their game.

We identified three strategic goals, and then articulated tactical goals to support the growth and development of each one.

While all this sounds, and is, rational and systematic, my primary interest was not in the strategy or tactics but rather on Tony himself, especially his willingness to learn and capacity to adapt. These two factors would be instrumental to how quickly he would feel the impact of coaching and how effective the coaching would prove to be in the long term.

GOAL 1

Adapt to working strategically, moving away from an operational mindset and approach.

It's no easy feat to change how you've been doing things successfully for a couple of decades. It's not just about changing your approach, your processes. There are many underlying emotions that may quietly impede your rational desire for change. The problems, what's wrong, tend to be top of mind.

We're inclined to focus on what's wrong – it's instinctive because our ancestors were always on alert to danger. Back then, it was literally a matter of life or death. Although that isn't the case anymore, self-preservation remains a strong instinct. But when the brain is focused only on what's wrong, all the energy channels into that, becoming stuck, unable to reach the frontal lobe of the brain where the functions of creativity and problem-solving reside.

My first step, therefore, was to gently guide Tony to reframe his challenges into what he wanted to achieve – in other words, goals – by changing the conversation into an exploration of what it would look and feel like being where he wanted to be. His energy, his chi (the Chinese expression for the vital force forming part of any living being), shifted quite quickly and excitement was clear in his eyes. He could visualize himself in that role and, at the same time, he saw that he needed to start thinking differently in order to develop the new behaviours that he recognized as necessary for an MD but were uncomfortable for him. The new perception of how he saw himself meant that his inner self could then readily search for and apply the new approach he needed. Once the brain makes a perceptual shift, acquiring new skills becomes a delight, not a drudge.

In order to make all this successful, so that Tony was not only able to transition well but also to transform his way of working and being in the MD role, it was vital for me to get to know him at a deeper level – his values and beliefs, his formative experiences that had made him the man he was today, how he made sense of the world or, simply put, 'his self'. I was interested in the whole person, not just 'work Tony'. Understanding him at his core would help me co-create a path with him that would be sustainable, not unduly difficult for him, and mean that he wouldn't drop off mid-way – in short, to create real long-term change.

So, Tony and I talked broadly about his life, what was important to him, the different kinds of relationships he had had throughout childhood and as an adult, his interests and passions, his fears, how he expressed himself. Among other things, I learned that he was close to his family back home, that he was a Newcastle United supporter and that his spirit of adventure had brought him to Asia where he had found a new home, somewhere to put roots down again. He did not have the expatriate mindset of moving from country to country every three years and, with it, a level of detachment.

Having got to know Tony, I decided to use a football metaphor to bring the transformation work to life. We imagined together that he was currently the captain of his football team, leading but also very much playing in the field. He was fully involved at a pass-to-pass level of the match. His team looked to him for guidance, for him to make every important decision – basically, for him to tell them what to do. The transformation we were envisaging was to get off the field – not just to coach from the sidelines but to become the football manager in its entirety, making high-level decisions and letting go of on-the-field daily operational details.

Putting the transformation in such terms made it very real: something Tony could not only picture rationally but also feel emotionally. My intention was to inspire excitement

– to make it visceral for him, not just cognitive. The head can decide but the heart is where the transformation happens.

With us both feeling the wonder of energy starting to flow between us, we set to work.

Perhaps the biggest stretch for Tony was letting go of his control of daily operations. The feeling can be akin to jumping out of a plane. Even with training and a parachute, you need to have a sufficient degree of trust and confidence in yourself and others around you to let go of control. Unlike skydiving though, this is a process, not an immediate action.

We started by assessing the existing positives. Tony had a capable team and very good working relationships with its members individually. He was the type of leader who was ready to interact with everyone and to be available, regardless of seniority or newness to the organization. His affable nature, coupled with a broad and deep knowledge of the work, made him well-liked and respected.

We then identified members of the team who were capable of more responsibility but perhaps had not yet had the opportunity. Tony committed to taking little steps to let go and transfer responsibility to those members he felt were ready. He would empower them to take greater accountability for daily operations, to make decisions and come to him with solutions, not problems. He would support them through missteps and help them gain the confidence that would help him gain confidence too. In doing this, his brain was starting its adaptation process while managing the stress that comes with change.

Starting this way was feasible and Tony felt a clear sense that it would work. The goal was that, eventually, he would be released from the minute details and gain time to work on the bigger picture and strategic goals.

Easier said than done, of course: Tony was always busy.

He was renowned for being available 24 hours a day, 7 days a week, something many colleagues in North America and Latin America took advantage of on a regular basis. In fact, he thrived on being busy. He enjoyed the hustle and bustle of operations, firefighting and sorting things out.

So, there was a concern that Tony would fill up his time with different operational work. To counter that very well-established behaviour that had also made him as successful as he had been, he agreed to set aside time every day to reflect and jot down what his future could look like as a well-rounded MD. We called it his 'Vision of Greatness'. He embraced this exercise whole-heartedly. Setting aside this time was in itself a breakthrough for him – it was the beginning of creating new neural pathways.

At the same time, Tony was aware that he found it difficult to concentrate. He was so used to 'busy-ness', dealing with multiple tasks at once, and always being available to his team and colleagues. We agreed that he would start to practise concentrating on one task, one problem or one piece of work in 15-minute slots every day. And, during this practice, his door would be shut. He shared what he was doing with his team and got their commitment to let him have those short breaks from them. He was training his brain to focus more deeply, shift from the constant 'noise' to moments of calm to think. He also began practising little moments of mindfulness throughout the day. After some time, he started to feel the difference, not just in his mind but also in his body. He recognized that he was no longer rushing headlong into a situation but, instead, taking a step back and assessing it before taking considered action.

Tony noticed that he was getting better results from his managers, who were also getting better at both delegation and managing upwards. His behaviour was having a ripple effect and a positive impact on his team.

TONY: I have pretty much stepped back from the nitty-gritty of the day-to-day operations now, although I am still involved in kick-off calls, discussions around challenges we are facing, or if we need to think out-of-the-box for some solutions and still have the final approval when needed. The only time I really get involved in the weeds these days is when we need to rally the troops, have a 'call to arms' to get everyone on the same page, to work extra hours, to get us through an important project or over a peak period. I have seen a huge difference in the team's response to me: on the one hand, less familiar with me; on the other hand, having gained more respect and I have seen them want to perform to higher levels.

GOAL 2

Craft and communicate his (new) 'managing director' brand and emerge from his predecessor's shadow.

Colleagues had known Tony as an operations man and continued to treat him as such. It was time to be clear about who the visionary MD was.

Tony wanted to remain true to himself as an MD but was struggling with that a little because he felt he needed to be what his predecessor was. In him, Tony had a model of what a successful MD did, how he led, how he behaved, how he got results. The trouble was that the two men had different personalities and ways of doing things. Trying to be like someone else was proving to be stressful and not at all helpful for Tony to make the leap from operations. It appeared that buried inside him was a conflict of identity.

Naturally, my professional curiosity was piqued. How large a factor was the identity conflict in Tony's potential to move comfortably from the football field to the boardroom, so to speak?

To find out, we crafted a few core questions for Tony to reflect on: What was unique about him? What were his personal values? What were his strengths? What value did he bring to the company as an MD?

We probed deeper into Tony's sense of identity, putting the focus entirely on him. By placing attention squarely on himself, he was able to directly challenge his long-held belief that he had to emulate someone else to be a successful MD. Answering the core questions over a period of time during our coaching sessions gave him the additional validation, comfort and confidence that he could be his authentic self, and did not need to strive to be like someone other than himself in order to be successful in his new role. He slowly but surely let go of the self-limiting belief he had been carrying both consciously and unconsciously.

Reflecting on those core questions gave Tony a deep awareness that brought about a resolution to his inner conflict and, with it, a renewed energy and purpose. He was a very creative man and his brain was bursting with ideas because his energy was now flowing, no longer restricted by misplaced beliefs.

While we were doing this foundational work, Tony continued to bring work issues to talk through. The open, honest and non-judgemental space we had established gave him the impetus to problem-solve creatively. Sometimes, I challenged his train of thought to nudge his perceived limits. Other times, we examined several ways to deal with situations, always concluding with clarity about the next course of action.

> TONY: At first, I wondered if what I was talking about in the sessions was relevant. I seemed to spend most of the time getting recent or

> current frustrations off my chest. Rita was a great sounding board and, unbeknown to me at that time, she was always watching and listening and posing questions that made me think about how I had the inner resources to overcome the frustrations. It's difficult to explain the impact this had on me and how I began to think differently about the challenges and frustrations that were having a negative impact on my performance and overall demeanour at work.

We also identified opportunities and forums for Tony to demonstrate his MD brand in action. He started to feel that his voice was equal to other non-operational colleagues' voices. He started to share his successes in managing difficult situations and engaging others to reflect and share as well. He initiated conversations about various projects, encouraging brainstorming and for people to learn from each other. And, through these considered actions, he found that he was gaining influence among his colleagues and senior leadership.

As he gathered momentum, Tony continued to build on his self-confidence and stood firm in his convictions. He also continued to be open and collaborative while putting his views forward.

> TONY: I have a brand and it's not just an operational brand. I am no longer in my former manager's shadow. I have a confidence in my abilities that has manifested in my additional roles and responsibilities at global levels. My current manager has confidence in me taking up his role one day and I am keen to do so. I am clearly taken a lot more seriously than I was previously.

GOAL 3

Develop a culture of innovation in the organization.

As we continued to delve deeper, Tony discovered that he viewed innovation as a threat. How could he instead view it as something positive, something to embrace?

When we perceive something to be a threat, we experience an amygdala threat response. The amygdala are two almond-shaped clusters of especially concentrated cells that are part of the limbic system of the brain, one on each side, inwards from the ear. They guard, control and manage the emotional system. They both monitor and transmit emotional signals of all kinds.

When the threat response kicks in, cortisol, the main human stress hormone, is released. And, when this happens, the normal creative process is prevented from flowing.

My challenge was to safely guide Tony to a shift from his unhelpful perception. The awareness of how he viewed innovation made it possible. Questioning what, in his previous experience, made him form the perception in the first place allowed us to examine deeply embedded beliefs and then to release them as purposeless.

One of the methods we used that proved to be powerful was a brain (or mind) dump: essentially to dump all the roving thoughts, conflicting emotions, clatter of conflicting voices on to paper in a combination of drawings and words. Tony had loved art from a young age and had excelled in the subject in school. The exercise of creating pictures of his thoughts and feelings felt natural and energized him.

The brain dump exercise not only freed Tony from his old beliefs around innovation but also opened up excitement and the many possibilities from innovating at work. We captured his excitement and the possibilities in a future-focused structure on paper. The shift had occurred. Tony's brain had adapted to thinking differently. And he has been able to influence his colleagues and teams in the same way.

> TONY: I have always been operationally sound, and now I feel I can more than hold my own when strategizing, analyzing and planning for the future. I have put aside time each week to give me the best opportunity to be a success at this. I work closely with colleagues across the region and the globe on the planning and steps needed to be successful. I am confident in my abilities and have overcome my fear of delegation. I now empower the right people in the right roles and find the balance between strategizing and supporting the operations team.

Tony's growth continued after our formal engagement ended. His new way of thinking and being continues to drive performance and innovation in his organization. He now deals with new challenges in a calm and considered way, no longer letting situations overwhelm him.

> TONY: The COVID-19 pandemic has sent a lot of additional tasks my way, needing good communications with the employees. And it was important someone who the team trusted delivered the important messages on the work from home and return to office procedures and expectations, as well as the difficult news on a return to Manila for our Filipino expats. I received a lot of good feedback from the employees on the way I handled some sensitive topics. For me though, it was not something I

even needed to try at, as I genuinely feel at one with the employees and this evidently came across to them all. We have ended up with no pandemic-related issues. People followed accordingly and trusted the company to do the right thing; and, as for the repatriation programme, we achieved over 90% retention rate when most people forecast a mass exodus.

I have come a long way in the past five or six years and a lot of that is down to the foundation laid down in better understanding myself and how to be more confident, and having the insight to look at things from a different perspective. I gained all of this from working with Rita.

Reflecting now on the two years that I was Tony's executive coach, I feel an immense sense of joy and contentment that the time spent had such a huge impact on Tony and that he continues to benefit from it to this day. Our journey together deepened my conviction that real and lasting change – in beliefs, behaviours and outcomes – can happen when working with or channelling, rather than going against, an individual's energy or chi.

I've tried to encapsulate the work in such a way as to give you, the reader, the essence, and to bring you on the journey with us. I hope you enjoyed reading our story.

Biography

Rita Shah is a Master Certified Coach (International Coaching Federation) and CEO of The Success Lab, a boutique executive coaching consultancy with a focus on supporting CEOs, C-Suite executives and women leaders. She is a Partner of the International Organizational Neuroscience Partnership (ION).

Rita specializes in one-to-one and team executive coaching, working with senior leaders to navigate the complexity of the ever-challenging and competitive business environment by strengthening their creativity, agility and resilience. She is an objective sounding board for organizational transformation initiatives and a trusted partner in her clients' personal growth. She goes the extra mile to support her clients and is appreciated for taking a holistic view of their lives. Her international corporate and commercial experience, and understanding of different cultures and motivations, enrich her work with leaders of all nationalities. She was honoured as a Global Coaching Leader in 2017.

Rita is also an abstract expressionist artist. She creates vibrant, joyful artwork that reveals something new with every gaze. Just as each piece is personal and unique to Rita, it also has the quality of evoking personal meaning for the viewer, as collectors who own her work have shared. Rita's artwork is in collections around the world from the UK to Japan to New Zealand.

CHAPTER 5

Trust and Excitement at Work: making a deliberate choice.

Emma Skitt

'Together at last'

There's nothing distinctive about the room we're in – a standard hotel conference room. Twenty people sit roughly two metres apart from each other. It's the first time this team has occupied the same space for 18 months, despite working together daily. It is, after all, late 2021 and normal life is still a bit odd. What's holding everyone's attention is the guy standing at the front of the room. A few minutes ago, I asked him to tell his team what he's proud of. His emotion is contagious and you feel your hair stand on end a little as he looks round the room. The relationships he has here range from 2 years to 20 years, yet their depth has accelerated in the past 18 months.

What would you say to this group, which has delivered astonishing performance in the food industry through one of the most challenging periods of the organization's history? They became 'key workers' in the UK's COVID-19 pandemic response, operating against an inescapable backdrop of fear and uncertainty, and delivering 'Christmas week volumes' over sustained periods while much of the country's population found themselves 'dining at home' 24/7. Record absence levels, paired with valuable loyalty, hooked the discretionary effort of every person to enable legendary performance numbers as well as flexibility of thought and action. Crisis management – delivering what we already know how to do well so that we survive the emergency – only gets you so far. This has been something else. On top of the record demand for food produced here on high-speed lines, the site has delivered the two biggest capital installation projects the company has had for over a decade. Handling any one of them – COVID-19 or either project – would have made the past two years 'momentous'.

As the guy at the front says, "We've done all three at the same time. It's staggering."

The guy at the front is Adam, the Site Director of a key manufacturing site at one of the UK's largest food producers. He talks to his team about their "incredible resilience", acknowledging that they may not feel it but he sees them as "thriving in the most difficult circumstances". He describes how overwhelmed he is by their commitment and dedication, and "the heart that comes to work" when it is so tough. He describes admiration and respect for the way they "care, passionately" about what they do, and for their functional expertise that he can always rely on. Yet, he emphasizes something else: despite the very different personalities across the group, he brings attention to their "interactions with other people". He pauses: "It's no coincidence that people stay here: it's how they feel about the place they work. That makes them stay."

At this stage, I had been working with Adam and his management team for 18 months. We didn't plan our work to be through a pandemic – in fact, the plans we made in February 2020 were turned on their head before we even started. But, here we are, with our goal to reflect on the successes, crystallize the learning and look ahead to how the site will continue without him. At 53 years old, he's been headhunted, unexpectedly, and will leave by the end of the year. I ask him to share what's important to him.

People perform better when they feel good about *themselves*

Before I tell you what he said, I'll ask you a question: one that I will be forever grateful to a colleague for posing during a breakout session in a neuroscience seminar (thank you to Catherine Doherty from the coaching consultancy, Fields of Learning): "If your salary was based on the amount of Trust and Excitement you generated in yourself, and others, how would you behave?"

This question has helped me to work more effectively with leaders and teams across a range of industries, and enabled them to make better choices around their actions. It connects with a working framework of the brain and, fundamentally, draws you to the principle that 'people perform better when they feel good about themselves'.

If we assume that we make choices based on our view and experience of the world – both the outside and the inner worlds that our brain interprets and creates for us – then having a framework to understand and manage those choices helps us deliver a future that we want – and one that excites us.

When I met Adam in February 2020, he had been Site Director for eight years at a large site where, previously, he'd been the Finance Director for 12 years – a numbers man, if job titles are to be believed.

If you have worked in manufacturing in the past 30 years, you will know the pressures inherent in leadership – the choices made by parent organizations to streamline, reduce costs, rationalize. This site was no exception. Over the past 25 years, Adam's site had survived downsizing, change of ownership, change in product portfolio, investment and growth. The employee profile was significantly local, often with a couple of generations of the same family passing through. Historically unionized, and modernized over the decades, it still had the feel of unspoken, quiet, passed-on collectivism that I had encountered 25 years earlier when I worked there, briefly, in the engineering team.

"I just don't know what it is that stops people," Adam had said to me at our first meeting – a statement that held genuine curiosity rather than being an impatient huff.

I was intrigued by Adam: energized by him. He talked about wanting people's lives to be enriched through working at the site. That didn't negate the fact that he wanted delivery, or that he'd spent eight years looking for a key to engagement. His frustration around people not fulfilling their potential was clear. And he'd explored theory after theory about management style, team working, culture building, looking (in a sense) for a 'unifying theory' that would unlock the invisible barriers that created ceilings, repeatedly, when performance on site reached a certain 'place'.

I'd shared with him the key principles I held close when working with any organization, and how I loved helping leadership teams to create the conditions for these to come alive. In other words, that:

- when you behave in ways that make people feel as if they matter, you increase the probability of their delivering great results ('People perform better when they feel good about themselves');
- the science helps you have an idea of what might be going on so that you can make choices that help you ('create Trust and Excitement in yourselves and others'); and
- it's not a logical 'A plus B equals C' – it's fuzzier than that and it's about how you talk to people in an everyday way.

We talked initially for just an hour. The site was fortunate to have had a history of investment in people's development and, being part of a large British plc, had some excellent working practices and forward-thinking influences. It became clear in our discussion, though, that there were some divides and barriers in the site population.

Nothing unusual in this, I have found over the years. The dynamics of the social webs that stay with us from school days continue to characterize workplaces. They're grown-up versions of 'he said, she said', the invisible (but quietly gripping) judgement of human hierarchies and power balances, and the excruciating (silent) embarrassment of being 'outside' the cool gang. Superimpose on to this the almost arbitrary allocation of an organizational hierarchy, with occupants holding a range of life-shaped response patterns, then give them responsibility for 'motivating' and 'assessing' the rest of the social web – and you've a melting pot of misunderstood intentions and off-the-mark communication. However, it sometimes works remarkably well, all things considered.

We arrived at two clear aims that Adam wanted to hold as the goals for his site:

1. People can have whatever conversation they need to create delivery.
2. People's lives are enriched by working here.

In the 'before' world that was February 2020, we had planned a set of interventions over the year to help create the conditions that would enable those goals. The site teams were not failing teams; nor were they in any particular crisis. But how to 'unlock' them? That was Adam's holy grail. Those few key 'things we think we know about the brain' that underpin the work I choose to do with clients had made sense to Adam in our first conversation – and helped him see that I wasn't selling him a 'mysterious blueprint to follow and achieve your dreams'. Instead, I was offering the view that it can be hard to find the key, because people are people. What we aim for is to change how people feel about themselves and each other – changing their brains, even? And I sensed that that thought caught his imagination.

Over the past 20 years, I have seen, increasingly, with clients that they know we don't do things 'to' people. We don't bring in a consultant to 'do this thing' or 'apply this' to them. Instead, they see that we're changing how we have conversations with people, so that it becomes possible to say what we need to say to each other – with the goal that we perform at our best.

My own, original, corporate employment history was with Unilever in the UK. This part of Unilever was known for pushing the boundaries in understanding engagement of people and what creates very different performance. From the age of 22, I was immersed in a world that expected cooperation, respect, honesty and high performance. It wasn't perfect – we got plenty wrong – but it had a thread running through it that viewed people as capable entities who could grow and deliver. This became my default or guiding view as I worked, freelance, with a wide range of corporate teams and individuals in my 30s and 40s. The neuroscience-based understanding I gained brought clarity to why the approach worked.

The activities and interventions I work on with clients are framed around 'getting good at creating Trust and Excitement' in the context of delivering the future they desire. We explore practical ways to do this, guided by the specifics of the organization, team and leader.

After many years of working in this field, I am still struck by how 'simple' is not 'easy', and how translating clear principles into human interaction in the real world is more likely to result in the Escape / Avoidance emotions than in the aimed-for Trust and Excitement. In reality, this shouldn't come as a surprise: our evolution as humans, with a brain that is trying to keep us safe – physically and psychologically – means that detection of threat is far more valuable for immediate survival. Yet, the resultant narrow focus and reduced perspective of the survival mode, with its accompanying short-term decision making and lack of new ideas in both innovation and problem solving, don't serve our increasingly fast-changing, competitive business world. Managing by fear just doesn't do the job anymore. Having a framework with a brain-based viewpoint helps us work out, individually and collectively, how to create the alternative.

Optimum operating conditions for humans

My long-ago study area was engineering – the cause and effect of anything fascinates me. I love to explore the 'human being' mystery in different business environments. In a manufacturing environment, you know – deep in your gut – that increasing production performance comes partly through exploring and finding out the optimum operating conditions for equipment and product. High-speed production lines – whether technically advanced or not – rarely operate on a 'press button and walk away' basis. They require familiarity, time, a lot of listening and much attention to small details, even when you understand the core principles upon which they work. This is pretty much the only way you can guarantee that your output will be anywhere near the design capability or specification. No matter how much you tell yourself that "It shouldn't be like this", that the massive investment you made in the kit means it "should work every time", you know, deep down, that that's not the case. Your relationships with that fact, with this machinery and with the humans who operate it, are what will make the difference. It follows that, if we cannot expect push-button operating excellence from something as 'designable' as high-speed packing machinery, then how can we expect it from the far more nuanced and complex beings who operate the machinery, or set the production plan, or recruit the teams or ensure product safety; or do every other important task that is required to produce food that's safe for people to eat. Adam and I hit one of my favourite areas of exploration – how you can get 'optimum operating conditions for humans', the people you lead, who work together on a large site.

What do we think we know about the brain that helps us become familiar with the nuances of people and understand their detail? Can it help us make the most of the 'illogical', and beautiful, way that people behave when they operate in the social web that is an organization?

I described to Adam how, as a leader (together with his leadership team), he could see it as the team's responsibility to understand, and to manage, their own neurochemistry. The goal of this is to have a further impact on the neurochemistry of wider teams and to create an environment in which everybody can be at their best. We (believe that we) understand that experiencing the emotions of Trust and Excitement creates a different set of conditions in the brain. It helps the brain to register less threat. It calms the response of the amygdala and creates a set of conditions in which the power of the prefrontal cortex can be more focused and, in consequence, effective.

Adam wanted himself and his teams to be more proactive, more creative; to communicate more openly, and to share ideas for solving challenges and grabbing opportunities. These are activities that we attribute to the executive functioning of the brain. I can recall the energy of the conversation when Adam saw how some of his teams' current ways of working were regularly, and unintentionally, creating the Escape / Avoidance emotions, thereby getting in the way of the brain's effectiveness in achieving everything they wanted. If he really wanted people – including himself – to take a risk in changing how they normally behaved, then we would have to find ways to make the environment one in which people's interactions generated more Trust and Excitement.

It was exciting in itself to talk about how this change would not come via a leadership statement, or a change programme that people had to sign up to, or even from skills training and team-building activities alone. It would come from one conversation at a time – one powerful relationship or partnership at a time – repeated and repeated to create different responses in people's brains. It would come through changing how they interacted with each other, regardless of hierarchy, or job title, or physical place on site.

The simple clarity of Adam's goal for 'people to be able to have whatever conversations are needed to deliver performance on the site' encompassed so many aspects and focused attention. The site needed to improve standards and make changes constantly. Could conversations help with this – with skills improvement, for example? Our growing understanding of the brain tells us that we build our skills more effectively when we feel psychologically free to adapt and when our neurochemistry is less cortisol-heavy, with higher oxytocin levels to connect us to others and enable us to trust ourselves more. Could conversations reduce the level of threat experienced? We learn and change better when our brain senses that "there is no threat so it is safe to try something new". In a threat situation we want certainty of outcome. Instinctively we know that, when being 'chased by a lion', we don't choose that moment to devise a new way to run; instead we rely on tried and trusted methods rather than be eaten whilst considering our choice.

Adam wanted to know what was creating the threats that triggered the Escape / Avoidance emotions in his teams. More importantly, could changing the way people talked and interacted reduce threat and influence delivery?

In keeping you safe, your brain will alert you to large and small changes in your physiology. It attaches meaning to this – meaning that has been formed and shaped over your entire lifetime. Much of this meaning is common to the wider social group, but yours has your personal 'flavour' shaped by your own life experiences.

The people on Adam's site faced the usual, tangible 'threats' that come from being part of any large business – a pressure on efficiencies and profit, and the need for the site to generate ever more money for the organization. In most large manufacturing organizations, the comparison between sites can give rise to a league table mentality, looking at efficiency, quality, safety and more in a comparative, and constant, drive to generate a bigger return on investment. In addition, at this time in the UK, Brexit was an unquantifiable threat to businesses whose logistics and materials supply relied on smooth exchange across the continent.

We explored more deeply into the real, but less visible, 'social threats' that exist in any group dynamic – the aforementioned social web – and our corresponding (human species) need to be accepted. The social web of belonging creates an inner narrative, which the brain assesses for safety as it would any other input. Our narrative contains our personal version of many questions:

Am I significant? Who listens to my opinions? Am I competent? Am I useful? Do my ideas carry weight? Am I influential? Am I good at my job? Do people like working with me? Do I get included in projects that are of interest to me?

The core of this is 'Do I matter to this group / team / organization?' If 'yes', then I can feel safer. I can feel more confident in predicting their responses. I can trust in myself and others. I can, maybe, let myself feel excited about the work I do, or the future I have. This 'yes' frees consideration of 'thriving' – 'Do I have interactions that make my day enjoyable and give me the stimulus I need?'

Because social dynamics can be with us from our early experiences, a team in a business can, under the surface, seem like a grown-up version of school. We can remember the positioning and the group dynamics of the playground, the classroom and the sports field. Who is important? Who is 'the best at x'? Who is in control? And who do people like?

The evolutionary success of social belonging is played out in the corporate world. In the brains of adults sit memories and patterns of what it was like to be a child in that social web, and what it took to thrive or survive.

In our organizations, we do things, mainly unintentionally, that generate the same Escape / Avoidance emotions. We can fear that we will lose our job. We can feel shame if we make mistakes or do not know how to do a task. We can feel a sense of disgust when people are treated in ways that conflict with our values. We can feel frustrated and angry when we are not listened to. And we can feel a sense of sadness when problems arise in the lives of work colleagues we care about. Similar emotions are triggered by events outside the workplace as well, of course. Every stimulus – a news article, a piece of music, a traffic light, an argument, a happy event, even the weather – is processed by our brain, alongside inputs from our 'constant companion', our inner narrative, where we express our meaning-making.

Exploring all this, Adam could see that he and his leadership team could play a part in changing the social dynamic within their organization. This could produce the tangible business deliverables for which they were accountable, and could have an impact on the second part of Adam's goal – that people's lives be enriched through working there.

We'd planned a set of interventions to get people together to learn about the brain-based framework that we could experiment with, and to practise how to generate Trust and Excitement in self and others. COVID-19 put the UK into lockdown before we could start.

What should we do? This was an unprecedented crisis situation: unknown, unpredictable and with potentially devastating real-world consequences for people's health and family life. It wasn't the time for 'culture change initiatives'. But, between Adam, his HR Manager, me and Mark (Adam's newest recruit who had worked with me while closing a large factory site two years earlier), we decided that this work was needed more than ever. Crisis throws people into the Escape / Avoidance emotions quite naturally anyway, which reduces performance if not managed well at the very time it is needed most.

We would take it step-by-step and see what happened.

If you had asked me, right then, whether I could be confident of results in an environment where we'd have to measure two-metre chair-to-chair distances, mark floors with tape to create safe zones and watch, like hawks, the air-quality meter in the meeting room before closing any window, I'd have hesitated. I knew my results were often sparked by my own ability to create an easy 'feeling' in the room with a team. I am known to build warmth and connection so that people allow themselves to engage with each other in a way they may not have done before. How could I be at my best in such a restrictive setting? A particular horror, for me, was the thought of working virtually. How could I commit to running team sessions on a virtual platform, when my Escape / Avoidance emotions felt like a temper-tantrum toddler, convincing me that I wouldn't be able to 'tune into' my clients, effectively enough, in front of a screen?

My own fear response told me that I would fail. My anger railed at the world for spoiling what we had planned. I saw these emotions reflected all around me as no-one 'knew' how to do safe and successful pandemic working. I had to extract myself from the Escape / Avoidance emotions before I could help anyone else.

Using the brain-based framework, I did a mini-version of the client work on myself. Trust and Excitement were needed – every piece of client work in my 18-month pipeline had been cancelled or put on hold in the space of two weeks. So, I did what I knew. I reminded myself of what I was great at, and what that felt like – re-reading feedback I'd received to tune into the impact I would create. Like a demon, I listed past successes and connected them to my strengths. And I reflected on what I did, regularly, to create Trust and Excitement in myself and others. I was building back a sense of Trust in myself.

The generation of Excitement was harder – it often is when you 'don't want' to do something. So I used some of

Dan Cable's *Alive at Work* (2018) ideas, taking 'short-cut' reminders for ways to activate, in his words, the brain's "seeking system" – thereby generating the Attach emotions. I used the "I wonder ..." prompt and talked with my close colleagues and friends, some of whom were in a similar situation seeing their freelance work fall away across the world as lockdowns continued. Our exploration was around 'I wonder what it would take to create magic with clients virtually?' My initial fear on hearing the experiences of those who had already done some virtual working gradually shifted into a (resigned) curiosity. I signed up as a participant on virtual courses to observe and experience their impact, imagining how my own strengths would translate in that medium. And I sought out experts in my network, acknowledging my apprehension and curiosity fighting each other. I realized that I was doing what I get clients to do – build certainty and safety, bit by bit and quickly – so my brain could let the shift happen in a messy, wobbly line. And then, as with most 'change' steps, you start before you're quite ready, knowing this is a live experiment that will teach you something for the next step.

How I work

My central approach with a leadership team is to start with their own understanding, habits and behaviours. Their impact feels like the lid of the organization, releasing / enhancing or blocking the delivery of others, so awareness of this is vital.

We start with learning the principles of the brain-based framework, practising ways to generate Trust and Excitement in self and others. Team members identify real places to experiment with these in their regular meetings and interactions – building them into their 'infrastructure' so that they are expected and normalized, and can be adapted as needed.

This is a truly simple approach that aims to minimize the 'tell' in favour of the 'show'. It has to be simple because the social dynamic is not. Every brain in a leadership team is reminding its human to stay exactly as they are. Only when conditions are socially 'safe' enough, as evaluated by the brain, can changes be made. Treating the new practices as experiments can help speed this up. It can reduce the 'pass / fail' feeling that triggers Escape / Avoidance emotions, which then reinforce their impact by reminding leaders that they 'should' already know how to do this. With experimentation, they can share the approach with their teams, working together for input and ideas. This unlabelled vulnerability of the leader is powerful. Silently, it acknowledges that their own performance relies on the performance and contribution of their team. It can build Trust, clearly, as it offers people a feeling that 'I matter to my manager'. It's also safe enough to trigger Excitement with a leader who will listen and collaborate when the answers are unknown, rather than inducing fear with an 'incompetent skipper in the storm'. This prepares the way for the leader to make more challenging requests of the team members as they build their goals.

Leaders listening and collaborating with their teams is not a new or ground-breaking strategy. My experience is that when someone understands their brain's framework and what their own, and others', responses indicate, then they will stay with the experimental behaviours longer, giving these a chance to be adapted and normalized. This offers more opportunity for the behaviours to be experienced as safe enough for more people to try, even after the novelty wears off, which can help to remove the 'change initiative' cycle that can leave people weary and cynical.

The broader 'frame' that I hold in my mind is, I believe, quite standard as a change process. Describe the desired future state; identify the current reality starting point; and create the pathways from there to the future. Seeing each part of this through a specific Trust and Excitement lens, though, shapes the methods and activities you choose, ensuring that you mix playfulness with stretch, encourage an emotional and vibrant connection to the future, and handle the current reality in a way that recognizes the scale of any obstacles and the resources the group can trust itself to rely on.

In team interventions, short or full day, I try to link an 'arc' of non-complex or straightforward activities to build connection and promote safety. I start with the self ("What have I done well?"), connect with others in the room (sharing strengths and listing successes and progress steps), look outwards at the team ("What did we do to create these successes?"), then look outside and more broadly to see what's possible. This is brought back into the team, partnerships and self to create the next steps. In this arc, the goal is to match safety with stretch at each stage – Support and Challenge always; Trust and Excitement always. It's never perfect – you feel like you're holding fizzy ideas and inputs as the group works together. It always adapts as the session progresses and you can't predict how much of either Support or Challenge there will be. And, as the Escape / Avoidance emotions are so readily present in all of us, getting used to each person's version of them and how you might help them shift towards Trust and Excitement in any moment is a delightful part of the job.

The simple activities

I'll share a few of these here – I used all of them with Adam's team, several times, both in person and virtually. They are always positioned as activities that can be done again, at any point, without facilitation. In this way, you help build the internal capacity of the team members to generate Trust and Excitement independently.

"What have I done well recently?"

In pairs, take one minute each to share the following (with no response other than listening):
- Something I did well recently: What did I do? What was the impact? How did it feel?

  Repeat with another partner: just 30 seconds each this time. What do you notice? Through repeated 'exposure' to this activity, people find it easier to think of things they did well. It's a seemingly simple, short interaction that does so much to build connection. Also, it brings the attention to people's own view of their capability and strengths. I find it a powerful foundation.

Successes

In small groups (3–5), take 7 minutes to list as many successes, accomplishments and progress steps as possible from the past 'x' months (often 3). Each group then shares their list with the others and I ask them a variety of questions about it:
- Do the people responsible for these successes know that each one is considered a success? Who needs a thank you?
- Which of these successes did you contribute most

to? Who gave you the most help in making them happen? Did you know about all of them (often no!)?

A powerful reflection is asking the group members to describe some of the team's characteristics or strengths that enabled the successes as a whole. This is often an eye-opener.

The 'successes' part is a key component in getting a shared, realistic view of a team's current reality.

Speed feedback

This activity needs connection to be in place for it to flow well. I always do it late on in a longer team session.

Pair people up: have them sit or stand opposite each other and take it in turns, 1 or 2 minutes each, to tell the other person what they love about working with them. I use the 'love' word deliberately in my briefing, thereby letting them know that they can go as near or distant to that usage as feels comfortable!

This activity does need a timekeeper to be strict(!) and to encourage people to either fill the 1 or 2 minutes or to finish on time if they are in flow. After the allotted time, they change partners.

If you're thoughtful in your planning and use 2 minutes per pair, each person in a 10-person team can share with every other person in about 20 minutes (9 conversations) if you manage the pair swaps well.

This activity often triggers quiet, nervous laughter the first time it's briefed. Once you start, the energy and noise in the room rise with each subsequent pair move and, by the end, it's hard to stop people. There is different laughter, more eye contact and usually a real 'buzz' in the room. People have usually heard comments about personal traits of which they were unaware and the 'giving' part has pushed them to bring the best of others to front of mind. In our brain-based framework, we would say it's likely that people's oxytocin levels rise during this activity – they feel connected and trusted / trusting. This feeling can last for a few hours and it's great to draw people's attention to what they've created.

In more than ten years of using this activity, I've had only one or two occasions where people have mentally 'opted out'. You need to handle this with lightness and experimentation so that they can stay out of the Escape / Avoidance emotions as much as possible. With Adam's team, I experienced both extremes. One pair couldn't offer more than 15 seconds to each other the first time. Other pairs had worked together for many years, yet acknowledged conversations during these speed sessions that both clarified the powerful meaning they had in their working relationships and reinforced the way they had supported each other through the difficulties of 2020.

Support and Challenge trios

This is an ongoing process that I usually set up as 'first practice' during a team session. We group the team into trios as far as possible (with a pair, or a group of four, if numbers dictate). After the session, the trios continue to meet as part of day-to-day work.

The aim is to create 'different' conversations between colleagues so that, over time, they grow their partnerships to enhance delivery. These centre around making progress on a specific problem or opportunity – sometimes individual, sometimes shared.

The process is named deliberately – Support comes first (feed back about strengths, "What I like about what I heard is …") to build Trust before Challenge is offered. This way, it's more likely that Challenge creates Excitement rather than creating fear / shame / anger, etc. Challenge is in the form of stretch questions based on what's been done well already. It isn't a standard action learning set: its power comes from what the trio learn about each other's strengths, motivations and thought patterns over time – rather than from ideas to solve the issue – and how they use this in their relationship to help each other's capability grow.

Trios are encouraged to meet for 1 hour every 4–6 weeks minimum, in addition to any other ways they work together. The meeting is framed as an experiment to make it safer to request contributions from each other. The 'conversation templates' I offer to ease the initial process are more like stabilisers, reducing the threat of failure or awkwardness as relationships form. One email I was delighted to get from one group, when I asked how their trios were doing, said, "Emma, we're so sorry. In our trio, we didn't follow your template at all. We just used the conversations to help each other manage everything that was going on." The trio described how they wouldn't previously have requested help from each other: they didn't have 'that kind' of relationship. The pandemic brought very tough issues to handle – both personal and work – and, for some, the trio sessions provided a lifeline to refuel and feel capable, trusting they could rely on each other as well as gaining Excitement and curiosity from what they had learned.

"How do I generate Trust and Excitement in myself and others?"

This is an awareness activity that also connects the group to each person's 'Best Self' understanding. Each person, in turn, shares for a few minutes the specific ways they have seen themself generate Trust and Excitement in their role as a leader. On balance, I would say that Trust examples are easier for people to access. This is not always the case, but maybe we are used to seeing Trust as a leadership characteristic. Excitement often has to be framed in terms of curiosity, involvement or engagement – sometimes joy – for people to feel it is *their* leadership 'thing'. Excitement can clash with the notion of 'gravitas' that people often carry as a leadership 'should' – it's often valuable to remind them of the brain-based framework and the role Excitement plays in delivering optimum operating conditions for humans!

With this group, we had both in-person and virtual experiences of this activity – the latter being surprisingly intimate, prompting sharing both ways. People described, verbally, their own behaviours with great insight and openness. The buzz that followed in the Chat when their colleagues added back-up examples to reinforce the individual's 'best self' moments was really something to experience.

Being a partner with Trust and Excitement

As a change partner, you get to walk alongside people at their messiest times, when the Escape / Avoidance emotions are the most probable. I think it's vital for you to be excited by what they experience. If you walk without that sense of curiosity, then you're missing out on one of the most powerful tools that you can offer, reflecting back your own Trust and Excitement response. Watching a group of people connecting with each other in the simple task of listing all the successes that they have achieved in the past three months offers a mini-masterclass. You take in the body language, and tone change, as someone proposes an achievement to be considered, or an area they haven't thought of, or one they've been involved in. You see what it means to people to have somebody recognize (even accidentally) who they are and what they do. This is not an earnest, considered strategic debate. It's often a '7-minute moment', scribbled on a flipchart or in the Chat of a virtual call, that feels unfinished and haphazard. Yet, it raises people's awareness of what they are actually delivering on a day-to-day basis – something that usually remains taken for granted or 'just doing my job'. You learn from them and respond to it. I love how, when people share across the small groups, they start to build: 'Don't forget this part' or 'Remember how bad that was at the start'. I love drawing their attention to how they do that. I enjoy the playful – yet deadly serious – way you have to keep them focused on what they've done well; even in 7 minutes. Our brains are so attuned to looking out for danger that the gaps and outstanding tasks sit front of mind. You help people to see that they do great stuff when they are 'just' doing their job – part of the Excitement is when they feel the value. This output gives them a chance to see the helpful patterns and the characteristic ways of working that they use automatically, and it builds Trust and confidence in their own, and their colleagues', abilities.

The path to the future that people want to build together is always bigger, longer and rockier than you would want it to be – this was no exception with Adam's team. The simple act of reviewing successes and working out how people made them happen starts to chip away at any learned helplessness within a group – reducing the tense fear that they may not be capable of making the next few steps along the way. It refuels energy and optimism if it is responded to, and guided, in ways that help people feel excited about what's possible and to trust in the contribution they make.

When I reflect on being a change partner, I notice many "I wish ..." thoughts. For example, I wish I had:
- picked up on one or two conversations, or voiced some of my observations earlier;
- prompted Adam more frequently to weave the practices into all his regular meetings;
- pushed harder on the planned brainstorming of the performance management process; and
- followed my gut more strongly with one of the less successful Support and Challenge trios.

There is another aspect of working alongside, not inside, a team. Maybe your own brain shows you the 'threats' to your position more readily than the successes you are enabling. Both you, and the team, get used to the 'new normal', so the three-way accountability balance between you, the leader and the team itself can be blurred and shaped by the relationships you build – or don't build. It's a further 'parallel play' of the social web, requiring a deliberateness that is sometimes slippery to hold onto. It continues to stretch my learning and curiosity.

Trust and Excitement in the middle of the change path

I was reflecting, recently, on one of the many unexpected bonuses of working virtually (no longer something that generates in me the Escape / Avoidance emotions). On virtual platforms, some meetings were recorded (for people missing) and most had Chat enabled, making it reviewable afterwards.

I could re-watch one of the group's (virtual) leadership team sessions we did in January 2021 and see it through a different lens. Everyone was exhausted after nine pandemic months. The seven minutes of success sharing was hard to stop – describing ways that people had adapted to run a 'socially distanced' factory, noting specific Support from each other with innovative problem solving and citing those incredible production delivery achievements against record absence levels. Re-watching it, I was taken back to their energy at the 'pockets of excellence' that were showing up through their experiments in building Trust and Excitement – they were starting to talk and listen more to help people feel they mattered. This was reflected in audit scores. The group delighted in sharing the turnaround of key individuals – some previous 'overt blockers' or 'cynics'; some anxious or nervous 'stay unseens' – who were driving solutions, passing on skills, speaking up in reviews and making a difference. Adam verbalized the real Challenge they faced. The benefits to working in this way were 'undeniable' and he wanted to find a way to embed them. I'm glad I have the recording. He said, "We want people to live in a fear-free world. How do we live and breathe it? How does it become who we are so it influences how the whole place operates?"

The goal was exciting – and potentially exhausting on top of what they had already created.

My role at this point was to hold the group in that see-saw place on the path where you've given everything, you've made great progress – but still the future you're going for seems far and impossible. It was important to balance the fear of that daunting gap with the Trust that they could make it possible and the Excitement of being part of something successful. I'd wanted to bring some confidence and certainty for the brain to register 'less threat', without tripping into the (well-meaning but sometimes toxic) positivity that can arise when teams are in the middle of building new habits around Trust and

Excitement. Focusing their attention on the magnitude of their achievements in a pandemic helped to bring realism. Sustaining new habits takes time even when you're fully staffed and not fighting a major crisis. To establish some of their 'new' practices (like regularly sharing successes or good news) as 'normal' (even if not yet 'permanent') during the intensity of 2020 was something to view with deep pride and was a reliable representation of their capability. It brought a tangible reason to be more sure of success, reducing threat signals for the brain, and building Trust in themselves and their surroundings.

My role was to help the group see these shifts as predictable ways that we respond, based on the brain-based framework. It is normal at this stage to feel exhausted and anxious and angry when the goal still seems so far away. Like a raised heartbeat as a response to exercise, the Escape / Avoidance emotions signal our brain's absolute commitment to keeping us safe (i.e., unchanged from what we 'are' now). The more familiar and accepting we can be with this pattern, the more we can learn our individual responses and 'recovery' habits to create safety for ourselves and our teams. Their initial frustration in 'We should shout more about the good stuff' could become, simply, the set-up for increased practice of drawing people's attention to what is going well. As one of the team noted in the meeting, "If we forget we're creating this, then so will everyone else." Habits take time as the brain adapts to what is considered safe.

Adam described, in this meeting, how much he was looking forward to his boss's upcoming site visit – the first in 18 months. It struck me how his straightforward, positive anticipation of how the ways of working and levels of engagement would be experienced by his boss demonstrated to his team that this mattered to him. By default, then, his team must matter to him, too. I wonder how often leaders miss this step and don't realize the power in showing their personal enjoyment when something is important to them.

Back to the Conference Room, Q4 2021

Let's return to Adam and how he talked to his team about what was important to him as he reached the conclusion of his years with the company and at this site.

On top of the tangible, site-specific delivery results achieved in extreme circumstances, he shared the company's recent, significant, supplier-ratings 'leap' awarded by one of its biggest national retail customers and how the site had contributed to that.

He also shared the acknowledgement he'd sent to everyone on site the previous day: "When you're going home and thinking you're not getting anything done, remember the challenges you are overcoming every single day, just to keep the site running."

He described how understanding the framework of the brain was "like a light switch going on" for him and how, right now, he could see the progress made in using it – a cultural shift that was "significantly changing the lives of a large number of people" built on how they were treated at work. The many examples of involvement and contribution he had seen across the site showed him that there were "many lives enriched by working here" and that this aligned with the responsibility he saw people taking for delivery of the bottom line and service.

He said how important it felt that his team realized what he saw in them – how they understood and accepted the fact that they were responsible for creating conditions for people. And that they knew the link between their successes and how other people felt about being at work. He loved that they knew what they were influencing, and the part they'd played in people's growth.

He concluded with a request as they looked ahead to their next phase with a different leader: "Think of Trust and Excitement. Please be excited about your future. Keep on the journey of engagement. Be proud of what you've achieved, believe in yourselves and your people and take this forward."

It felt like a brilliant conclusion.

The poet, David Whyte, in *Crossing the Unknown Sea* (2001), wrote that "the antidote to exhaustion is not necessarily rest. The antidote to exhaustion is wholeheartedness". I think that in this statement, without knowing, he showed what this working framework of the brain looks like in practice. You can't be wholehearted without feeling a sense of Trust in what you're doing. You can't throw yourself into being wholehearted if you're not Excited or curious. Wholeheartedness helps you feel alive.

Trust and Excitement may have no primary survival value compared with the Escape / Avoidance emotions but they help us thrive and grow. We want that in our organizations.

Let's conclude with considering that question again:
- If your salary was based on the amount of Trust and Excitement you generated in yourself, and in those around you, how would you be – and behave?
- What would be the impact if you chose to be, or do, that in your organization?

In continuation ...

On finishing the final draft of this – my first formal writing about what I do, so a first contributing chapter in any book – I reflected on the 'portrait' I had created of Adam and the work we had done together. I've always spoken easily about my work, but choosing what, and how, to write for this book has been a mammoth task, through which I've learned much about the heart of what I do for a living. Out of courtesy, curiosity and some nervous excitement, I sent the draft to Adam. Now, four months into his new organization and role, he read it and responded that night: "Absolutely wonderful", his reply began, and he described how reading it had made him feel quite emotional and re-inspired to engage this way with his new teams.

As a return on investment, I'll take that and celebrate.

References

Cable, D. (2018) *Alive at work: The neuroscience of helping your people love what they do.* Boston: Harvard University Press.

Whyte, D. (2001) *Crossing the unknown sea: Work as a pilgrimage of identity.* London: Penguin Books Ltd.

Biography

Emma's career has been in two distinct parts, connected by her fascination for results and the ways people deliver in organizations.

Her initial ten years, spent with Unilever via its Fast Track development programme, included leadership roles in manufacturing and HR, concluding as a European HR Director, aged 31. This formative experience sparked an appetite for working with human behaviours and the organizational strategies they shape. Since 2001, she has combined these through independent consulting work with national and global organizations.

Emma finds that joy at work comes through a delightful in-person and virtual mix of:
- coaching individual leadership teams to drive growth and transition; and
- designing, and delivering, engaging global programmes to build organizational culture change capability.

Emma's original academic area (Chemical Engineering, Imperial College, London) has broadened over 30 years with studies in HR and Business Strategy, plus the application of Neuroscience and Neurobehavioural Modelling.

CHAPTER 6

Soft Skills Through the Lens of Hard Science: insights into why leaders need to know about the brain

Gerrit Pelzer

Habe nun, ach! Philosophie,	Ah! Now I've done Philosophy,
Juristerei und Medizin,	I've finished Law and Medicine,
Und leider auch Theologie	And sadly even Theology:
Durchaus studiert, mit heißem Bemühn.	Taken fierce pains, from end to end.
Da steh ich nun, ich armer Tor!	Now here I am, a fool for sure!
Und bin so klug als wie zuvor;	No wiser than I was before:
Heiße Magister, heiße Doktor gar	Master, Doctor's what they call me,
Und ziehe schon an die zehen Jahr	And I've been ten years, already,
Herauf, herab und quer und krumm	Crosswise, arcing, to and fro,
Meine Schüler an der Nase herum-	Leading my students by the nose,
Und sehe, daß wir nichts wissen können!	And see that we can know – nothing!
Das will mir schier das Herz verbrennen.	It almost sets my heart burning.
Zwar bin ich gescheiter als all die Laffen,	I'm cleverer than all these teachers,
Doktoren, Magister, Schreiber und Pfaffen;	Doctors, Masters, scribes, preachers:
Mich plagen keine Skrupel noch Zweifel,	I'm not plagued by doubt or scruple,
Fürchte mich weder vor Hölle noch Teufel-	Scared by neither Hell nor Devil –
Dafür ist mir auch alle Freud entrissen,	Instead all Joy is snatched away,
Bilde mir nicht ein, was Rechts zu wissen,	What's worth knowing, I can't say,
Bilde mir nicht ein, ich könnte was lehren,	I can't say what I should teach
Die Menschen zu bessern und zu bekehren.	To make men better or convert each.
Auch hab' ich weder Gut noch Geld,	And then I've neither goods nor gold,
Noch Ehr' und Herrlichkeit der Welt;	No worldly honour, or splendour hold:
Es möchte kein Hund so länger leben!	Not even a dog would play this part!
Drum hab' ich mich der Magie ergeben,	So I've given myself to Magic art,
Ob mir durch Geistes Kraft und Mund	To see if, through Spirit powers and lips,
Nicht manch Geheimnis würde kund;	I might have all secrets at my fingertips.
Dass ich nicht mehr mit sauerm Schweiß	And no longer, with rancid sweat, so,
Zu sagen brauche, was ich nicht weiß;	Still have to speak what I cannot know:
Dass ich erkenne, was die Welt	That I may understand whatever
Im Innersten zusammenhält,	Binds the world's innermost core together,
Schau' alle Wirkenskraft und Samen,	See all its workings, and its seeds,
Und tu' nicht mehr in Worten kramen.	Deal no more in words' empty reeds.

Johann Wolfgang von Goethe, Faust

We are in one of the most beautiful seminar locations on this planet: a stunning castle at the foot of the Alps. In the room are experienced managers. They are looking at me with eyes full of expectation, hoping to finally receive *the* formula that will help them become even better leaders.

I am here to teach the leadership module of Salzburg's Institute for Management's Executive MBA programme. And I am dreading this moment when, after introductions, I will crush the hopes of my eager students by telling them that I do not have the formula they are craving. There *is* no simple 'how-to' solution for outstanding leadership.

However, the good news is that there are ways to become a better leader without 'giving ourselves to magic art'. It's not as simple as applying a formula and so it takes some work.

But let's take a step back and put things into context.

A burning desire to 'understand whatever binds the world's most inner core together' has always been a major driving force in my life. As a young man, I studied chemistry and received a doctoral degree in the natural sciences. I loved the accuracy, objectivity and predictability that I found in science.

Understanding 'the laws of nature' has brought humanity much progress. And, while we often complain about how bad the world is today, I am incredibly grateful to be on this planet now and not when Goethe wrote his *Faust*. Despite a global pandemic and many armed conflicts, we have never had a higher life expectancy, we can treat diseases that would certainly have killed us some hundred years ago and we can predict the weather in almost any place in the world with astonishing accuracy.

Mathematics is often described as the language of the natural sciences and it is amazing to see how mathematical formulae can describe almost anything from the flight curve of a ball thrown by a five-year-old child to the energy states of electrons in a complex molecule.

However, this focus on science, particularly in the Western world, has come at a price: we attempt to describe *everything* in mathematical terms; we try to see *everything* in simple cause-and-effect relationships; and we like to believe that we have the ability to control outcomes in any given situation.

I experienced this intensely while I held senior positions in the chemical industry in Europe and in Asia.

Imagine an organization dominated by engineers and natural scientists – like myself. We had all learned to apply the laws of nature and mathematics to control outcomes. We had also all learned to produce powerful but safe ingredients for your shampoo so that you can use it daily, if you wish, with no harm. It is critical to be able to produce this compound any time with the same quality at minimum cost in a safe manner, and so we worked out the best process that ensured just that. We would write down all the steps and all the details meticulously in *standard operating procedures*, which, naturally then, we wanted *everybody*, from purchasing over to manufacturing to packaging and delivery, to *always* follow. And, for chemical manufacturing, this worked quite well.

So far, so good. But, then, organizations often make a critical mistake. What we have learned from engineering, the natural sciences and mathematics, and what works so well in a manufacturing process, we then try to apply to all parts of the organization. (Interestingly, this is true for practically any organization, not only those driven by the engineers and scientists mentioned above). We like to look at *everything* that happens in an organization as a process. All processes have defined inputs and outputs, and, *Faustian-like*, we want to be in control of these processes. By following the ideal processes, we believe, we will always be able to achieve the desired outputs.

Strategic management in corporations is typically concerned with identifying where the organization is now and where it shall be in the future. Then, we develop the steps that help us to get from where we are now to where we want to be. We 'roll out' the corporate strategy believing in *simple, often linear, cause-and-effect dynamics*. A causes B and then, inevitably, C will follow. All we need to do is to lay out the process and make sure that everyone follows it. We believe we are in control of outcomes and, consequently, managers and leaders are held accountable for such outcomes. Hence, leaders attempt to run their organizations like machines, as if we were producing chemicals or running computer programs.

This approach has several shortcomings. One is that we typically do not know all the variables. Staying with the example of chemical manufacturing, we may know enough of the key parameters like temperature, pH, flow, etc. that enable us to produce the desired ingredients for your shampoo in a predictable manner. However, the overall organizational 'processes' are much more complex, if not complicated.

I recall a time when the company I worked for was about to be sold and I was put in charge of predicting manufacturing costs for the next five years. You can imagine that there is a massive number of variables that have an impact on the costs of hundreds of products over an extended period of time: demand forecast for each product, raw material costs development, labour costs, anticipated process improvements, currency exchange rates... Merely *collecting* this data took a couple of weeks. By the time the data was available, some circumstances had already changed and many of the initial predictions and assumptions had to be corrected.

How can one possibly expect to forecast costs over five years when the critical parameters cannot be reliably predicted for just a few weeks?

Nevertheless, estimating cost developments is still a relatively simple example. There is something that is even harder to predict in organizations: human behaviours!

I learned soon in my corporate career that an organization's success is critically dependent on the people working within that organization. This is true for any business in any sector. Strategy matters, but strategy does not drive results: people do. People create a company's success or failure.

When we ask, "How can I motivate my team?" or "How can we improve employee engagement?", the challenge is that people do not operate according to simple processes with inputs that guarantee certain outputs. They do not follow simple Newtonian mechanics or if-then rules. The process approach that works so well in chemical manufacturing does not work when it comes to 'managing' people. You can't operate an organization like a machine. (For more in-depth exploration of this subject, I strongly recommend *Strategic Management and Organizational Dynamics* (Stacey and Mowles, 2015).

Whether people thrive or fail depends largely on leadership quality within an organization. During 12 years in the corporate world, I had 8 different bosses. Some brought out the best in me and I enjoyed my work. Others, however, triggered in me a dread coming to work on a Monday morning.

Leaders can create the conditions in which people can be their best, where human energy can flow without restrictions. When human energy flows, people can achieve amazing results. Their creativity is unleashed, and energy flows into creative solutions and innovation. If human energy is blocked, people will put up a show at work. They will avoid risks and, if a situation goes wrong, they will blame others. Their performance will remain below their potential. Eventually, the most talented people will resign.

So, if there is no simple "how-to" operational procedure for people, what makes good leadership? What makes good teamwork? What motivates people? What makes us get up in the morning and do the things we do? And, perhaps more importantly, what *stops* us doing the things we say we want to do (like eating more healthily, exercising more or being nicer to the people we live with)?

After a corporate career, questions like these got me into executive coaching over a decade ago. However, I soon learned that coaching schools did not have all the answers and I became rather disappointed with over-simplistic approaches to 'behavioural change' or 'reaching one's goals'. Simple models like GROW (e.g. Whitmore, 2009) may be a useful starting point for beginner coaches and the GROW structure, of course, comes in handy in helping someone think through options and then define actions for the way forward to achieve specific goals. But, for the most part, this is a rational process that only works when the coachee already has the abilities to do what needs to be done.

What if a person knows what to do but something, what used to be called 'irrational', is constantly holding them back from just doing it? What if a leader truly wants to be more assertive or less micromanaging, but they are deeply stuck in old habits despite best intentions? Throughout the 20th century, psychologists have tried to find answers to such questions but with limited success. (Indeed, some psychologist friends of mine advised me against going back to university to study psychology because they were concerned I would not find the answers I was looking for.)

So, in my quest to 'understand whatever binds the world's innermost core together', I turned back to science and the field of *applied neuroscience*. There is still much we don't yet know about the brain. However, tremendous progress has been made over the past few decades since nuclear magnetic resonance spectroscopy enabled us in the 1980s to observe the brain functioning while its owner was still alive.

I started this chapter with the Executive MBA students and the bad news that there is no simple formula for effective leadership and motivating people. However, leaders can learn to become better at creating the conditions under which people can be their best more often – resulting in both higher engagement and improved individual and organizational performance – by better understanding individual human nature. Neuroscience leads the way, offering us insights into the mechanisms of human behaviour that psychology was unable to resolve.

This does not mean that 21st-century executives need degrees in neuroscience. In my experience as an executive coach, it suffices to understand some core concepts, which I elaborate on below.

There are three essential aspects that all leaders should know about the brain and the mind:

- *every brain, and thus every person, is unique* as a consequence of the way all individuals adapt to their own particular circumstances;

- *emotional processes play a more important role in human behaviour than most people think*; and
- *human relationships are fundamental to health, well-being and performance at work.*

I will be necessarily brief in my explanations below. The interested reader who would like to deepen their understanding may want to have a closer look at the following titles: *The Fear-Free Organization* (Brown, Kingsley and Paterson, 2015), *Buddha's Brain* (Hanson, 2009), *The Developing Mind* (Siegel, 2020), *Pocket Guide to Interpersonal Neurobiology* (Siegel, 2012), *The Emotional Brain* (LeDoux, 1998), *Rethinking the Emotional Brain* (LeDoux, 2012) and *The Deep History of Ourselves* (LeDoux, 2020).

Uniqueness

When we try to run an organization like a machine, or even when we take a more comprehensive point of view and look at an organization as a complex adaptive system, we take the approach of the natural scientist who believes that, if we know all the parameters that influence a situation, we ought to be able to predict, with reasonable if not mathematical accuracy, the future outcomes – like the chemist who can predict the properties of a compound when they know the manufacturing parameters such as pH, temperature and flow.

But this is where things go wrong in organizations: we assume that we can control outcomes. We have a theory – a strategy – that, if we do A, B will follow. This includes defining processes and procedures that, if only people followed these procedures, we would get the desired outcomes. But people do not always follow others' procedures: they have their own – well-embedded.

Or we apply a one-size-fits-all approach: we assume that what motivates Jane will motivate Tony, too. We assume that the conditions under which John is at his best will also be the conditions under which Jirapon is at her best.

You see where this is going. Nevertheless, it is worth highlighting that the uniqueness of each person is often neglected in organizational (and many other) contexts, although we basically know that every person is different. Nowadays, we even have the neuroscientific evidence for the uniqueness of each brain.

What is the brain for? Obviously, the brain is in charge of a plethora of tasks, from controlling all bodily functions such as breathing and digesting to complex decision making and planning for the future. A primary task is ensuring survival. But what is often overlooked is the importance of the brain as *the organ of adaptation*.

If we want to consider human development to the top of the food chain a success, this success is largely attributed to our adaptability to different circumstances. As its primary task, the brain has to ensure survival and survival depends on circumstances. This may be obvious when we think of survival in the context of our hunter-gatherer ancestors (our brains haven't changed much since then) in different climates or regions with different food supplies. But the task of adaptation goes much further and is much more individualistic than this.

We come into this world with brains that have no universal concept of what is right and what is wrong. We are born into this world and we need to find ways to survive under very variable circumstances. From day one, we need to find ways to make sure that we are fed. We cry and our mother, or whoever our primary carer is, will feed us – or not. Based on the responses of our primary carer – not only when it comes to feeding but also over the course of the following years in a variety of situations – our brains will learn to adapt to these situations, to form our personal models of what works and what does not, and to anticipate how to respond in any new situation (based on our unique experience of the past) in establishing what will help us to survive.

Each person's circumstances are unique and defined by genetic predisposition, the environment and the people they grow up with. As a young child, you experiment to find out what works and what doesn't in your unique circumstances – and so you learn.

To survive as a species over millions of years of evolution, it is critical for any living creature to identify and react to threats as quickly as possible. Also, in modern times (again, the human brain has not changed much since we were hunter-gatherers), your brain constantly scans for danger cues. With the priority on survival, your brain is not looking for optimum solutions by default. Its priority is to respond to circumstances as quickly as possible. It assesses situations constantly and decides in an instant, often without our conscious awareness (!), how to respond. If a situation seems familiar, the brain tends to choose a response that led to survival in the past. This is one of the reasons why we are 'creatures of habit' and why some habits are so difficult to change, even when, on a cognitive level, we *know* they are limiting our growth, damaging our relationships or keeping us from being the person we want to be. Survival, in terms of the individual brain's experience, trumps other desirable outcomes.

This also explains why, whether we like it or not, early childhood experiences can shape us for the rest of our lives. As we can see from Attachment Theory (cf. e.g. Sroufe and Siegel, 2011), the adaptations we make in the interactions with our primary carers have an impact on our attitudes, thinking and behaviours as adults, and can lead to behavioural patterns that are eventually incredibly difficult to change.

In conclusion, each brain, each person, is not only unique: each person perceives, interprets and responds to the same situation differently. That is why one-size-fits-all solutions do not work when you are in a leadership position, working with different people. Human behaviours are complex and do not follow Newtonian mechanics. What motivates you does not necessarily motivate everyone else. Circumstances under which Angelique thrives may totally overwhelm James.

When I coach leaders, they often bring up questions such as "How can I motivate my team?" or "How can I increase employee engagement?" I usually respond by asking these leaders what motivates *them*. Often, even experienced executives have a sense of what motivates them, but they have never actively sat down, reflected and put into writing the key factors that motivate them personally and professionally. This often leads to reflection questions such as in Box 6.1 below. While values are just one aspect of motivation, my coaching clients quickly realize the *uniqueness* of their 'set of motivational factors'. This leads to the insight that motivation at work is highly individual and the question, "How do I motivate my team?", too generic. In the best case, we can answer the question, "What motivates *this particular person*?" It may be a challenging task for leaders to understand what motivates each individual, but it is well worth exploring – at least for one's direct reports and other key stakeholders.

Box 6.1 Reflection questions for leaders – values and motivation

- What are the core values in my life that define me as a person? What makes me judge things as right or wrong, good or bad?
- What makes me get up in the morning and do the things I do?
- What gives me fulfilment and makes my life meaningful? What is my purpose in life and how is this aligned with my role as a leader?
- How well do I know the people I work with?
- How much do I know about their life circumstances and what motivates them?
- Why do they come to work?

Once you know these individual motivators, the art is in linking them to the organization's vision, mission and goals. Suppose there is congruence between the individual's and the organization's goals and values. In that case, the question of how to motivate people (including yourself) becomes obsolete: people who find meaning and fulfilment in their daily work do not need to be motivated – they are motivated. This intrinsic motivation makes the carrot and the stick dispensable because people will love their work. And it is this intrinsic motivation that keeps people going even when times are tough. Therefore, setting your company up for success begins with the recruiting process: by ensuring that you hire the right people whose values and ambitions match your organization's. When you make the wrong choice, you hire people for a job only. They will find meaning and fulfilment outside work. You will grow grey hair trying to figure out how to engage them. Eventually, they will jump ship the moment the opportunity presents itself.

Emotions at work

As *homo sapiens*, we tend to see ourselves as rational beings. Especially in what we call the 'developed world', we value 'rational' decision making and, particularly in the workplace, there seems to be no room for emotions. Once again, the focus on 'science' and mathematics as its language has led most people in the corporate world to become obsessed with numbers expressed in key performance indicators (KPIs), logic and a 'mechanistic' process focus as outlined earlier. When someone is labelled as emotional, it's not a compliment. More likely, it implies that the person does not have the necessary qualities to succeed in the organization. When a person expresses their feelings, we say things like "Don't be so emotional", or, when it comes to decision making, "Emotions have clouded your judgement."

Surprisingly, so far, neither neuroscientists nor psychologists have established any agreement as to what 'the emotions' are, and how to distinguish them from feelings, moods and states (cf. LeDoux, 2012; Brown and Dzendrowskyj, 2018; Siegel, 2020, pp. 230–271). However, neuroscience has provided evidence that emotional processes in the brain take place much faster than cognitive processes – and often without conscious awareness and as the underpinning of all 'rational' decision making.

Paul Brown has offered a working concept of eight basic emotions, described here and illustrated in Figure 6.1 below.

> Of the eight basic emotions, five keep us safe and let us know about danger, two get us closely involved positively with people and objects and action, and one pushes us in either direction. The emotions of fear, anger,

disgust, shame and sadness keep us safe or make us ready to deal with danger. They are the flight/fight/fright/freeze emotions related to escape/avoidance. Excitement/joy and trust/love are the two emotions to do with growth through attachment and belonging. Startle/surprise can take us in the direction of either escape/avoidance or attachment. If the likelihood is that it's going to go in the direction of avoidance, then surprise appears as 'shock-horror' startle. If on the other hand the likelihood is that surprise is going in the direction of attachment, then it appears as 'oh-my-gosh' delight (Brown, Kingsley and Paterson 2015, p. 9).

It is essential to understand that emotional processes occur in the brain all the time – and, again, much faster than rational processes and often without conscious awareness: our body can physically respond to fear in an instant without our feeling afraid. As Paul Brown frames it: "We are continuously emotional. The bedrock of everything we do and are is emotional."

Thus, scientifically, it does not make any sense to try to put emotions aside in the workplace but to focus instead solely on the rational aspects of our being and thinking. Not only are our emotions our permanent companions: they are critical to allocating the body's energy to where it's needed to ensure survival and build productive relationships. Hyphenating the spelling of 'emotion' *to* 'e-motion' emphasizes that emotions provide the *energy for action.*

Allocation of energy is critical for survival and for performance. The moment the brain perceives a threat, the biological fear response prepares your whole biological

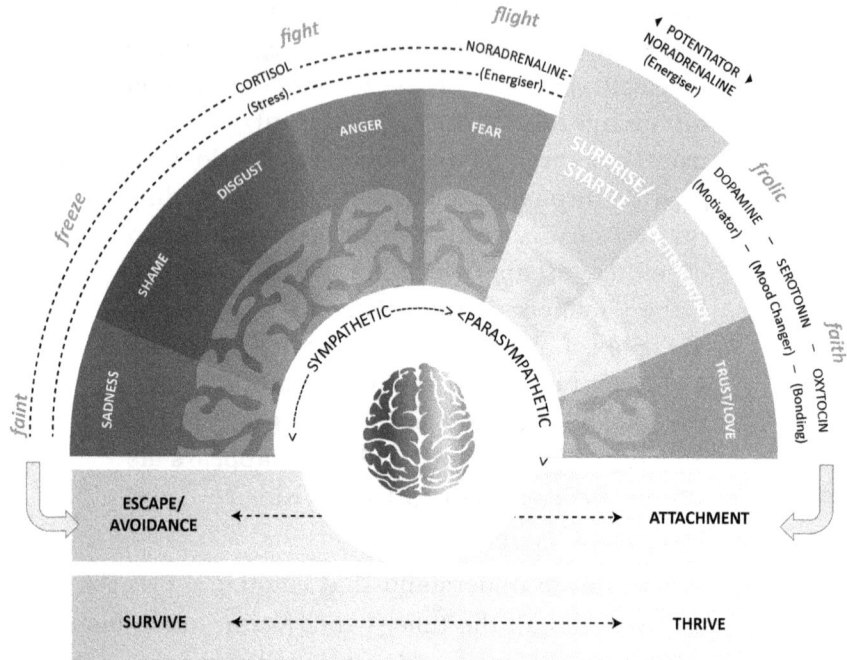

Figure 6.1 The London Protocol of the Emotions
ION Consulting International Pte Ltd 2023
see colour representation of this diagram on inside front and rear cover pages

system for fight, flight, freeze or faint – in an instant and, at least initially, without awareness and without cognitive control over the process. When our ancestors had to run for their lives from a predator, all available energy would be allocated to running as fast as possible. In parallel, other functions, like digestion, are shut down. When you are running from a tiger, you are not thinking about food or sex, and you are not thinking creatively.

Today, however, most of us encounter life-threatening situations less frequently than our hunter-gatherer ancestors. But, because our brains are basically still the same, they are continuously on the outlook for signs of danger. A threat does not always come in the form of a predator. Threats can also come from other human beings. So, we are also continuously, but largely non-consciously, scanning for potential signs of danger from others – in their tone of voice, for instance, or their facial expressions. The boss's angry voice or look is processed in the same areas of the brain and evokes similar physiological responses as the tiger in the bushes behind us when we were hunting mammoths.

Similar processes apply for the other basic emotions – for instance, sadness. When someone has lost a loved one or is going through a divorce, the brain, whether we like it or not, will allocate energy to processing these events. We can't 'control' or set these emotions aside by sheer willpower. Under such circumstances, people are simply *unable* to deliver optimum performance at work. Those enduring these encounters, as well as their leaders, need to understand that their responses to sadness are inevitable biological processes, not signs of weakness.

As Brown, Kingsley and Paterson (2015) lay out in detail in *The Fear-Free Organization*, leaders are wise to establish a work environment free from fear and instead nurture the attachment emotions of excitement/joy and love/trust. The *perception* of fear evokes modern variations of the fight-or-flight response, expressed, for example, in low employee engagement, absenteeism, high voluntary employee turnover rate, risk aversion or a blame culture. Conversely, tapping into excitement and joy in an environment of trust enables creativity and innovation, unleashes potential, and can make work meaningful and fulfilling.

How well do you understand and regulate your own emotions? And how do you nurture emotions of excitement, joy and trust in your organization? More reflection questions to help you explore your relationship with emotions are in Box 6.2 below.

Box 6.2 Reflection questions for leaders – emotions

- How aware am I of my emotions?
- How well am I able to regulate my emotions?
- What are my fears and how might fear hold me back or trigger unproductive behaviours?
- How well is my ability for 'empathic resonance' developed? Can I get a sense of the emotional experience of another person whom I am interacting with?
- How might my behaviour evoke fear in others, and what can I do about it?
- How can I trigger emotions of joy and excitement in the people I work with?
- How do I typically respond when a mistake is made?
- Am I giving feedback in ways that are perceived as well-intended and constructive? How open am I to receiving candid feedback from others?
- How passionate am I about my work or our corporate vision? Am I expressing my passion in ways that are 'contagious'?

The power of relationships

Another aspect of human nature that is regularly underestimated in corporations is the critical importance of relationships. Here, I am not talking about relationships in the form of 'networks'. Many leaders do in fact know that it is vital for their career and their company's success to 'know the right people', to maintain relationships with them and to know whom to talk to in order to achieve their goals.

I am referring here to relationships that establish and nurture human connections that are at the core of our being. This may sound esoteric to some. Talking about human connection in the corporate world is readily rejected or ridiculed, just like when talking about emotions in the workplace. The focus is on getting the job done. Human relationships and connections are to be kept outside the workplace. But making a connection with another human being is neither esoteric nor soft. It is a biological prerequisite for well-being and performance at work. It is also the foundation of mental health.

Deep in our core, we are social beings. As humans, we have always lived in groups. Relationships ensured the survival of our species over at least the past 200,000 years of our evolution. For our hunter-gatherer ancestors, hunting in groups was so much more effective than hunting as individuals. Relationships also enabled effective alloparenting – i.e. raising children by a group of caregivers in addition to the biological parents. Lacking hospitals and homes for elderly people during hunter-gatherer times, one depended on others to take care of them when they were sick. Being left alone or sent into exile was basically a death sentence.

Even in our modern times today, relationships are critical for survival. The moment we are born, we depend on others to feed and take care of us for an extended period of time. This caretaking goes far beyond nutritional needs. For instance, in the 1940s, Austrian psychologist René Spitz found that love and care are critical for survival. He compared children in an orphanage, cared for by professional nurses, with children who grew up in prison, cared for by their imprisoned mothers. Although the physical conditions in the orphanage were better, the death rates were significantly higher than for the children in prison: within two years, 37% of the orphans died, whereas all the 'imprisoned' children were still alive after five years. (Spitz, 1945, 1946). Did Maslow (1943) get it wrong when he put love and belonging in the middle of his pyramid instead of at the bottom?

After eight decades of research, the Harvard Study of Adult Development concluded that "People who are more socially connected to family, friends, and community are happier, healthier, and live longer than people who are less well connected" (Harvard Health, 2017). In contrast, loneliness leads to less happiness, earlier health decline and decline in brain function.

The COVID–19 pandemic has painfully demonstrated how the inability to maintain relationships with others due to imposed isolation has an impact on our well-being. And there is a reason why solitary confinement is considered the worst punishment for prisoners. Even the toughest criminals crave human connection.

The importance of relationships is also found in various theories about motivation at work. For instance, Sirota and Klein, in their three-factor theory of human motivation, recognized 'camaraderie', defined as "having warm, interesting, and cooperative relations with others in the workplace" as one of the primary goals of people at work (the other two factors were 'equity' and 'achievement') (Sirota and Klein, 2013).

According to Blickle and Hogan (2017), 'getting along' is a basic human motive besides getting ahead and finding meaning "because people always live in groups, they are inherently social and, at a deep and often unconscious level, need companionship and social acceptance – and dread rejection and isolation"

Furthermore, the quality of relationships in how we interact with others has an impact on our performance: in

1964, Harvard professor Robert Rosenthal had elementary school students perform the Harvard Test of Inflected Acquisition. Teachers were later told which students were expected to bloom academically and intellectually based on the test results. And, indeed, when re-tested a year later, those students showed intellectual gains and their teachers described them in many positive ways.

The irony was, though, that the 'growth spurters' were purely randomly assigned, not based on their actual test results. In other words, this is an example of a self-fulfilling prophecy: it was the behaviours of the teachers, based on their expectations of the spurters, that lead to improved test results, not the predisposition of the children (Rosenthal and Jacobson, 1968).

In other words, if you *treat* people at work like heroes, it may increase the chances that they *become* heroes. If you treat people like children, don't be surprised if they behave like children. If you treat them like idiots...

Modern neuroscience nowadays confirms what psychology and the social sciences long postulated: we are deeply social beings.

Daniel J. Siegel, Clinical Professor of Psychiatry at the UCLA School of Medicine and the founding co-director of the Mindful Awareness Research Center at UCLA, brought together various scientific disciplines, thereby laying the foundation for the consilient field of Interpersonal Neurobiology (IPNB). IPNB "explores the ways in which relationships and the brain interact to shape our mental lives. IPNB is meant to convey the embracing of everything in life from society (interpersonal) to synapses (neurobiology)" (Siegel, 2012, p. AI-42).

In this interdisciplinary approach, Siegel proposes that the mind operates like a complex system as the brain dynamically processes the flow of energy, information and the immediate experience of relationships – and does so not only in the brain but throughout the body (intra) and within our relationships with others *and* our environment (inter):

> The mind is an emergent, self-organizing process that shapes how energy and information move across time. This aspect of mind is a natural, emerging, and self-organizing dynamic process that arises as a fundamental property of the system of energy and information flow that is created in both the body and in interactions with others and our environment. (...) The way we are thinking here is that the complex system in question is not merely our head-based brain, but the system of energy and information flow that is distributed throughout the body and that is exchanged in our relationships. Mental life is an emergent, self-organizing process of this embodied and relational flow of energy and information. The mind is not separate from our bodies or from our relationships – it both arises from them and it regulates them (Siegel, 2012, ch. 1, p. 6).

So, what we call 'social' or 'psychological' is, at its core, 'biological'. Nothing 'soft' but 'hard' science.

Remember that an essential function of the brain is to ensure survival. Consequently, our brains are permanently scanning the environment for danger. The brain is continuously asking, "Am I safe or not? Am I safe or not?" This process includes the scanning of the signals sent out by other people. The sending process by one person, and the perception and interpretation of such signals by another, do not require conscious awareness: they are largely non-conscious processes.

On the most basic level, our nervous system helps us answer the question, "Am I safe or not?" or "Can I trust this person?" On a deeper level, it enables empathy – for example, *feeling*: the feelings of the other person. John receives Linda's signals. John begins to have a subjective experience of Linda's feelings in his mind. In an ideal case, this allows for a person to be *felt*, to be *seen*, to be *appreciated* and to be *joined*.

Think of a deep conversation with your best friend. Perhaps you are discussing a serious challenge that you are facing. The *trust* you have established with your friend, perhaps over years, and their *presence, authenticity* and *attunement*, enable you to feel *safe, seen* and *felt*. In the absence of perceived threats, your brain can make new connections and you can see things from a different perspective. This is why we get so much value from conversations with close friends.

Now, leaders do not need to become best friends with the people they work with. But, in any human interaction, the same neurobiological processes outlined above are at play: as a leader, your behaviours (including the non-conscious transmission of verbal and non-verbal signals) are interpreted by the people you work with. They are either indicating danger or safety. The absence of fear and the presence of trust prevent people from activating their natural survival responses (fight, flight, freeze or faint). When they feel *seen*, they become enabled to think more creatively and find new solutions to complex problems. *Nurturing the emotions of excitement and joy on a basis of trustful human connections is perhaps the strongest but completely underestimated motivational factor at work.*

In the 'science-driven' and 'rational' corporate world, the aspect of human relationships and connection is often neglected, if not belittled. Financial results remain the priority and human connection, empathy and compassion are almost considered irrelevant. However, the corporate focus on goals, KPIs and processes is neglecting human nature at its core. Therefore, my hope is that, with a better understanding of applied neuroscience, more and more corporations will create more human workplaces where people can enjoy their work more *and* develop the sense of flow that produces great results.

The third and last set of reflection questions in this chapter aim to help you explore your capacity to establish and maintain productive relationships in the workplace – see Box 6.3 below.

Box 6.3 Reflection questions for leaders – relationships

- At work today, have I made genuine connections with people? How?
- How do I think about individuals at work? Do I believe in their potential? If not, how might my attitude towards them, non-consciously expressed through my verbal and non-verbal cues and behaviours, limit them in utilising their full potential?
- How aware am I of the verbal and non-verbal signals that I am sending?
- How authentic am I in my interactions with others? Am I building trust?
- How can I help employees maintain healthy relationships when working from home and interacting with team members remotely?

Conclusion

To deal effectively with today's challenges, corporations will have to make use of the collective intelligence of the people working for them. The leader's job is to create the conditions in which people can be their best. This requires an understanding of how humans operate, which in turn requires an understanding of how the human brain and mind operate. Leaders do not have to become fully fledged neuroscientists, but they do need to understand and apply – at minimum – three key aspects of human nature:

First, each person is a unique individual. Therefore, what motivates one person is different from what motivates another. Leaders need to understand their own motivations and those of the people they work with. Intrinsic motivation is based on having one's values regularly fulfilled at work.

Second, emotions are critical to releasing or blocking human energy at work. Leaders need to avoid behaviours that trigger fear responses. Instead, they need to nurture feelings of excitement, joy and trust.

Third, relationships matter. Genuine human connections at work based on trust enable people to be their best.

References

Blickle G. and Hogan R. (2017) 'Socioanalytic Perspective' in Zeigler-Hill, V. and Shackelford T. (eds) *Encyclopedia of Personality and Individual Differences*. Springer, Cham, pp. 1–5. Available at: https://doi.org/10.1007/978-3-319-28099-8_1186-1 (Accessed 2 November 2022).

Brown, P. and Dzendrowskyj, T. (2018) 'Sorting out an emotional muddle: Insights from neuroscience on the organizational value of emotions', *Developing Leaders*, Issue 29. Available at: https://www.developingleadersquarterly.com/fb/Developing-Leaders-issue-29-Spring-2018/26/

Brown, P., Kingsley, J. and Paterson, S. (2015) *The fear-free organization: Vital insights from neuroscience to transform your business culture*. London: Kogan Page.

Hanson, R. (2009) *Buddha's brain. The practical neuroscience of happiness, love, and wisdom*. Oakland: New Harbinger Publications.

Harvard Health (2017) 'Can relationships boost longevity and well-being?' Available at: https://www.health.harvard.edu/mental-health/can-relationships-boost-longevity-and-well-being (Accessed 2 November 2022).

LeDoux, J. (1998) *The emotional brain. The mysterious underpinnings of emotional life*. New York: Simon & Schuster.

LeDoux, J. (2012) 'Rethinking the emotional brain', *Neuron* 73, Elsevier Inc., pp. 653–676.

LeDoux, J. (2019) *The deep history of ourselves. The four-billion-year story of how we got conscious brains*. New York: Viking.

Maslow, A.H. (1943) 'A theory of human motivation', *Psychological Review*, 50(4), pp. 370–396.

Rosenthal, R. and Jacobson, L. (1968) 'Pygmalion in the classroom', *The Urban Review*, 3(1), pp. 16–20. Available at: https://doi.org/10.1007/BF02322211 (Accessed 2 November 2022).

Siegel, D.J. (2012) *Pocket guide to Interpersonal Neurobiology: An integrative handbook of the mind*. New York: W.W. Norton.

Siegel, D.J. (2020) *The developing mind: how relationships and the brain interact to shape who we are,* 3rd edn. New York: The Guilford Press.

Sirota, D. and Klein, D.A. (2013) *The enthusiastic employee: How companies profit by giving workers what they want,* 2nd edn. Upper Saddle River, New Jersey: Pearson Education.

Spitz, R.Á. (1945) 'Hospitalism', in. Eissler, R.S. (ed.) *The psychoanalytic study of the child (Vol. I).* New York: International Universities Press, pp. 53–74.

Spitz, R. Á. (1946) 'Hospitalism: A follow-up report' in Eissler, R.S. (ed.) *The psychoanalytic study of the child* (Vol. II). New York: International Universities Press, pp. 113–117.

Sroufe, A. and Siegel, D.J. (2011) 'The verdict is in. The case for attachment theory', *Psychotherapy Networker,* March/April, 35, pp. 34–39.

Stacey, R.D. and Mowles, C. (2015) *Strategic management and organizational dynamics,* 7th edn. Harlow: Pearson Education.

von Goethe, J.W. (2019; original text ca. 1808) *Faust.* 2nd edn. Schöne, A. ed. City: Deutscher Klassiker Verlag, pp. 33–34. English translation from https://www.poetryintranslation.com/PITBR/German/FaustIScenesItoIII.php (Accessed 2 November 2022).

Whitmore, J. (2009) *Coaching for Performance: GROWing human potential and purpose.* 4th edn. London: Nicholas Brealey.

Biography

Dr Gerrit Pelzer is passionate about helping leaders in multinational corporations to create the conditions under which people can be their very best.

Gerrit is an Executive Coach, a Coach Supervisor and an Adjunct Professor of Leadership. He co-hosts 'Second Crack – The Leadership Podcast' and is a Founding Partner of 'The ION Partnership'.

He combines over 12 years of coaching executives with his own leadership experience in Europe and Asia. Thus, he can relate to today's leaders' issues, speak their language, and provide practical steps to help them and their teams grow.

With a background in the natural sciences, Gerrit also takes a scientific approach to coaching, especially in using the latest insights from applied neuroscience to achieve positive behavioural changes that last. Spending many years in Asia, however, has led him to add wisdom from Zen Buddhism to his practice, thereby creating a unique and holistic approach to executive coaching

CHAPTER 7

The Transience of Teams

Sim Peng Thia

Naïve and in a new world

I started my working life as a weapons systems engineer. Six months into the job, and together with three other engineers, I was sent to the US on a technology transfer assignment. The goal of our assignment was clear – we were to return with a full grasp of this new technology system that our company had acquired. It was a technically challenging and exciting project, especially for an engineer fresh out of school. In hindsight, however, what made it interesting was how the four of us – practically strangers – were thrown into a 'team', and expected to simply deliver the stated goal. We had to form, storm, norm (and eventually mourn), all within six months (which turned into nine). We simply had to 'get on with it'.

Our team consisted of four engineers across different disciplines. I was the most inexperienced and the only woman. Two others were in their mid- to late-20s, and the most senior, who would become our de facto team leader, was in his early 30s. Two of us were new to the organization and no-one knew each other well or at all. After a short meet-up and briefing by the project head, we packed our bags and headed to the US.

As the youngest in my family, I had always been told: "Just focus on your studies, don't worry about anything else." It was a comfortable and protected place to be in, but it also meant that I seldom looked at the world beyond my own narrow focus on self. Even when I tried to offer up my two cents on a situation, I was often silenced or my suggestion would be mocked, and I learned never to speak up. In order to gain approval (to survive, really, as a young child) among the adults in my life, I had to keep within the narrow bounds of the known rules in my behaviour and minimize my outbursts.

Accustomed to merging with the wallpaper as my primary survival tactic, I panicked on arriving in the US. I was thrust into a role that required me to proactively probe and ask – to stand out and to be heard (horrors!) – in an environment that was by default defensive and wary of my presence. Exacerbating this, I was in a foreign country, living and working with a bunch of practically strangers, away from my very protective family. I had an amygdala hijack and my brain went into fight mode (and on many occasions contemplated flight mode).

The next youngest member of the team was in his early 20s and this was also his first job out of university. He and I were both electrical and electronics engineers. He came across as a serious person and a diligent worker. I found him distant and intimidating at first but, after our first month in the US, I saw his more playful, personable side: he was a young man trying to do his best in his job.

We also had an aeronautical engineer on our team. He had joined us from another firm around the same time I had. Friendly and open, he was kind but also candid with his comments. It is fair to say that, while his IQ was likely quite high, his EQ needed some work. However, he took his work seriously and wanted to do what he thought was the right thing. I could connect with him quite easily from the start, but I could tell there were some tensions with some of the others in the office as he tried to find his way around the new office dynamics.

Thankfully, we had in our team Alan, a mechanical engineer. In his early 30s, he was newly married and looking forward to building a family and life with his wife. He had been an officer within an elite unit of the Singapore Armed Forces during his National Service years and he became the de facto leader of our team. With his natural inclination to lead and his seniority both in years and work experience, it was easy for the rest of us to fall in line. For the boys, Alan's rank and vocation during his National Service days helped. But I don't think it was necessary – Alan led by example, holding himself to high standards, both morally and professionally. I never truly appreciated him for his leadership, but in hindsight this was not only critical to the success of the assignment but also enabled our shared experience as a team to be a positive one.

How did we perform? Thrown into a foreign culture and an environment that viewed us as alien, at best a nuisance and at worst unreasonably probing, the cultural challenges and tension in dynamics resulted in our being firmly positioned as 'outsiders'. We had to watch one another's backs and we constantly checked-in with one another to make sure that we were in agreement throughout. We also had to ensure that we presented a common and united front to the host company. We had to get to know a system that cut across each of our disciplines because our roles were interdependent and our common purpose clear. But, to achieve our stated goal, we *needed* each other. If we had tried to simply go about our roles in parallel, we could not have reached our joint goal. Looking back, the set-up of our circumstances accelerated our coalescence as a team. It was an intense period, living and working together, and we were able to storm and reach a workable norm within our team dynamic.

But Alan's presence and style were critical in making this happen. As an effective team leader, he was like the musical conductor, guiding us along and helping to ensure that we were coherent as a whole. He released our energies. If emotions are energy in motion and energy flows to where we place our attention, then Alan successfully regulated our emotions and directed our energies towards constructively achieving our mission.

For me personally, Alan created a safe place that calmed those parts of the brain that are constantly on the lookout for danger – the amygdala. His leadership style was non-directive – surprising, perhaps, given his military background. While he had great self-discipline, he was patient with the rest of us, resolving many of our conflicts. He was nurturing and open to feedback. If there was anything more I wished he could have done, it might have been that he could have been firmer with us, more demanding, which could have driven us all to achieve an even higher standard of delivery. Having said that, he was in the early stages of his own career and who knows what he has since achieved.

Just as suddenly as we were thrown into forming a team, once we landed back in Singapore, we said our goodbyes at the airport: we went back to the families we had not seen for nine months, to our separate departments, and individual lives. Apart from a series of meetings to close off the project, which were very much task-oriented, the four of us never kept in touch. Perhaps our lives back home were so different that there really wasn't any common ground for our lives to be intertwined in any way.

Back at base, there wasn't any formal debrief as a team, to say goodbyes, thank you, good job, good luck; to review what went well, what we learned as a team, how the team developed and matured; and how it had an impact on each and every one of us. Perhaps, if we had had the organizational maturity then to do a proper review and closure of the team, each of us could have taken more from the experience and been more intentional about how we could apply the value of the experience to our continued personal and career development. Also, if we had documented best practices and put them (and worst practices to avoid!) into institutional memory, this could have served the organization going forward with future staff and teams.

The internet start-up

Singapore was riding on an internet "tech" boom in the late 1990s. I took up an offer to join a relatively young company that had secured funding from some blue-chip investors and was looking to list on the local bourse within 12 to 18 months of my joining. The company was growing rapidly and had started to expand regionally.

On the first day I reported for work, the company had just moved into a new office in the middle of town. The furniture and furnishings were new and bright, and most of the staff young and energetic. There was a buzz in the air and I felt uplifted just being there, eager to start work and get moving. There was even an 'Inspiration Room' taking up the 'corner office', filled with brightly coloured beanbags, games, snacks and drinks, and a huge whiteboard. There was always someone in the 'I-Room' as it was referred to.

The company had an impressive portfolio of big-name customers and a healthy pipeline of repeat and new clients. However, there was an urgent need to ramp up its revenue quickly to achieve the valuation it desired at listing. Around the time I joined, the company hired two 'heavyweights' as chief financial officer (CFO) and chief marketing officer (CMO). Both were seasoned multinational corporation (MNC) veterans at the peak of their illustrious careers, and had been mandated to boost the company's image and financial figures to prepare for the listing. Yes: 'the listing' was front and centre in the minds of both management and investors.

The new CFO took pains to get to know and connect with staff. He organized company barbeques at his home and would often be seen having chats with staff, simply to understand their role and how they were doing. He did not hire any new staff after he joined, working instead with the existing finance team – two accountants and a financial analyst.

The CMO was brought in amid much fanfare and anticipation because she was key to achieving the company's revenue targets and, consequently, its valuation. She had a reputation as one of the top sales women in the tech industry in Singapore. From the very beginning, she and the two staff she hired on joining were constantly away from the office, wining and dining, and meeting clients. Apart from an initial introduction to the staff during a company meeting, her presence in the office was rarely felt. Any interactions required were mostly done via her subordinates.

As the months passed, things started to change. What was once a bright, energetic buzz slowly changed into frustrated, pent-up energy. Staff were beginning to complain – at first to their managers and then among themselves. Subtle verbal 'warnings' were meted out by managers to not speculate and spread rumours based on hearsay. Consequently, staff took their conversations outside the office over 'coffee'. What was all the speculation about?

The management team was increasingly absent from the office, always in meetings to discuss the listing. Only the CFO made it a point to routinely meet with his staff. Rumours were rife that the CMO had burned a hole in the company's budget by entertaining potential clients but that new contracts were not forthcoming. In fact, revenue growth was slowing to a halt and much of the existing work was maintenance. Project managers were busy pitching for new business, and designers and programmers were underutilized. Resources sat idle. In a project-driven environment, not having a project to work on, or in the pipeline, is unnerving. Without clear communication from the top as to what was happening in the company, staff were left to speculate and ruminate. The negativity bias, innate to us as human beings, reinforced their increasingly fearful emotions as their brains scrambled to put together stories of impending doom in an attempt to make sense of the situation.

At some point, snacks and drinks in the I-Room were no longer replenished. As people spent more time out 'having coffee', the room was left mostly vacant. Soon 'they' closed the space off to use it as a storeroom, stacking old or unused laptops and other IT equipment up along the walls.

Rumours abounded that the company was burning cash faster than it was being generated and that investors were unhappy with the company's trajectory. Speculations went unchecked and no attempts were made by management to engage with staff. Energy levels dipped alongside the quality of the work. Staff were distracted and, because most were quite young and early in their careers, they started to get restless. More rumours suggested that the company might not list.

At a Town Hall meeting, the CEO announced management's plans to postpone the listing, citing an unfavourable market. After so much time and effort spent on this single objective, there was no Plan B. The company was rudderless and floundering. It was a short meeting. There was no game plan, no question-and- answer session. And the CEO's own disappointment and exhaustion were palpable.

Today, I am convinced that the CEO had given up hopes of a listing when he walked into that meeting. That was certainly the message everyone got. The meeting served as a confirmation of 'the end' for many. Most started looking for jobs outside, including many of the project managers. If the company had had any real hopes of turning things around before the meeting, it had none left after. Almost everyone was looking to jump ship. Not long after that meeting, the CMO announced her resignation.

As staff left, I had to take over the running of some projects – and some very disgruntled customers. One stood out in particular. An MNC, who was also a long-time customer, had been very patient with the company because of the goodwill built up from past engagements. Unfortunately, repeated delays had exhausted the relationship. The stress and uncertainty faced by the previous project manager from the internal workings of the company had had an inevitable impact on her engagement with the customer. Like dominoes, as the internal workings of the company started to fall, connected systems and stakeholders – customers, suppliers, investors – were all affected. As the interface with customers started to fray, the destiny of the company seemed doomed. There was a sense that everyone had given up.

In the midst of this panic was the finance team. The four of them had stood steady throughout, holding silent while attempting to calm false rumours as best they could. They had up-to-date and realistic information with regards to the situation of the company. The CFO – their team leader

– had made sure that they were kept informed as much as possible. However, they were also bound by confidentiality and sensitivity, and could never share much with the rest of us.

By the time I left the company, it was essentially in scale-down mode. The only team left intact was the finance team, although its members were clearly stressed out. The regional offices were being closed down and there was much to be done to close the books.

I have always wondered if things might have turned out differently if the management team had kept in constant communication with the staff? At the beginning, the staff were hugely engaged and had a stake in the future of the company. There was a clear and common purpose – to get the company listed. Everyone knew what their roles were and what they had to do – the roles and processes were clear. At the core of the business, staff were constantly co-creating with clients as to the best outcome desired by them, leveraging on the expertise and systems within the company to support those outcomes. However, management kept the engagement with investors separate from 'business as usual'. Would the outcome have been different if management had engaged the rest of the staff actively instead and worked as a whole, larger team, interfacing with clients and investors as a coordinated entity?

Looking at it from another angle – again, if emotion is energy in motion and energy flows where we place our attention – the unanswered questions of the staff had increasingly generated the experience of uncertainty and, behind that, the emotion of fear. And, as they placed their attention on the worst-case scenario (of the listing falling through and the company failing), blocked energy was not flowing towards the best possible outcome. If that collective energy could have been unblocked, somehow, and channelled towards co-creating a common desired outcome, could things have been different?

Great manager, high-performing team

When I joined a large multinational corporation in the finance sector, I was lucky to have an amazing team manager, Nick. He was technically outstanding in his field, smart, communicated clearly and elegantly, and was a true people manager. He genuinely cared about his staff and everyone knew it.

As global head of his business area and leader of a fast-growing team, Nick was kept busy managing senior management stakeholders as well as establishing our credibility and standing with other teams in the organization. However, he always had time for his staff, up and down the ranks, no matter how junior. He was accessible and friendly, and yet never shied away from a difficult conversation or decision.

The mandate of our team was rapidly growing and we had always delivered to a high standard. There was no room for free riders, and at some point we had to put one of our colleagues on performance watch. This was after multiple warnings and many hours of counselling by senior staff, including Nick himself. The staff member eventually left after finding another role elsewhere. While we were in the process, it was awkward, frustrating and energy-consuming at times, as such processes usually are, but in hindsight the whole incident was handled very well. In fact, the person who left never said a bad word about Nick. He had called her out on her attitude and underwhelming performance but also put together a robust support structure for her as she went through the performance watch period. I was one of the team members tasked with supporting her through that process. My instructions were to be fair and candid, yet supportive whenever I could be. The whole situation was handled with such positivity (in spite of the context) and everyone involved had a genuine desire to help that member of staff succeed. It was a difficult, sensitive and potentially messy situation. Nick had to balance the demands of the organization with what he felt was the right thing to do by his staff, and he executed it skillfully.

The incident only served to illustrate the degree of psychological security members of Nick's team felt. There was a high level of trust among the team members, such that everyone felt safe to focus on doing what was right by the team. Of course, there were still pseudo cliques and individuals who were overly concerned with their own performance and ambitions. But, somehow, Nick's energy and sense of rightness kept these in check and enabled the rest to focus and move on productively. Overall, it was a high-performing team, swiftly achieving the mandate it was given.

When I joined, the team was almost 2 years old with over 30 members globally. The mandate given to the team was clear, and many of the internal systems, processes and ways of working had been established by then. The team's reputation and credibility within the organization was on the rise, and by all measures it was growing and on the upswing. Each member of the team knew what was expected of them and had the skills to do what they had to do. The pieces were in place.

It felt 'right' at that time. However, there was also always a sense that the management of senior stakeholders in the organization and other stakeholders outside the team were the responsibilities of Nick and his top team. The rest of us wanted the team to look good, but it was never our 'job' and we did not take a proactive role in it. Our views and our loyalty were to Nick and our team. We all knew that Nick had created a safe zone within the team for us to do our job. He handled the management demands that were not always reasonable. However he, and sometimes his top team, would filter these out and we were often protected from the unpleasantries.

In 2008, the global financial crisis hit and, while the survival of the larger organization was intact, the activity on which the team's existence relied was no longer viable. The function of the team was still needed but the original planned growth trajectory was not. As global head of the team, Nick's own career path was greatly circumscribed. The senior management bench of the organization went through a radical change and, consequently, so did the team's key internal stakeholders.

The team had to undergo a radical rethink of its place and identity within the organization. I know for a fact that Nick and his top team worked hard at trying to figure out the next best steps for the larger team. Somehow, they concluded that it was time for Nick to move on and for a new leader to take over to see how best to reinvent the team. The decision was made behind closed doors, among Nick and those who reported directly to him. None of the wider team members were consulted.

Without taking away from the strengths and value that Nick's successor brought to the team, Nick's departure was sorely felt. There were many staff movements thereafter and, while the functional team remained, many of the characters changed. From my conversations with Nick afterwards, I gathered that leaving was not his preferred choice. However, he could not see any other way forward that was best for the team or himself. He felt that, while we were well on our way to delivering on the original mandate, the unexpected sudden and deep changes brought on by the global financial crisis required a radical repositioning of the team's purpose. And he also felt that he was unable to come up with a convincing value proposition that could do the team justice.

In hindsight, I wonder again if Nick and his top team could have engaged with the rest of us as events were unfolding, sharing with us the uncertainty and the facts as they evolved, and discussing with the team as a whole how we might want to proceed from there – as opposed to thinking that they had to either come up with a full and complete solution or give up. If Nick had taken a whole-team view and recognized that the team, in its entirety, needed to step-up and take on collective leadership – and responsibility – for the way forward, things might have taken a different trajectory altogether.

While the original mandate was no longer valid and new stakeholders were in place, perhaps steering through this phase as a collective whole might have kept the team agile through the sea of change. And who knows what might have emerged on the other side when we finally reached the new-found land? It could have enabled Nick to continue longer in his leadership of the team and even kept the team intact.

Nick was a great team leader and people manager because of his particular personality and, of course, his own life experiences. However, like most other managers promoted to lead teams and even organizations, there was no intentional and proper support given to him as his role expanded beyond individual contributor to being accountable for a global team. There was no purposeful training available to him to develop his awareness about teams, the dynamics of their functioning *as a whole team*, and the team's own consciousness of itself and its interaction with the various systems and stakeholders within and beyond the organization.

If Nick and his top team (and eventually the larger team) had been made aware of how to view the team and its environment from a systemic viewpoint, would that have made a difference? And while everyone had their role within the team, if the team had acquired a sense of leadership and ownership with which to thrive and learn, would that have made a difference? If the team had recognized that, as a whole, it was greater than the sum of its parts, would that have afforded a more agile mindset as the team, together and in consultation, reacted to the changes in its external environment?

Who knows? Nick might have been an even more effective team leader and still be the captain steering the ship for many years after.

Biography

Born and bred in Singapore, Sim Peng studied engineering in London before returning home to embark on her first job. She was posted to the US for a job attachment soon after starting work, which in hindsight made for a great adventure. She has since moved on from engineering to dabble in business development, finance and coaching.

CHAPTER 8

The Joy of Mindfulness

Nandini Das Ghoshal

Getting Started

It is 9 pm at night. I light my little tea lamp and pour a few drops of frankincense into the water holder of the lighting apparatus. Within a few seconds, a familiar relaxing scent floods my senses. I then take my position, legs crossed and comfortable, closing my eyes softly and yielding to the experience.

I bring my awareness to the room, focusing on the present. Some thoughts stray in. I hold them for a while and let them go. I focus on my breathing. Breathing in through the nose and released from the mouth. There is no rule here. Only the focus matters. And the awareness. My exhalation is longer than the inhalation. I visualize a blue sky and that always relaxes me. I notice the sensations in my body.

I bring my focused awareness to the spine and imagine every disc in the spine stacked comfortably on top of each other. My awareness runs up and down the length of my spine, like a gentle light sabre caressing every muscle, bone and tissue.

I then start a body scan – focusing my attention on each foot, each digit of each foot, the soles of the feet and the ankles, and working my way up. Sometimes, I encounter discomfort at the base of my spine or in the joints of my left hip. I engage with that feeling and then let go. Strangely, the discomfort eases.

When I finish, I relax every part of my face, shoulder and back. My body obeys the intent. I breathe evenly.

As I open my eyes, my watch shows 9.35 pm.

Mindfulness and meditation

Mindfulness is a state of mind where one is present, in the moment, and able to engage non-judgementally with whatever is arising. It is about being aware of one's body and mind by paying attention to the present moment, the thoughts and feelings, noticing what is emerging and cultivating a non-striving, non-judgemental and non-doing stance.

Meditation is focused practice whereby one learns to direct one's attention and awareness with one's breath as one focuses inward. The breath is the instrument – the tool that is being used to control one's attention. Mindfulness is a state of mind whereas meditation is a practice, an inner act. The two terms are used interchangeably these days, much to the annoyance of purist practitioners who follow the original philosophy, depending on their foundational experiences. *The key point to note is that mindfulness is an outcome whereas meditation is inner action that the individual can take.*

When we sit down in the recommended posture, we make a beginning towards mindfulness and start the journey into the Self. Mindfulness training programmes insist on the posture and for good reason. In my own experience, following the discipline leads to a better outcome and eventually we are able to access the state of mindfulness faster, even without the posture.

For the purposes of our exploration here, we will talk about mindfulness using meditation techniques. We shall refer to the practice as 'mindfulness meditation', which is the first level of practice, at the point of entry, and takes years to master. Practised consistently, it yields disproportionately beneficial results. It is where one starts, a place where the beginner experiences their mind.

It is important to mention that everyone has different states of mind and hence each of us starts at a different level. Some people find it easier than others to get into meditation and attain mindfulness states. It is an immensely personal experience and hence almost impossible to dimensionalize. The meaning that is derived from this journey within is so unique for everyone that having common metrics for measurement does not really capture the essence of the practice nor does it any justice. The resultant joy is perhaps the shared experience that meditators and mindfulness practitioners can connect on. It is my attempt to explore here why it is worth the effort and discipline.

Meditation practices have existed for thousands of years. Meditation derives from the word 'meditari', which means to think, contemplate, devise or ponder. In the Yoga Sutras, the most ancient Hindu source text on the philosophy and practice of yoga, there is reference to the word 'dhyana', which means to contemplate or focus. Some early written accounts of the different states of meditation in Buddhism in India can be found in the sutras of the Pāli Canon, which dates back to the first century BCE. The Pāli Canon is a collection of scriptures from the Theravada Buddhist tradition.

One of the original texts of meditation is in the Yoga Sutras of Patanjali, a compilation of 195 (some say 196) aphorisms or 'sutras'. This ancient text dates back to 400 CE but masters claim that the practices existed even before 3000 BCE. The purpose of the practice of yoga and meditation, as discussed in one of the English translations from Sanskrit, is explained thus: yoga helps the individual to attain "mastery and integration of the activities of the mind field. Resulting from that mastery and integration, the seer, the Self rests in its true nature." There are eight limbs of yoga and the five of them have to do with the regulation of awareness, attention and breath. In a nutshell, to be contemplative or to meditate is perhaps as old as humankind.

Meditation approaches can be attentional, whereby one trains to regulate attention by zeroing in on the breath, a mindful observation of an experience, or the chanting of a mantra or meta-awareness, as in open presence. It can be constructive, whereby one cultivates virtuous qualities like loving-kindness. Or it can be deconstructive, whereby one uses self-observation to understand the nature of experience; or a combination of some of these. Long-term meditators may be able to share even more sophisticated techniques.

For thousands of years, the root texts of meditation have been aiming to help individuals gain mastery of their minds – the ultimate aim, no matter what approach one chooses. We are still in the same pursuit.

Having examined the origins of mindfulness and meditation, let us try to understand mindfulness as it is being taught and practised in the modern, contemporary context. When you are being actively mindful, you are noticing the world around you, as well as your thoughts, feelings, behaviours, movements and the effect you are having on others around you. Patience, acceptance, having a beginner's mind, generosity, gratitude and letting go are the recommended attitudinal foundations of mindfulness. Cultivating these is a journey.

In my experience, the practice of mindfulness meditation itself can reframe the mindset. One often gets asked, 'Does the mindset have to be developed first, before the practice?'

I would say the practice creates the mindset. And hence the important thing is to begin.

One can practise mindfulness anytime, anywhere, and with anyone by being fully engaged in the here and now. Many people go about their daily lives with their minds wandering from the actual activity they are participating in to other thoughts, desires, fears or wishes. When one is mindful, one is actively involved in the activity with all the senses, in the present moment, gently bringing oneself back to the conversation or task at hand, instead of allowing the mind to wander. The question arises, how do you develop this state of mind? After all, most people find themselves thinking about the past or the future in stubborn whorls of thought waves that refuse to quieten down. This default state of mind has been referred to as the 'monkey mind' by meditators.

The act of meditation can resolve this for us. One needs to just start. Sitting still in the correct posture, focusing on the breath, while bringing one's attention back to the present moment when it wanders unconsciously. Sounds simple? I invite the reader to try it for ten minutes every day. A large number of people give up even before a few days have lapsed. But those who do manage to ride through then stay there for life. What are the rewards for this practice? We will explore some of these in this chapter.

I asked Subba Vaidyanathan, a marathon meditator who calls himself a 'mind athlete', what the joy of mindfulness meant for him. Previously a senior banker, Subba has been on the path of discovering himself through meditative practices since 2004. He is also a spiritual guide and a teacher of the Yoga Sutras. The art and spirit of meditation go back centuries and are at the root of all practices – Hindu and Buddhist.

Subba described his own experience of joy beautifully:

> It is the space where I feel that I do not have to achieve anything. More importantly it is that space where I am nobody. I am here and I am sitting in service. In the spirit of trust and surrender. I surrender. And I am willing to be guided.

He added that, if you can explain what has happened to you, then you have not experienced it.

I asked Anita Eicke, a senior executive coach and a trainer for mindfulness in Germany about her personal experience with the practice of mindfulness. She said she appreciated the sense of curiosity this practice had created in her. The joy is to know what is going on within ourselves: being aware. The mind and body unit come together into a recovery mode: being still with oneself, especially with the digital world always pushing us into some kind of reaction mode. Mindfulness inculcates a sense of being non-judgemental, being a witness instead of a reactive element in whatever is going on. Anita recommends regular practice of ten minutes a day, so that it is doable and can be integrated into one's daily life as a habit.

In the current days of the 'mental health epidemic', people have attributed their most natural emotional upheaval to the rude snatching away of what was 'normal living' by COVID-19 as a mental health issue. This in turn has led to many more people turning towards meditation and mindfulness to try and reclaim some normalcy. Millions have experienced the impact of fear and anxiety not only in their minds but also their bodies. This is perhaps a watershed moment for 'mindfulness' to be accepted as a mainstream therapeutic practice.

Interest in meditation in the West seems to have started rising in the 1970s, not so much as an aid to mental health but more as a practice that led to an altered state of mind. A number of technology students, academicians and scientists in that decade – Daniel Goleman, Richard J. Davidson and Jon Kabat-Zinn being some of the prominent names among them – became interested in meditation as a practice and the results it produced in the mind. They were active meditators already, as students, and perhaps meditation evangelists in the making.

The credit for putting mindfulness meditation as a salve for overall stress and anxiety, on the map of the Western world, goes to Jon Kabat-Zinn. He is an American professor of medicine and a molecular biologist from the Massachusetts Institute of Technology (MIT). In his youth, he pursued meditative practices and was guided by teachers of Zen Buddhism such as Philip Kapleau and Thich Naht Hanh. He is now popularly known for his contribution to chronic pain reduction via mindfulness and meditation, and he has worked through the pain and pleasure of intense practice to create Mindfulness-Based Stress Reduction (MBSR). MBSR was introduced in 1979 at the University of Massachusetts Medical School (UMASS) from where it continues to spread worldwide. The UMASS Memorial Health website[1] claims that more than 25,000 people have gone through the programme since then. There are more than 1,000 instructors worldwide and growing in number every day. More importantly, the programme has allowed for a significant amount of evidence to be collected by meditation enthusiasts on the benefits of this practice. Jon Kabat-Zinn's book, *Full Catastrophe Living*, which was first published in 1990 and then revised in 2013, describes

---

[1] https://www.umassmed.edu/about/clinical

the philosophy, science and practice of the MBSR along with the research on the medical benefits of mindfulness-based techniques.

For those who value evidence, one of the best compilations and summary of scientific data on the benefits of mindfulness and meditation is documented in the book, *Altered Traits*, written by Daniel Goleman and Richard J. Davidson. The former is a renowned psychologist and author, best known for his book, *Emotional Intelligence*. The latter is the William James and Vilas Professor of Psychology and Psychiatry at the University of Wisconsin-Madison as well as the founder director of the Center for Healthy Minds.

Both authors travelled extensively within India during their youth and spent time with various meditation gurus to learn and experience techniques of meditation. They had teachers from Buddhist and other ancient traditions. Their experiences led to an explosion of research measurement and evidence collection in the elite universities to which they were attached. At the beginning of the 1970s decade, there were very few published scientific reports on meditation. By 2016 alone, there were 1,113 such reports in the scientific literature worldwide; and by another report more than 1500. The scientific community's interest and attention towards mindful meditation as a practice and mind tool are now unstoppable.

Another study that gives a comprehensive overview of the benefits of mindfulness and meditation is one by Tang, Holzel and Posner. Since then, innumerable papers have been published that discuss the good and bad of mindfulness and meditation. Tang et al. (2015) categorized the benefits of the practice under three broad headings – attention control, emotion regulation and self-awareness.

These in turn lead to innumerable health benefits. There is also evidence that the structure of the brain itself changes in long-term meditators – a remarkable finding per se.

We shall explore the benefits of mindfulness meditation later in the chapter, although it is not possible to fully keep up with the exploding literature on the topic.

Subjects studied have reported improvement of focus, attention, emotional control, awareness, memory and mood at one level, and even claimed deeper therapeutic benefits such as alleviation of depression, anxiety and trauma. These benefits are not independent of each other. What ties them all together is the neural training that the brain goes through. And, most importantly, is how all of this comes together in the consciousness of the meditator, resulting in the joy, bliss or an altered consciousness that the meditators of the West were seeking in the 1970s and 1980s from Eastern spiritual masters.

Mindfulness allows the individual to go within their Self and understand their unique 'me'. In an age where the norm is noise and notification, cultivating a refuge for the 'me' might be a pursuit that can actively build self-knowledge and in turn wholesomeness, self-worth and confidence. In fact, it has given rise to a term called 'interoception'.

In my own journey with mindfulness, there were some important stages to traverse before I could actually experience the feeling of joy. I feel these are important to know for a beginner because they help them to stay on course. Even though the experience is different for different people. I have observed that mindfulness has its fair share of quitters and we will also try to understand why this could be happening.

Each of our minds is unique and works in a truly individual way. It is almost impossible to tell how one person's mindfulness practice is similar to or different from another's. Some outward signs of success are, however, the ability to sit in a pose for many minutes, to be still, to be completely and totally present in the moment and to engage with all the senses (self-declared). Some people liken it to experiencing a sense of flow, whereby they lose all sense of time. Who is to say that this is not mindfulness – to be in full awareness and flow? For artists, it happens when they are totally immersed in their art; for musicians, in their music; for poets, in their words. The attention is not wavering: it is uninterrupted by thoughts. It is indeed bliss.

Stages before the joy

The Unrest

This is the most formidable challenge that one has to overcome in order to be a habitual mindfulness practitioner. In the beginning, there is always 'unrest': the restlessness, the noise in the mind that constantly pulls you away, the voices in the head, the distraction from others and the Self. Sometimes, it is our body that rebels against this forced stillness. Sometimes, it is the mind. It is incredibly tough to spend time with oneself. When one enters the practice, this realization shocks the Self. I have had many nights of restless legs, sweat break-outs and similar physical responses attributable to a session.

The trick is small practice sessions, consistently and persistently, allowing for breaks when they need to happen and then going back to a session again. I am now able to sit with ease, without any guiding voice or focused thought, or any other such crutch. To me, this is an achievement. And I have been practising for more than four years.

The noting

The biggest training that the brain goes through in all of this is one of noting: noting the body, the energy and the feelings in different parts; engaging with the pain or discomfort; and observing the emotions that arise and how they manifest physically: not judging but staying with the emotions, with a beginner's mindset and curiosity – a deep and authentic curiosity. Eventually, this trains our mind to note at a higher level: our reactions to events, our triggers for stress, how we cope and what we do, the attentional blinks, reactions without judgement. In real life, I still slip. But I recover faster. We note best when we do not judge ourselves or others. Our brain is an adaptive organ. At all points of time, it is capable of adapting to the situation. But, for that, it needs training and that training is this ease with noting. The noting comes before the reframing of the reaction that wise people call 'response'. Understanding the difference between reaction and response happens with ease and joy in this practice.

The intensity

Some way into the journey, one may experience acute discomfort. This is different from the 'unrest' phase. It could come in the form of heightened disturbing emotions or dreams, unresolved emotional issues, uncontrolled movements and other such experiences. In Buddhist meditation practices, this is considered progress. The West is seeing a proliferation of Buddhist-inspired meditation practices being offered in workplaces, social groups and other settings too. However, there are side effects. In Zen Buddhist traditions, the term 'makyō' refers to a class of largely perceptual 'side effects' or 'disturbing conditions' that arise during the course of practice. To me, this is a point where one may even reconsider whether to maintain the practice. I persist with mine, even though I have had some disturbing nights. I am happy to report that good sleep is back again.

It is well known that in the journey of mindful meditation, one goes through discomfort of the body and mind.

Without going too deeply into these reports, from a practitioner's point of view, I can confirm that you may have some uncomfortable nights. However, staying and persisting can yield benefits. Adjusting your own practice to what works best for you is entirely up to your own appetite for this. Like everything else, moderation is a good thing. It will not be all smooth sailing and that shows that you have reached an important milestone in this journey.

The ease

Ability to feel ease in the process and get into a meditative state is a milestone. There are various methods for it. If one explores different meditative practices, one will find one that works. Working with the breath is usually where one starts. However, success comes with practice – building the muscle, as it were, for mindful practices, although there is no guarantee as to the time it may take for the individual to get there.

The clarity

Once you start experiencing perceptible clarity after a sitting is when you know that this is really wonderful. For me, better sleep was also an indicator of progress. However, in my lived experience, none of the above phases were sequential. I could have days of clarity followed by unrest. One also has to remember that we are mere mortals and our brains are always working to respond to external circumstances and protect us. This has a profound effect on how one's body responds to meditation or mindfulness. In extremely stressful or trying conditions, a trained brain gets back into equanimity faster. However, blocking emotions completely is not really a desired outcome. And, in situations of extreme emotional disturbance, one may not be able to sit for ten seconds, let alone ten minutes. At that time, suggesting mindfulness in postured elegance would be fallacious, unless initiated by the Self.

Starting your own practice

Getting started with a mindfulness practice is the first and most important step. Can we make it a normal activity, like brushing our teeth? Yes, we can. The evidence of the benefits of mindfulness and meditation is overwhelming.

We can start with sitting for ten minutes every day for a guided meditation. Apps like Calm and Headspace provide that initial help, which is much needed. YouTube has thousands of recorded meditations. I find people spend a lot of time trying to assess which one is the best. In my experience, there is no such thing – finding one type with which you personally resonate and sticking to it is good enough. The point is to do it every day, with joy.

Building a little ritual around the meditation helps tremendously. When I created a time, a place and a physical activity around it – a space in the house, a kind of fragrance, lighting a lamp in a certain way, my body slipped into the state more easily. By the 21st day, it had become a habit I would look forward to: my daily 'me space', which allowed me to tune out of the hundred tasks that needed to be done.

Finally, if it helps you, work in a group with other people. The collective commitment towards a practice embeds the habit.

A word of caution here. Masters say that it is impossible to make progress without a guru or a teacher. Subba, the deep meditator and teacher explains: "You are working with the most important sense of your body and being – the mind. It is dangerous if you are not able to process the key stages with someone experienced. Good meditators take years of practice – 10 or 20...".

Mindfulness for leaders

It is not uncommon to find leaders who evangelize some form of mindfulness. Either they are habitual meditators or they are mindfulness snackers, consistently doing about 15 to 30 minutes a day. In any case, they swear by their practice.

In further discussions with Anita Eicke, I discovered that she links the benefits of mindfulness with those of leadership. She reflected on how we can lead with a clear mind and make better decisions if we calm our monkey mind. However, even though mindfulness has exploded in popularity, it has not necessarily led to the creation of a large number of mindful leaders.

Anita explains her idea of mindful leadership in detail. First, it comprises leadership resilience, which comes when a leader is more self-aware, aware of their emotions and able to regulate them; second, the building of better attention and focus, an outcome of meditation and mindfulness – leaders can better focus on the task at hand, concentrate better and be more aware of their biases; and, third, inspiring others into action by adopting a calming demeanour where there is emphasis on response and not reaction.

Measuring the benefits of mindfulness

Even though meditation techniques have existed for thousands of years, some key events in the Western universities of repute fuelled actual laboratory studies that measured the benefits of mindfulness. This was further fuelled by the emergence of the functional magnetic resonance imaging (fMRI) and electroencephalogram (EEG) techniques, coupled with his Holiness the Dalai Lama's personal interest in cooperating with labs at MIT and Stanford in studies that looked into the brains of habitual meditators to understand what exactly was going on.

Daniel Goleman and Richard J. Davidson , in *Altered Traits* (2017), bring forth evidence to say that some of our behavioural traits change permanently with long-time meditation. Even two weeks of practice make a difference. The evidence comes from fMRI and EEG studies that have observed actual changes in the physical components of the brain in long-term meditators. This evidence is further supported by claims made and surveys completed by study subjects.

Chronic stress has a debilitating effect on the body. It equates to poor healthfulness. In numerous studies, it has been found that a meditator's brain shows less amygdala reactivity to stress. Improvements in attention have been recorded after just two weeks of practice, producing better focus, less mind-wandering and improved working memory. Markers for inflammation lessen a little with just 30 hours of practice.

Jon Kabat-Zinn, the meditator, physician and lifelong crusader against stress, revised his seminal book, *Full Catastrophe Living*, in 2013, 23 years after it was first published in 1990. The book is essentially about the MSBR method. In the revised version, Kabat-Zinn referenced a lot of the evidence that had emerged from thousands of studies across universities in the United States. In the chapter, 'Introduction to the Paradigm', he summarized thus:

> Perhaps the most fundamental development in medicine over the past decades is the recognition that we can no longer think about health as being solely a characteristic of the body or the mind, because body and mind are not two separate domains – they are intimately connected and completed integrated. Science will never be able to describe a complex dynamical process such as health, or even a relatively chronic disease, without looking at the functioning of the whole organism, rather than restricting itself solely to an analysis of parts and components (2013, Kindle version).

This statement from Kabat-Zinn is a declaration of a new paradigm in medicine and healing. It is based on more than 40 years of serious medical practice and working with thousands of patients with chronic conditions of pain, anxiety, skin diseases, cancer and other inflammatory conditions.

For long-term meditators, the evidence of transformation in the biology of the body is compelling. As noted, in those who have done 1,000 hours or more, lab observation has recorded significant alteration of the brain biology – lowered reactivity to stress, lessened inflammation, a strengthening of the prefrontal circuits for managing distress, and lower levels of the stress hormone, cortisol, signalling less reactivity. Add, also, stronger selective attention and decreased attentional blink, along with less mind wandering. Those with marathon records of over

27,000 lifetime hours of meditation exhibit a different brain pattern altogether as well as slower ageing. All this Western fascination with the measurement of benefits has given rise to the academic discipline of 'contemplative neuroscience'.

For long-term meditators, it has been observed that there is an increase in cortical thickness, hippocampal gray matter density and the size itself of the hippocampus. This is an important finding because the hippocampus is sensitive to emotions and has a role in regulating emotional response. It is also the centre of long-term memory storage and retrieval (Public Health Nigeria, 2020).

The other areas of the brain that record changes have to do with the control of attention, self-regulation and staying focused. This has far-reaching consequences in helping humans to age better, controlling depression and anxiety, and increasing their memory and cognitive abilities.

In the 2015 study by Yi-Yuan Tang and his colleagues referred to earlier, meditation is defined as "a kind of mental training to improve the individual's core psychological capacities". The findings provide evidence to say that mindfulness practice leads to better self-regulation in meditators. Self-regulation improves as it impacts attention control, emotional regulation and self-awareness.

The imaging studied in this paper indicates that meditation actually changes large-scale brain networks and is not restricted to particular areas. The brain diagram below (Figure 8.1) is adapted from the source paper, visualizing the areas of the brain that are involved in attention control (the anterior cingulate cortex and the striatum), emotion regulation (multiple prefrontal regions and the striatum which are limbic regions) and self-awareness (the insula, medial prefrontal cortex and posterior cingulate cortex and precuneus).

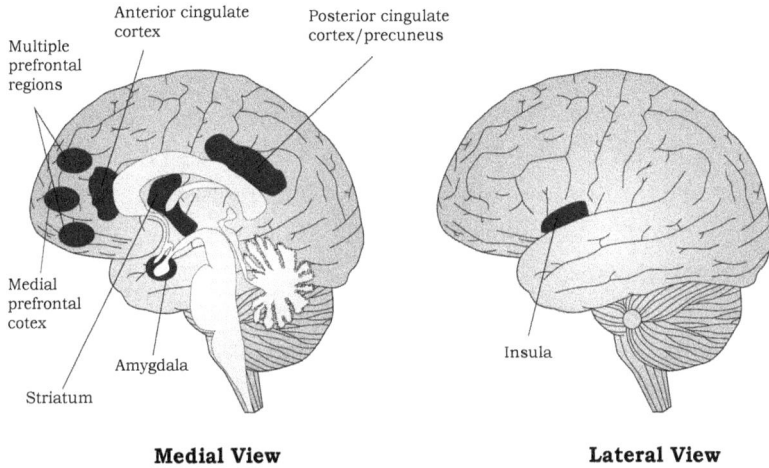

Figure 8.1 Schematic representation of brain regions influenced by meditation

Tang, Posner and Holzel (2015) further state that the structures of up to eight brain regions were found altered in long-term meditators: the frontopolar cortex, which the researchers suggest might be related to enhanced meta-awareness following meditation practice; the sensory cortices and insula, areas that have been related to body awareness; the hippocampus, a region that has been related to memory processes; the anterior cingulate cortex, mid-cingulate cortex and orbitofrontal cortex, areas known to be related to the Self and emotion regulation; and the superior longitudinal fasciculus and corpus callosum, areas involved in intra- and inter-hemispherical communication. Even though the biological names seem confusing, it is worth noting that they are significant parts of the 'emotional brain'.

Mindfulness training has been shown to enhance gray matter density in the hippocampus. Furthermore, after mindfulness training, reductions in perceived stress correlate with reductions in amygdala gray matter density, a fact reported by Richard J. Davidson as well.

This particular report is worth considering because the results have been collected from a cross-sectional group of meditators and not just Buddhist monks. Hence, the applicability of the findings to the ordinary person becomes more relevant.

So, it appears that, while the measurement of the brain's activities through fMRI and EEG methods is giving new insights into the benefits of mindfulness, revealing which parts of the brain receive an impact, the evidence is undeniable that mindfulness practices are perhaps the only conscious activity, capable of being undertaken by an individual, that can induce self-healing by bringing about actual structural changes in the brain. This is encouraging enough to make trying it seem worthwhile.

Perhaps one of the biggest benefits of meditation is the change that we experience in our inner narrative. Goleman and Davidson describe how meditation in a focused way helps us to reconstruct our inner narrative, which is forever playing in our do-nothing mode:

> Our sense of self gets woven in an ongoing personal narrative that threads together disparate parts of our life into a coherent story line. This mainly happens in the default mode. We construct our experience around a narrative where we are the star – and that we can deconstruct that story we centre on ourselves by applying the right kind of awareness. The stuff of our lives become less 'sticky' as we shift into a less attached relationship toward all that.

Marcus Raichle (2015) has observed that there is really nothing called 'doing nothing'. When we are apparently 'doing nothing', some parts of our brain become highly active, even more active than when engaged on a difficult cognitive task. While the brain has only 3%–4% of the body's mass, it consumes nearly 25% of the body's energy and this remains constant no matter what we are doing, even if we are doing nothing at all. The brain stays busy even when we are relaxing.

So what is the brain doing when we are relaxing? Raichle identified that the medial prefrontal cortex and the posterior cingulate cortex get particularly busy – he calls this the 'default mode network'. It was typically self-reported that, in these times of 'doing nothing', the mind wandered off and focused on the Self: the mental activity focused on 'I' and 'me'. Typically – my thoughts, my emotions, my relationships, who likes me, etc. – all the minutiae of my life story. Our default mode continually replays a movie where each of us stars, replaying particularly favourite or upsetting scenes over and over.

Managing attention is the essential ingredient of every variety of meditation. The wandering mind therefore comes under control when we do meditation. A basic instruction in all meditation urges us to notice when our mind has wandered and then return the focus to the chosen target – say, a mantra or breathing.

Deep meditators work on continuously deconstructing their sense of Self and dismissing attachment. However, this kind of pursuit may not be the joy of every meditator.

Is there too much mindfulness?

Might there be a risk of having too much mindfulness? Willoughby Britton, Assistant Professor of Psychiatry and Human Behaviour at Brown University Medical School, cautions us that too much mindfulness can be messy. In her paper entitled 'Can mindfulness be too much of a good thing?', written and revised in 2019, she explores this mess in depth.

In this paper, Britton elucidates that the qualities that are enhanced due to mindfulness are non-judgement, acceptance, curiosity, open-mindedness, optimism, self-efficacy, courage, trust, patience, persistence, kindness, empathy, generosity, gratitude, social intelligence, freedom, autonomy and choice. But can too much meditation be good for the human being? She reports studies showing that meditators who go beyond 30 minutes a day experience emotional blunting and dissociation. Low practice amounts in Mindfulness-Based Cognitive Therapy (MBCT) participants increased sleep duration but, as the practice amount approached 30 minutes per day, sleep duration and depth began to decrease and cortical arousal (awakenings and microarousals) began to increase. Hence, if your objective is to improve sleep, stick to a 30-minute period or less. However, reaching this stage is a long way off for a lot of us.

Britton goes on to stay with her scepticism about mindfulness being a panacea for all issues related to chronic physical health or emotional well-being. In another chapter titled 'Challenging and adverse meditation experiences: Toward a person-centered approach' (Lindahl et al., 2021), the authors assert that in religion and science, the notion that extremely challenging and adverse experiences can arise during or as a result of meditation has been downplayed or ignored. Most scientific research in this area does not even report the effects. However, in religious literature as well as contemporary psychological research the challenges to the mind and body are well documented.

Meditators are known to hit a phase called the 'dark night' where they may experience disturbed sleep, morbid emotions, anger, guilt and anxiety in an extremely physical way. Britton aids such people to deal with this phenomenon. Many who experience it are known to have left their 'practice' out of fear. However, meditation continues to grow in popularity in the West and also now as a tool in psychotherapy.

In 2022, Britton continued to be a researcher in contemplative practices and talked about the dark side of meditation. However, this is not deterring anyone from taking up the practice more. She herself is an MBSR and MBCT instructor. Clearly, she is in this with her eyes open.

And, finally

Let us pause from the science and take a moment to appreciate what the joy of being mindful really is. One way to look at it is as done from the Eastern philosophy of becoming a 'nobody' and just enjoying the 'being'. The other way is to approach it is as a mind tool to enjoy the benefits, many of which are being constantly discovered and validated from research and measurement labs of premier universities of the world. The continuum of literature is vast and one can explore it for one's entire lifetime. There is no one perfect approach. Whichever path you take, the constant practice will be beneficial and yield joy in a compounded immeasurable way.

My own experience has enabled me to create a safe space where I can be 'me' and feel my awareness of life and living more deeply. My practice has helped me work on my emotional stress. I find that, in any situation that would have set my internal cortisol levels off the charts, I am able to control or reset equanimity much faster. And this happens because my brain has been trained through mindfulness practice. In a stressful situation, I do not have to sit cross-legged in a meditative pose for the effect to come on. When facilitating mindfulness sessions for groups or clients, I have received the same feedback. People enjoy the sense of being 'me' and not having to do anything to feel joyful.

Pursuing mindfulness has done wonders for my level of awareness. My engagement with life around me, in the present moment, has improved vastly. And it is a developing phenomenon.

Finally, my somatic joy from everyday experiences has increased hugely. To me, this has been a magical transformation. For someone who was always in a hurry, deeply impatient, supressing stress and unable to process inner anger, these transformative traits are a gift and a discovery. I am so grateful to be able to report them here.

Mindfulness really is the most credible non-pharmacological, non-invasive and self-directed brain tool that one can call upon in moments of stress and anxiety. No one will recognize you for achievements in meditation or mindfulness, but you will know how you have changed if you can deal with stress better, sleep better and experience the little pleasures in life more joyfully. You will know you are mindful if that new bloom in your garden gives you joy, or a conversation with a friend over coffee makes you happy, or you feel love and gratitude for all the goodness you receive from the world more wholeheartedly. Mindfulness is an entry to a better life, not a path for disconnecting from it. Instead of trying to find the perfect path, we need to just begin.

References

Britton, W.B. (2019) 'Can mindfulness be too much of a good thing? The value of a middle way', *Current Opinion in Psychology*, 28, pp. 159–165. Available at: https://doi.org/10.1016/j.copsyc.2018.12.011 (Accessed 27 October 2022).

Goleman, D. and Davidson R.J. (2017) *Altered traits: Science reveals how meditation changes your mind, brain, and body*. New York: Avery Publishing Group/Penguin Group.

Kabat-Zinn, J. (1990, 2013) *Full catastrophe living: How to cope with stress, pain and illness using mindfulness meditation*. London: Piatkus Books.

Lindahl, J.L. et al. (2021) 'Challenging and adverse meditation experiences: Toward a person-centered approach', in Farias, M., Brazier, D. and Laljee., M. (eds). *The Oxford Handbook of Meditation*. Oxford: Oxford University Press, pp. 841–864.

Public Health Nigeria (2020) 'The key functions of the hippocampus', 22 August. Available at: https://www.publichealth.com.ng/the-key-functions-of-the-hippocampus (Accessed 27 October 2022).

Raichle M.E. (2015) 'The brain's default mode network', *Annual Review of Neuroscience*, 38, pp. 433–447. Available at: https://doi.org/10.1146/annurev-neuro-071013-014030 (Accessed 27 October 2022).

Swami Jnaneshvara Bharati. *Yoga Sutras of Patanjali*. Available at: https://www.swamij.com/yoga-sutras-list.htm (Accessed 20 January 2023).

Tang, Y.-Y., Hölzel, B.K., and Posner, M.I. (2015) 'The neuroscience of mindfulness meditation', *Nature Reviews Neuroscience*, 16(4), pp. 213–225. Available at: https://doi.org/10.1038/nrn3916 (Accessed 27 October 2022).

Biography

Nandini Das Ghoshal is an experienced executive coach and corporate trainer based out of Singapore. She works with leaders, executives and entrepreneurs to help them discover the best version of the Self. She has been a corporate leader, entrepreneur and bespoke learning content creator in her professional journey. She is committed to exploring the nature of the mind, mechanisms of brain and behaviour, and applying her research and practices to help clients experience a more flourishing professional and personal life. She is the co-founder of ION Consulting, Singapore, based on the work of Dr Paul Brown. She has explored and trained in various modalities of mindfulness meditation including yogic breathing, app-based, Silva meditation, Reiki and Mindfulness-Based Stress Reduction. She aims to work with youngsters and help them find their own mindfulness mojo.

CHAPTER 9

The Welcoming Organization: being your true Self at work

Khyati Kapai

From fear to freedom

I was having a conversation with Paul Brown about his co-authored book, *The Fear-Free Organization*, and asked him what a *fear-free* organization would be *full of* instead. He elaborated that a fear-free organization is where individuals would have the psychological freedom to bring their whole selves to work. So, when I asked him what he would call such an organization, after a 'generative pause'[1] in his thinking, he offered, 'The Welcoming Organization'.

Drawing on my executive coaching and facilitation experience, I share my thoughts here on what would make a 'Welcoming Organization'. I present it as a 'true and liberating alternative'[2] to the unsustainable working conditions of fear-based organizations. It seems that we are ready to replace the assumption of using fear as a performance motivator with a more accurate, sustainable and freeing alternative.

Fear-based organizations tap into survival instincts and basic human motivators such as fear, or emotions like anxiety that proximate to 'fear' to push employees to perform. Fear-based organizations are still prevalent.

In a coaching session with a client, we were reviewing feedback from her supervisor who had encouraged my client to use more fear with her team because the supervisor saw it as a powerful motivating tool. Where do we even begin in such a coaching situation? In some

---

[1] A generative pause relates to a finding in the Thinking Environment that is described by Nancy Kline using the metaphor of waves and pauses: "The human mind seems to think in waves, and after a wave there is a pause. Inside the pause something almost Delphic happens that produces another wave of thinking." Notably, pauses in talking do not necessarily indicate pauses in thinking.

[2] The phrase, "true and liberating alternative", coined by Nancy Kline is a reference in the Thinking Environment to when an untrue limiting assumption is replaced with a true and liberating alternative in a breakthrough thinking process.

of the organizations I work with, employee engagement initiatives are data-driven versus being-driven: they are focused on measuring quantifiable indicators that apparently reflect the degree of employee engagement. In some cases, the frequency of these measurement exercises compounds the issue of poor employee experience because the focus is on measuring and reporting, which evokes a survival response. We cannot simply demand, measure and report performance. Instead, when the focus is on creating the conditions conducive for an attachment/ thrive response, then such circumstances automatically generate sustainable performance (Figure 9.1).

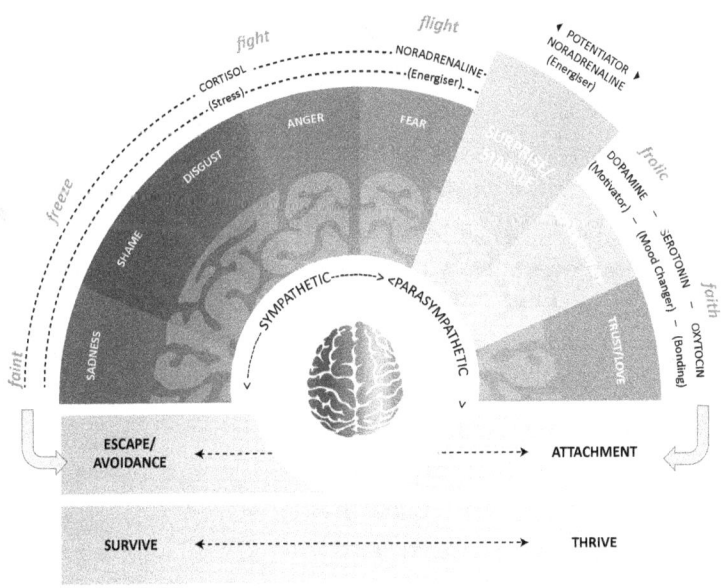

The London Protocol of the Emotions
ION Consulting International Pte Ltd 2023
see colour representation of this diagram on inside front and rear cover pages

Why psychological freedom?

In conversation, Dr Brown explained that individuals who can bring their whole selves to work enjoy psychological freedom and create psychological safety for Self[3] and others. Currently, because of a fear-based approach, many organizations are restricted to a concept of psychological safety that can create a victim mentality on the part of the individual employee – that is, where they believe that the responsibility for employee well-being is someone else's, not 'theirs' – in other words, someone else can be blamed for what is happening to 'me'. Instead, we need to embrace the concept of psychological freedom – the freedom to be wholly 'me' – which underpins the capacity to adapt appropriately and is the basis of resilience. From this all sorts of thrive-based feelings and actions can result, of which 'safety' may be only one.

Fast-tracked by the hybrid nature of work during the pandemic, we are witnessing a change in the psychological contract between employees and their organizations in which employees want the freedom of not just where and how they work but also ownership over *why* they work. I was first introduced to an evolution of organizations when reading Frederic Laloux's *Reinventing Organizations*. In writing that book, Laloux explored whether it was possible to structure and run organizations in entirely new, more life-giving ways. The book has inspired organizations to explore more soulful and purposeful management practices. In it, Laloux describes 'evolutionary purpose' as one of three breakthroughs of a 'teal' organization:

> ... (such) organizations are seen as having a life and a sense of direction of their own. Instead

---

[3] Self is capitalised throughout to convey an individual's idea of their 'true' self.

of trying to predict and control the future, members of the organization are invited to listen and understand what the organization is drawn to become, where it naturally wants to go (Laloux, 2016, p. 55).

Laloux's reference to such organizations as 'teal' is shorthand to typify the next phase of the development of organizational consciousness. It is contrasted with four organizational models that exist (impulsive, traditional, achievement and pluralist).

"Where it naturally wants to go" suggests to me where its members naturally want to go in flow with a sense of their true Self. Laloux outlines two other breakthroughs of teal organizations: *self-management* (powerful and fluid systems of distributed authority and collective intelligence) and *wholeness* (a reclamation of our inner wholeness whereby we bring all of whom we are to work).

In his book, Laloux provides examples of organizations that have adopted some teal-like breakthroughs – these include organizations like Morning Star and Buurtzorg[4]. The idea of wholeness has also appeared in the autobiographies of leaders such as Microsoft's CEO, Satya Nadella, and PepsiCo's former CEO, Indra Nooyi.

In Nadella's autobiography, *Hit Refresh*, we read:

> It's about helping employees live out their own personal mission in the context of Microsoft's. Microsoft no longer employs people, people employ Microsoft... Anybody at Microsoft can look at our constellation of assets and dream of

---

[4] The purpose of an organization reflects its calling in the world. For example, the healthcare organization Buurtzorg's purpose is "for patients to live rich and autonomous lives". (Laloux, F. [2016] *Reinventing Organizations: An illustrated invitation to join the conversation on next-stage organizations.* Brussels: Nelson Parker.)

what can be and bring it to bear on any problem in any geography... This culture needs to be a microcosm of the world we hope to create outside the company. One where builders, makers, and creators achieve great things. But, equally important, one where every individual can be their best self... (Nadella, 2017, p. 241).

In her autobiography, *My Life in Full*, Nooyi writes:

"I had adopted a philosophy that people should be able to bring their whole selves to work. I see this as fundamental to inclusivity in any organization", (Nooyi, 2021, p.193) and "If we didn't let people bring their whole selves to work, we wouldn't get the best employees" (Nooyi, 2021, p. 205).

The idea of being ourselves at work may raise this concern: how will the contributions of employees who enjoy psychological freedom serve the overall organizational objectives?

Psychological freedom and self-regulation

In a way, what we really want to know is: 'How can I both be "me" and also "belong"?' Coincidentally, the 'we' in an organizational context can also serve as an acronym for 'welcoming everyone'. And breaking down 'belonging' into its compound components can help us understand the compatibility of Self and We: 'belonging' is made up of 'be' and 'longing' – that is, 'be-longing' contains a longing to be and to go along with.

We can rely on self-regulation because belonging supports our instincts to survive (feeling safe in numbers) and thrive (flourishing through quality of relationships). Individuals are unlikely to stay part of organizations if this resonance is not there. Laloux observes that, when an interpersonal virus gets into the system (a person who feeds off the system, rather than contributes, and who absorbs energy rather than exchanging it), it can be excluded by a healthy system that seeks to repair the damage that has been done to it, as part of its natural capacity to do so. Like many biological functions, there is a circularity in the system that, functioning properly, reinforces itself (Laloux, as referenced in Brown and Lanz, 2020, pp. 131–132). According to Dr Brown, the employees are the cells of an organization, and the quality of relationships is the oxygen. According to Dr Siegel, a renowned psychiatrist and professor, energy and information flow throughout our human lives: that flow is regulated by the mind, shared in relationships, and passed through the embodied mechanisms of the nervous system and whole body that we are simply calling the 'brain'.

The following definitions[5] have been outlined by Dr Siegel:

- Energy: A term from physics that means the 'capacity to do something'. It comes in various forms, such as kinetic, thermal, nuclear, electrical and chemical. The nervous system functions by way of the flow of electrochemical energy.
- Information: Patterns of energy that carry meaning and 'stand for' or symbolize something other than the energy itself. Information is best considered a verb-like entity (not a noun) in that it gives rise to further processing in cascades of associations and linked meanings that emerge over time.

---

[5] Terminology source: Siegel, D. (2012) Pocket guide to interpersonal neurobiology: An integrative handbook of the mind. California: W.W. Norton & Company.

- Energy and information flow: The movement across time of energy and the swirls of energy that have symbolic value, that stand for something other than the pattern of energy flow alone. Energy and information can flow within the body (an embodied mechanism) and are transferred between people in relationships (sharing). The mind can be viewed as an emergent process that arises in the form of self-experience (subjectivity) and self-organization (regulation) as energy and information flow within and between people.

According to Dr Dan Siegel, becoming a part of a 'we' does not mean that you lose a 'me'. From an interpersonal neurobiology perspective, we work at promoting inner and interpersonal integration through the fundamental process of attuning to the internal subjective states of both Self and other that fill our lives with meaning and connection (Siegel, 2012, p. 19-8).

Paul Brown has observed that breaking down 'information' into its compound components 'in-formation' reveals that this dynamic information processing is in the service of forming our sense of Self. Given the conditions, we can positively integrate our brain's continuous management of information, energy, and relationship.

Creating the conditions of a Welcoming Organization – the Thinking Environment

We need to create the conditions in which individuals can continue to grow and flourish and enjoy 'inner and interpersonal integration'. The maturation of neural wiring in humans is not complete until approximately 24 years of age when the executive centres of the thinking brain come into their own (Bainbridge, 2008, as quoted in Brown et al., 2015, p. 43). The implications of this are significant for the talent development initiatives of organizations, particularly those initiatives designed for young talent in their early twenties. A learning culture approach to organizational performance has been outlined by Nadella:

> It's about a dynamic learning culture. In fact, the phrase we use to describe our emerging culture is 'growth mindset', because it's about every individual, every one of us having that attitude – that mindset – of being able to overcome any constraint, stand up to any challenge, making it possible for us to grow and, thereby, for the company to grow.
>
> I told my colleagues that I was not talking bottom-line growth. I was talking about our individual growth. We will grow as a company if everyone, individually, grows in their roles and in their lives (Nadella, 2017, pp. 93–94).

This is evident in Microsoft's success during Nadella's tenure. When the best of each of us continues to develop and is free to function at our best, then the organization, in turn, benefits from higher-than-expected returns. So, we need to focus on creating the conditions that welcome self-regulated performance.

Once a case is made for such a Welcoming Organization, this then raises the question, 'What practices would such a Welcoming Organization embrace?'

There are many thought leaders, including those mentioned earlier, who share insights on 'welcoming' practices. As a Time to Think practitioner, my closest experience is of how the Thinking Environment can help us create practices that provide working conditions fit for 'humans being'. I have consistently felt and observed the experience of 'be-longing' in such an environment.

The Thinking Environment and its Ten Components are the work of Nancy Kline (see Table 9.1). Her ongoing discoveries[6] over more than 35 years, in collaboration with her colleagues worldwide, have been about how we can create the conditions for individuals to think well *for* themselves. During her time at a Quaker school that she co-founded, Kline discovered that 'the most important factor in determining whether students could think for themselves, afresh, at any given moment, seemed to be how they were being treated by the people with them while they were thinking'. Eventually, the essential behaviours that helped people to think for themselves became clearer. Ten ways of being together have been identified thus far, specifically focused on how we treat one another. The Ten Components of a Thinking Environment refer to the conditions that manifest as behaviours and appear to consistently contribute to helping people think well for themselves. These ten components are Attention, Equality, Ease, Appreciation, Encouragement, Feelings, Information, Difference, Incisive Questions™ and Place.

Table 9.1 The Ten Components of a Thinking Environment

ATTENTION
Listening without interruption and with interest in where the person will go next in their thinking

EQUALITY
Regarding each other as thinking peers, giving equal time to think

---

[6] Kline encourages "a love for discovery that is marginally more than the love for the discoveries".

EASE
Discarding internal urgency

APPRECIATION
Noticing what is good and saying it

FEELINGS
Welcoming the release of emotion

ENCOURAGEMENT
Giving courage to go to the unexplored edge
of thinking by ceasing competition as thinkers

INFORMATION
Absorbing all the relevant facts

DIFFERENCE
Prioritizing diversity of group identities and
understanding their lived experience

INCISIVE QUESTIONS
Freeing the human mind of untrue
assumptions lived as true

PLACE
Producing a physical environment – the room, the
listener, your body – that says, 'You matter'

Kline, N. (2022) Available at: https://www.timetothink.com/thinking-environment/the-ten-components

Kline (2020) describes the Ten Components as "Nature at work. I think the human mind is looking for them all of the time". Any organizational culture can exhibit and embrace these behaviours to allow individual and corporate values to come to life. These behavioural components are actionable: we can offer generative attention, instil equality, restore ease, foster appreciation, provide encouragement, welcome feelings, absorb information, cultivate differences, craft incisive questions and establish place. They can be described distinctly yet are integral to one another. From my experience in introducing the Thinking Environment in organizations, the far-reaching effects of the Ten Components are often underestimated and even resisted because of their simplicity. Yet, it's a simplicity that sits on the far side of complexity.[7] And the principle of Occam's razor reminds us that the simplest proposition that requires the fewest assumptions is the most likely to be correct. One of my course participants, Natasha Dalmia, systems thinker and coach, observed that the components are Gestalt in nature, referring to an organized whole that is perceived as more than the sum of its parts.

An applied neuroscience (brain and behaviour) perspective supports Kline's ongoing observations and understanding that these ten behaviours not only work – they work every time. The reason for this dependable quality of thinking is that generative attention, uncorrupted and sustained, calms the amygdala, the emotional 'control centre' of the brain, making it possible for 'approach or attachment' hormones like serotonin and oxytocin to flow. These hormones then 'bathe' the cortex, the cognitive 'control centre' of the brain, allowing a perfect interplay between these hormones and cognition. And, because the

---

[7] Oliver Johnston observed that "the thinking environment holds the kind of simplicity that is to be found on the far side of complexity" (Kline, 2020, p. 117).

listener's attention doesn't waver, and we know it won't waver, the amygdala stays calm and thought-disturbing hormones like cortisol and adrenaline stay at bay (Brown as quoted in Kline, 2020, pp. 33–34). The bedrock practice that a Thinking Environment is built on is the promise of non-interruption in both its verbal and non-verbal nature. In fact, Kline concludes that the very first minute one of us in stark disagreement interrupts the other, the brain registers the interruption as a physical assault. Immediately, the brain hormones of adrenaline and cortisol bathe the cortex, the very centre of our thinking; the amygdala, dictator of feelings, instantly dispatches the triumvirate actions of freezing, fleeing, fighting. And, presto, we disconnect. Our thinking shrivels. And polarisation is born (Kline, 2020, p. 10). Laloux also mentions non-interruption in his ground rules for wholeness (Laloux, 2021).

The Thinking Environment can foster a whole way of organizational life in which individuals can go further in their thinking, recognizing the diverse convocation of lives that come together to form an organization. It creates the potential for individuals to grow into their best selves and employ the organizational context to pursue their individual passions while producing outcomes that reward the organization for creating such an environment; and so, the virtuous cycle continues. When people can be themselves, they have capacity for growth and development. In a conversation with Nancy Kline about this chapter, she shared that it's striking how many organizations say they have their values, the 'what', but they do not have the 'how'.

I think the Ten Components allow values to be lived. I don't see it as the culture of an organization but its consciousness, which has the power to cultivate an organizational culture and arrangements based on the widest possible welcome for one's whole and true sense of Self. I have observed and experienced that the Ten Components, when activated as a system, both harmonize the freedom enjoyed by individuals and commit them interpersonally through self-regulation.

In addition, the Thinking Environment provides liberating structures for all aspects of organizational activity to bring the Ten Components to life. In application, as further explained below in Table 9.2, the practical building blocks of Rounds, Thinking Pairs, Dialogue and Open Discussion support everyday conversations. Fuller applications support the way we problem solve (Time to Think Council[8]), hold meetings (Transforming Meetings), mediate (Timed Talk), interview, mentor and coach (Thinking Partnerships/Thinking Sessions).

All the building blocks and applications described below are held by the Ten Components, which is what allows them to create the conditions of a Thinking Environment. When the components are weak or missing, these approaches are not as liberating and may even be experienced as rules. With the support of the components, further bespoke applications can be developed for organizational life. At the same time, the components alone are sufficient to allow moment-to-moment interactions to flow.

Table 9.2 The building blocks and applications of a Thinking Environment

THINKING PAIR
A Thinking Pair refers to equal turns for two people to think for themselves about topics of their individual choices. There is no dialogue or comment on each other's turn unless requested by the thinker.

---

[8] Conceptualised by Nancy Kline in collaboration with Scott Farnsworth.

DIALOGUE

Dialogue at its best is not two people talking, it is two people thinking. Good dialogue could be described as thinking on the same topic with short, frequent, roughly equal turns back and forth as well as all the discipline of a Thinking Pair. Dialogue has a generative impact on independent thinking rather than making shared thinking explicit. In this way, it supports psychological freedom in an interdependent context.

ROUNDS

Rounds are a way of getting everyone thinking. A question is decided that people will be addressing in the round. The direction of the round (clockwise, counter-clockwise) is determined. A volunteer begins the round. No one speaks again until the round is completed.

OPEN DISCUSSION

Anyone can speak next in no particular order but without interruption and taking roughly equal turns. No one raises their hands to be put in a 'queue' of next speakers (in itself an interruption) and no one 'tailgates' the speaker.

TRANSFORMING MEETINGS

Transforming Meetings applies the Ten Components specifically through the Building Block Applications (of Thinking Pairs, Dialogue, Rounds and Open Discussion) to agenda items that are in the form of a question that focuses on the desired outcome from discussion of that item.

TIME TO THINK COUNCIL

The Time to Think Council allows for the wisdom of the group to make its ways non-intrusively into the problem-solving of one person. Each council member speaks in the language of experience and knowledge, not in the language of advice. The Presenter can access the knowledge, experience and information of colleagues without being told what to think.

TIMED TALK

This involves setting a timer and taking as many equal uninterrupted turns talking as necessary to resolve the issue.

MENTORING

Mentoring in a Thinking Environment has one goal: the independent thinking of the Mentee. This goal sets it apart from other mentoring models that rely heavily (and often unawarely) on advice and direction from the Mentor. The Mentoring Session begins with a Thinking Partnership Session for the Mentee. The Mentee is assured of uninterrupted Attention followed by 'incisive questions' to do their own thinking on a topic of their choice. This Session is then followed by the Interview, a period of questions from Mentee to Mentor.

The questions draw out life experience and knowledge from the Mentor that can both enrich the way the Mentee sees a situation and adds to their insights and framing of ways forward on their topic. However, this contribution from the Mentor is specifically not worded as advice so that the Mentee can continue to do their own thinking, come to their own conclusions and understanding, and agree to take responsibility for their own decisions and outcomes. Following the interview, the Mentee offers a Thinking Session to the Mentor. The expressly Mentee-focused aspect of the Mentoring process produces sustained confidence and self-esteem in the Mentee as well as successful problem-solving and achieving of goals. The Thinking Environment Mentoring Process communicates, in its very structure, genuine respect for the Mentee, and offers productive and often inspiring opportunity and time to think.

THINKING SESSION

A Thinking Session is a longer Thinking Pair during which more can happen including the building on assumptions and the possibility of exploring an incisive question. The process works well because it is grounded in the purpose of igniting independent thinking based on the principle that people make the most progress when they are self-motivated, autonomous and can feel respect from others.

PRESENTATION

The key skill for presentations is connection with the audience that determines the level of thinking the audience can do while the presenter speaks. A presenter thinks of the audience as a Thinking Partner, allowing their attention to encourage them. The use of slides involves a careful consideration of providing only supplementary and illustrative input without compromising the connection between the group and the presenter.

INTERVIEWS

The outcome is to elicit the best thinking from the interviewee and to create a liberating, not directive, experience for them through an embodiment of the Ten Components by the interviewer. The opening includes an invitation to share any questions or concerns about the interview. Note-taking is only after the interviewee has finished answering the question, and the interviewer shares who will read the notes and their use of them. The interviewer ends with an appreciation of a quality noticed in the interviewee.

DIVERSITY PROCESS

The component of difference includes both diversity of group identity and diversity of ideas. When we don't value each other's identity differences, we don't value our divergent thinking. The process explores ways to remove the blocks to pride in our diversity, so that we can think together – all of us – as ourselves. Participants learn about the place of assumptions in the creation and maintenance of our individual and group identities; and how to build incisive questions to replace untrue limiting assumptions about our individual and group identities with true and liberating ones, helping us to think better when working with each other. With the skill of building incisive questions and the Thinking Environment in general, the thinker can process well the limiting assumptions that surface and can create a very different life without them.

Source: Adapted from materials created by Nancy Kline, Time to Think Ltd.

These approaches overlap, and can be combined, with the insights of other thought leaders. For example, Laloux describes an empty chair practice whereby, in meetings, an empty chair is included that represents the organization and its purpose (Laloux, 2016, p. 123). By listening to themselves becoming the voice of the organization, employees can sense the interests of the organization by reflecting on questions such as whether the discussion and decisions serve the organization well.

Does the Thinking Environment work?

I propose that the Thinking Environment could be a blueprint for a Welcoming Organization based on how the future of work is evolving. Four organizational needs appear to be emerging:

1. Navigating work and work environments remotely requires even greater confidence in independent thinking because employees cannot rely solely on traditional avenues of on-the-job in-person induction, training, collaboration and networking, communication and relationship management.
2. Navigating work and the work environment remotely requires a renewed way of connecting with others that maintains a sense of belonging and inclusivity despite physical distancing.
3. With a psychological contract that balances the power between employer and employee, organizational environments will need to shift towards welcoming the whole Self of an employee (thoughts, feelings, personal aspirations, needs and preferred ways of working). However, this also leads to an integration challenge in the world of work. As we find more meaning in our work, and exercise more flexibility

in how we work, the boundaries between different aspects of our lives are blurring and we need a widely understood compass that helps create what I call 'integration margins' to prevent employees feeling overwhelmed and burnt out. Integration margins would help us create margins or spaces in our increasingly integrated lives to realign with Self.

4. Navigating organizational contexts from one acronym to the next (from VUCA – volatile, uncertain, complex, ambiguous to BANI – brittle, anxious, nonlinear, incomprehensible[9] to the next hopefully more positive acronym: WISER [see below]) will require an approach to organizational life that is not only discovery-based by nature but also open to exploration, and the organic emergence of an organizational culture and consciousness, based on the ongoing observations and experiences of those involved.

WISER is an acronym I have coined that stands for 'Welcoming, Integrated, Simplified, Easeful and Responsive'. It attempts to describe a positive experience of the dynamic integration of energy, information and relationships at both an individual and interpersonal level. In such a case, individuals would experience a welcome of Self resulting from an integrated flow of energy, information and relationships. I think this requires a simplifying of information exchange, processes, structures, number of relationships and systemic demands to facilitate this integration. Ease and space would create the conditions for us to evolve in our capacity to sense the subtleties of relationships and our environment, allowing us to respond continuously and optimally in a learning loop.

---

[9] VUCA appears to have been first used in 1987, drawing on the leadership theories of Warren Bennis and Burt Nanus. BANI is credited to American anthropologist, author and futurist, Jamais Cascio.

From my observations and experience of the Thinking Environment, it does support and create the space for independent thinking, self-awareness and coming to terms with oneself. I have consistently observed genuine humility that I believe is inculcated when individuals have a true sense of equality and allow themselves to experience something greater than themselves. Thinking Environment practitioners also strive to embrace the practice of discovery alongside their discoveries to date, reiterating Laloux's 'sense and respond' approach that is crucial to sustained organizational performance.

A look at the impact of the Thinking Environment on organizational life suggests that sustaining such an approach would support these emerging contexts.

Rebecca Timmins, Head of Operations at Emery Little and Time to Think practitioner, describes how, in team meetings conducted within a Thinking Environment, participants often examine assumptions that might be holding them back. They sometimes go as far as creating a specific incisive question but, more often, examining assumptions alone causes a shift that unlocks new potential. Box 9.1 describes a team meeting at Emery Little.

Box 9.1 Transforming meetings at Emery Little

As an example, Timmins described a team meeting to advance a quarterly goal set by the leadership team: "This new process needs to be business-as-usual by the end of the quarter." It was considered a big goal involving how client money was looked after and how clients were charged. They had some of the collateral ready to go, which included scripts and training for the financial planners and templates for two key documents that were in testing, but that was about it. They needed to create, train and embed a process, and quickly. And they felt totally stuck in their thinking because it just felt too big to make any progress on.

Then Rebecca asked, "What are we assuming that is keeping us stuck?" and the assumptions rolled in round after round. The team concluded that they were assuming they had to get it right, maybe even perfect, before they could take it to the wider team. They dismissed this as untrue and replaced it with: "Not only do they know better than us anyway, and need to be involved, but one of our core values is "progress" as in "progress, not perfection". So their incisive question was, "If we knew that we needed progress, not perfection, what would we do?" And the ideas came thick and fast.

Nine months later, they were 75% through the project. Clients were receiving a better service than ever and paying more for it. And the team was more engaged and committed than ever. The systems and processes were clearer and more efficient than ever before. Progress over perfection has become their normal, so they know they're not done, but every single person is committed to constant improvement.

Source: Produced with the kind permission of When We Think and Emery Little

Other research initiatives also support the positive impact of the Thinking Environment on organizational life. Emily Havers, who certified as a Time to Think consultant, conducted research into the effectiveness of the Transforming Meetings Programme (Havers, 2009). In her research on how meetings in a Thinking Environment have an impact on organizational life, she interviewed 15 senior officers from 11 organizations across 3 continents and found 95% consistency in the outcomes of meetings

held in a Thinking Environment. In particular, her research findings suggest that these meetings time and again:
- produced a measurable, positive impact on the performance indicators of organizations;
- generated better ideas, solutions and decisions;
- created an environment in which people felt valued and equal;
- achieved resolution faster;
- gave rise to greater participation and more involvement from everyone; and
- fostered productive working relationships.

A 2007 research initiative by Beverly Whitehead, an organizational psychologist and coaching practitioner, researched the effectiveness of the Time to Think mentoring programme involving 16 mentoring pairs in South Africa over 6 months. In her research, most participants reported that the programme:
- balanced the voices in the organization;
- increased respect for each other; and
- developed interpersonal skills.

And that, through it, people:
- shared knowledge and experience;
- generated good thinking, ideas and innovation;
- solved work problems; and
- resolved inner conflicts relating to self or career.

One of my participants, the head of a business line for a listed company, appreciated his Thinking Environment course experience by concluding that it is not the nature of the challenge that makes it difficult to think about our business problems, but the *way* we think about them.

Because the practical applications of a Thinking Environment are grounded in the Ten Components, they can be embedded pervasively in an organization and its everyday work practices rather than appearing as bursts of add-ons that we sometimes observe in the case of an event-based approach to diversity, inclusion and belonging. This is because the Thinking Environment is a way of being: all the components, including appreciation, difference-in-action and equality, are cultivated and embodied in every interaction. And such an environment need not be restricted to for-profit organizations.

The resulting paradigm shifts

Individuals come together to create an organization. As more individuals within an organization practise these ways of being in terms of the Ten Components, organizations can expect to observe the following behavioural shifts from:
- urgency to ease;
- feedback to appreciation;
- time management to attention and energy 'flowment' (a term I have coined to refer to our ability to generate and sustain a flow of energy in ourselves and those around us as we act in the service of truly human organizational goals that reflect conscientiousness for all stakeholders);
- competitive thinking to encouraging and championing independent cutting-edge thinking;[10] and
- too much information all the time to just enough information when needed.

And more expansive shifts including:
- expanding the notion of place to encompass internal place (Self) and external place (a physical and a

---

[10] Thinking independently is one of the four Paths described in Time to Think practitioner, Nick Chatrath's book *The Threshold: Leading in the Age of AI* which is dedicated to describing threshold leadership in the coming AI context. According to Chatrath, the four pathways (Cultivating Stillness, Thinking Independently, Embodying Intelligence and Maturing Consciousness) offer a way of being to progress in leading in the age of AI.

digital environment) to make everyone feel that they matter;
- acknowledging the mix of feelings and well-being that drive thoughts and behaviour, and recognizing that the treatment for well-being is 'treating others well to be';
- embodying and embedding difference and equality in organizational culture (that is, diversity and inclusion in action that allows for our humanness to transcend our social constructs and contexts); and
- expanding the notion of productivity to include the quality thinking that precedes activity.

In essence, workplace conditions and arrangements would be designed in human versus process terms, thereby creating sustainable organizations. The sustainability stems from the interplay of the Ten Components. For instance, equality and information harmonize difference; ease and place support both attention and encouragement to get things done without burnout.

Kline highlights the relationship between Self and organization as follows:

> In a thinking organization these Ten Components flow continuously through the individuals and the organization. Both thrive only if the Thinking Environment is reciprocal between them. This kind of reciprocity should be part of our definition of equality. Each of us matters but what we create matters too, and how we treat our creation determines how it will treat us. We depend on each other. We are both. (Kline, 1999, p. 140)

The behaviours and activities of individuals create an 'Organizational Self', a term I'm using to refer to an organization's essential being. The Organizational Self, in turn, creates the conditions for individuals to thrive (or not). And, like the working mind, the organization also seems to do this by integrating energy, information and relationships. The way the organization triangulates these three can be described as its *culture* ('the way we do things around here', especially as observed in the examples set by those enjoying positional hierarchy). The ends towards which the organization triangulates these three can be described as its *purpose*. The operating context in which the organization triangulates these three describes its *mission*. And the outcomes and means to accomplishing this triangulation can be described as its *vision* broken down into strategy and then operations. In these ways, the organization starts creating an identity for itself that differentiates it from others – namely, how individuals cooperate internally and how the organization competes or collaborates externally. And organizational performance, like individual performance, depends on how healthy the system is.

An individual's perception of this Organizational Self (how welcome they feel by it) determines whether they consider a particular organization worth giving of themselves (their Self) to. For individuals, the more positive the triangulation at the individual and organizational level, the more integrated their experience at work (and vice versa) as individuals see their own purpose in the shared purpose of the organization. Organizations successful at this integration, both internally and externally, would be committed to stakeholder consciousness rather than just shareholder capitalism. This would support the creation of a WISER[11] reality, which, in turn, the organization would benefit from. And I think what underpins the functioning of all this is 'generative flow'.

---

[11] Refers to the WISER acronym described earlier of 'welcoming, integrated, simplified, easeful and responsive'.

Generative flow

> Human resources are like natural resources: they're often buried beneath the surface and you have to make an effort to find them
>
> – Ken Robinson, TED Talk, 2010[12]

In conversation, Paul Brown explains that developments in neuroscience are confirming that we are primarily energy systems, and that our individual psychology comes from the way our brain is both shaped by and responds to the emotionally driven energy flowing through it. This energy-in-motion is profoundly 'e-motional' because it is emotions generating feelings that are attached to the stimuli of experience in the shaping of the individuality of the brain. And then language, via the cognitive system, begins to represent the emotionally signified experience to us, and from us to others, and so gives us an account of what our brain already knows. Modern neuroscience has shown us that, at any moment in time, through its emotional system, the brain has prepared itself and the rest of the body for action well in advance of that preparedness coming into conscious awareness. The brain can organize itself for action within 85 milliseconds. Awareness does not arise until 250 milliseconds (Brown and Dzendrowskyj, 2018).

From my experience, the Thinking Environment offers:
1. the widest welcome for the flow of our emotions; and
2. the least interruption of thoughts flowing into conscious awareness.

This is valuable because cognitive performance and brilliance are generated from the intelligence of emotions – that is, having an acute awareness of our e-motional

---

[12]https://www.ted.com/talks/sir_ken_robinson_bring_on_the_learning_revolution/transcript

experiences and thoughts, and the language[13] to describe the subtlety of those experiences.

Most importantly, how can we create the conditions for people to see themselves and things 'truthfully'?

You are welcome

One of my course participants, and co-contributor to this book, Nandini Das Ghoshal, executive and life coach, and co-founder of *The Story of Me*, coined a phrase for what she experienced in the Thinking Environment as 'the Uninterrupted Me'. I feel this phrase captures the essence of who we can be in the context of a Welcoming Organization.

I think the following describes the experience of the Uninterrupted Me in terms of the psychological freedoms[14] one would enjoy in a Welcoming Organization built on Thinking Environment principles that would allow us to see ourselves and things more truthfully:

1. I would have access to uninterrupted time to think alone and in the presence of someone's generative attention.[15]

---

[13] I think eloquence may be a "thinking enhancer" (term coined by Nancy Kline). Insights can be hard to express in language, but our lived experience of them makes them real for us. Some deep insights and experiences are ineffable for us because they challenge our limits of linguistic expression that would allow us to fully grasp them and extract meaning from them. The more an individual has the conceptual and linguistic precision to articulate an insight, the more clarity it holds for the individual. We are elated during an insight when we can ascribe apt words to that combination of feeling and thought that is arising within us. Those specific words resonate with us and are compelling for us. In this way, insights are personal in both substance and expression.

[14] These psychological freedoms contain expressions coined by Nancy Kline in the Thinking Environment.

[15] In the book, *You're Not Listening*, the author, Kate Murphy, has detailed the value of "the voluble inner voice" by sharing research-based insights into the importance of listening to yourself. Murphy includes a quote by physicist and Nobel Prize winner, Richard Feynman, who wrote in his book of essays, *The Pleasure of Finding Things Out*: "By trying to put the

2. I would have relevant information when needed to be able to do my best thinking.
3. I would not receive unsolicited advice.
4. I would be able to unlock my thinking from untrue assumptions that I've been living (with) as true.
5. I would be able to dismantle denial by facing what needs facing.
6. I would be encouraged to go further in my thinking.
7. I would be able to discard competitive thinking.
8. I would be able to absorb difference-in-action to think outside the constructs of identities.
9. I would be able to appreciate myself and others by looking for, noticing and acknowledging what is good.
10. I would be able sufficiently to release and restore my sense of well-being.

This may raise the concern, "How can an environment that allows me to be me also create the conditions for me to bring my best Self to work?"

In the TED talk series, *How to Be a Better Human*, Herminia Ibarra, the Charles Handy Professor of Organizational Behaviour at the London Business School, reminds us that whatever made us successful in the past may not make us successful going forward and might even get in the way. She explains that what's tricky about career transition points is not that the new skills are hard to learn – it's that the old ones have become core to our sense of who we are, our identity. As a result, not sticking with them feels like we are somehow being inauthentic and so we get stuck by staying with them (Ibarra, 2021).

To overcome the 'authenticity paradox' and embrace an 'adaptively authentic' way of being, concepts coined by

---

points of view that we have in our head together and comparing one to the other, we make some progress in understanding and appreciating where we are and what we are."

Ibarra (Ibarra, 2015), I have found Thinking Partnerships/ Sessions to be valuable. To develop a new way of thinking about ourselves, we need to come to terms with the underlying assumptions that are driving our existing behaviours so that we can change our perception of Self and life.

When you do things from your Soul, you feel a river moving in you, a joy.

– Rumi[16]

In a way, a Thinking Session unlocks one's confidence to be the best version of one's Self. This seems to be supported by findings explained by Ian Robertson in his 2021 book, *How Confidence Works: The new science of self-belief.* Unravelling the win of the British Open by golfer Padraig Harrington, Robertson describes the creation of a mental zone in which his attention was focused on a specific goal within a circle of control. Fuelling a turnaround, Harrington's caddy, Ronan Flood, offered the golfer words that allowed only memories linked to past successes with chipping and putting to come out of his memory banks. This "focused Harrington's attention into an almost trance-like state on this tiny hinterland of behaviour". Describing attention as a psychological regulator, Robertson highlights the powerful duo of attention and confidence with words being potent orchestrators of them. This amplifies the value of a Thinking Session in which all the 'content' is thinker-generated so the focus is on words that carry full context and significance for the thinker.[17]

---

[16] Source: Jeffrey Douglass (2008) *Living from your soul*, p. 45. Eustis, Florida: SPS Publications.

[17] I have a memorable experience of the significance of our words from a Thinking Session in which my outcome was: "I want to feel less challenged *by* this relationship." My Thinking Partner-in-training replayed my outcome as "... feel less challenged *in* the relationship", following which I felt and articulated a defensiveness that I had already made progress in

And the Thinking Partner offers valuable continuous attention: a psychological generator. The quality of an incisive question, offered as many times as it generates productive thinking, focuses one's thoughts on liberating possibilities within a circle of control or influence, thereby creating the necessary shift in emotions and thoughts. As Robertson describes, by allowing one to pay attention to the right things, you do them better, which in turn makes you more confident, which then makes you do them even better, and so on.

In a Thinking Session, the Uninterrupted Me can unleash a built-in confidence booster by deciding which personal truths can be dismissed, replaced and embedded in exploring new possibilities for the 'aspirational Self'. And when a session surfaces "bedrock assumptions about self or life" (Kline, 1999), it has a liberating effect on many aspects of life. This breakthrough process allows the thinker to rewrite (rewire) their "plot" through a shift in feelings. For me, assumptions seem to be part of the brain's working language for adaptation. It is interesting to observe and experience how assumptions that were liberating in a past context can be limiting in a current context, but this needs an opportunity to come up into our consciousness. From a coaching perspective, it is a very efficacious partnering expertise because the thinker journeys independently through the derivative of a biographical inquiry (examination of assumptions) but with a feedforward focus (moving towards the accomplishment of outcomes).

This practice has revived the word 'empowerment' for me – a word that in some contexts has been understood as giving power to others. An applied neuroscience

---

creating a distance in the relationship, so I no longer identified with being *in* it but still felt challenged *by* it.

perspective reveals what true empowerment would be. We each have a brain with the capacity – and inclination – to act in our best interests in terms of self-preservation and adaptation. At any point in time, although only within the framework and perhaps limitations of its own experience, our brain is causing us to act adaptively in a way that it has determined is in our best interests. We may make mistakes and regret our actions but that is a consequence of hindsight and reflection because we have moved on.[18] As we are reminded in the novel, *Midnight Library*, by Matt Haig, "the only way to learn is to live". Humanistic ideas of self-authoring and self-actualisation are in line with the Thinking Environment's commitment to empowerment by igniting independent thinking that allows for individuals to unleash the 'all-knowing' already within their system.

After taking participants through a Thinking Session exercise, one shared with the group: "After today, I'll never be lonely again, because I'll always have another me." This response reveals 'unstuck' and psychological freedom. Other participants have described their experience of the Thinking Environment as "wholesome", "soulful", "feeling true to myself" and "one of the few places in the world where others allow me to be me, and I allow myself to be me". This reinforces a discovery by Nancy Kline that "we can think *for* ourselves only if we can think *as* ourselves".

From freedom to fulfilment

Say not, "I have found the truth," but rather, "I have found a truth."

– Kahlil Gibran

In the beginning of this chapter, I shared a conversation that Paul Brown and I had on coming up with a title for this

---

[18] Heraclitus's insight that one can never step twice in the same river for neither the person nor the river is the same in time and space.

chapter. That was not the whole conversation because I had shared another idea for the title. I had been reading the book, *The Molecule of More*, by Lieberman and Long (2018), and learned of anandamide, which is an endocannabinoid (part of a collection of neurotransmitters they refer to as the 'Here and Now' molecules) and is named after a Sanskrit word that means joy, bliss and delight. Attracted to this description of a state where we could experience enough contentment with ourselves and our conditions, I had shared the possibility of a "Blissful Organization" with Dr Brown. He had replied, "We're not there yet." And after a generative pause in his thinking, he added, "But how lovely it would be. The idea that we could finish a day of work and, when asked how our day was, be able to reply, "It was blissful."

For organizations, perhaps the invitation is to cultivate a shift from fear to freedom and ultimately to fulfilment where, in bringing the best of our Self, we can experience the best of being human. As described in the London Protocol of the Emotions (see inside front cover), we can start experiencing our growing trust in Self and others as 'faith'. In terms of our evolution, it can be seen as expanding from surviving to thriving and, finally, to arriving.

> We shall not cease from exploration
> And the end of all our exploring
> Will be to arrive where we started
> And know the place for the first time.

– T.S. Eliot, 'Little Gidding', *The Four Quartets*, 1941.

As we invite in the Thinking Environment, "What do you think, or feel or want to say?"

I welcome you and your discovery of Self.

References

Brown, P. and Dzendrowskyj, T (2018) 'Sorting out an emotional muddle: Insights from neuroscience on the organizational value of emotions, *Developing Leaders*, Issue 29.

Brown, P., Kingsley, J. and Paterson, S. (2015) *The fear-free organization: Vital insights from neuroscience to transform your business culture*. London: Kogan Page.

Carlisle, C. (2011) *Spinoza, part 6: Understanding the emotions*, Guardian News & Media Limited. Available at:https://www.theguardian.com/commentisfree/belief/2011/mar/14/spinoza-understanding-emotions (Accessed 8 November 2022).

Chatrath, N. (2023) *The Threshold: Leading in the Age of AI*. United States of America: Diversion Books.

Haig, M. (2020) *Midnight library*. Canada: HarperCollins.

Havers, E. (2009) *A study of whether and how meetings in a thinking environment impact organizational life*. UK: University of Southampton.

Ibarra, H. (2015) *The authenticity paradox*. Available at: https://hbr.org/2015/01/the-authenticity-paradox (Accessed 8 November 2022).

Ibarra, H. (2021) *Yes, good leaders are authentic leaders – but here's what that actually means*. Available at: https://ideas.ted.com/yes-good-leaders-are-authentic-leaders-but-heres-what-that-actually-means/ (Accessed 8 November 2022).

Kline, N. (1999) *Time to think*. London: Cassell, Octopus Publishing Group Ltd.

Kline, N. (2015) *More time to think*. London: Cassell, Octopus Publishing Group Ltd.

Kline, N. (2020) *The promise that changes everything: I won't interrupt you*. UK: Penguin Life.

Laloux, F. (2016) *Reinventing organizations: an illustrated invitation to join the conversation on next-stage organizations.* Brussels: Nelson Parker.

Laloux, F. (2021) *Laloux's insights: A document with ground rules for wholeness.* Available on: https://enliveningedge.org/tools-practices/lalouxs-insights-document-ground-rules-wholeness/ (Accessed 8 November 2022).

Lanz, K. and Brown, P. (2020) *All the brains in the business: The engendered brain in the 21st century organization.* Switzerland: Palgrave Macmillan.

Lieberman, D. and Long, M. (2018) *The molecule of more: How a single chemical in your brain drives love, sex, and creativity – and will determine the fate of the human race.* Dallas: BenBella Books Inc.

Murphy, K. (2019) *You're not listening: What you're missing and why it matters.* New York: Celadon Books.

Nadella, S. (2017) *Hit refresh: The quest to rediscover Microsoft's soul and imagine a better future for everyone.* New York: HarperCollins.

Nooyi, I. (2021) *My life in full: Work, family, and our future.* New York: Portfolio/Penguin.

Robertson, I. (2021) *How confidence works: The new science of self-belief.* London: Bantam Press/Penguin Random House.

Robinson, K. (2011), *Out of our minds: Learning to be creative.* Oxford: Capstone Publishing Ltd (a Wiley company).

Robinson, K. and Aronica, L. (2013), *Finding your element: How to discover your talents and passions and transform your Life.* London: Penguin Books.

Robinson, K. and Robinson, K. (2022), *Imagine if... Creating a future for us all.* London: Penguin Books.

Siegel, D. (2012) *Pocket guide to interpersonal neurobiology: An integrative handbook of the mind.* California: W.W. Norton & Company.

Sternberg, P. and Dawe, F. (2018), *Integrating wellbeing and student engagement: Lessons from the Growing Creative Leaders of the Future Programme.* London: Leadership Foundation for Higher Education. Available at: https://www.timetothink.com/wp-content/uploads/2021/03/leadershipfoundationreportsept2018.pdf (Accessed 8 November 2022).

Whitehead, B. (2007) *Newlands Brewery pilot mentoring programme.* Cape Town, South Africa.

Acknowledgements

I'm grateful to Nancy Kline for your generosity of time and attention in sharing your thoughts on this chapter. I appreciate your integrity and rigour. Your discovery of the Thinking Environment is a gift to many for tuning in with confidence.

I'm also grateful to Dr Paul Brown for your mentorship during this chapter. I appreciate your patience and generosity. Your passion for understanding and applying neuroscience is a beautiful invitation to lead a life with greater awareness.

Biography

Khyati Kapai is the Founder of Yzer Solutions Pte Ltd (pronounced 'wiser'), a learning and development consultancy. Khyati has been teaching, facilitating, and coaching since 2001. Khyati is also a Faculty Member of Time to Think Ltd, offering courses in the Thinking Environment and supporting organizations in creating its conditions. Khyati has worked internationally supporting clients from diverse cultural and professional backgrounds including investment bankers in Shanghai, engineers in Singapore, ministry officials in Cambodia, and luxury retailers in Europe. Clients choose to work with Khyati for her rich thinking interventions and evidence-informed approach to learning and behavioural shifts.

Before moving to the talent development industry, Khyati worked in Hong Kong as a Financial Analyst for Citigroup and as an Auditor for Deloitte & Touche. She is based in Singapore and grew up in Hong Kong.

CHAPTER 10

Thinking of Others

Leanne Drew-McKain

Introduction

"I used to be terrified of flying," said the chatty man to my right as we passed 30,000 feet on our 5-hour flight to Perth, Western Australia. "I also used to be afraid of heights, but I'm not anymore." He had my instant attention in a way he could not have expected and I encouraged him to tell me more.

He continued:

A few years ago, on a walking holiday with my wife, I came across a viewing tower in a rainforest and decided to challenge myself to climb it. I really wanted to finally conquer my fear.

I started the climb; I was very scared – shaking. I got about halfway up the tower and just froze. I couldn't go any further up and was too scared to get down. I gripped onto the railings and I don't think I moved for at least 15 minutes. Eventually, I summoned the courage to loosen my grip and gingerly start the climb down. When I got to the ground, I was a mess.

I went on with the holiday, but my frustration and disappointment in my failure remained. So, on the last day of our holiday, I decided to go back and see if I could make it to the top of the tower.

There I was – at the bottom of the tower again. I started the climb, still just as scared; terrified. I got to the halfway mark again and stopped. I bumped into another man! He was stuck, frozen with fear. "I can't move, I'm too scared," he trembled.

"Right," I said. "Let's do this together. Come on, you can do it. You'll be okay, I promise. You start climbing and I'll be right behind you, so you can't fall."

You know what? We did it! We climbed all the way to the top, and back down again, without stopping.

This courageous climber's story begs a compelling question. What neural pathway-disrupting power could possibly be great enough to shift the brain out of a runaway panic attack in full flight?

Is it just possible that triggering a shift in our cortical circuitry that redirects our emotion from 'self' to 'other' is key to conquering what author H.P. Lovegrove calls "the oldest and strongest emotion of mankind" – fear?

Fear in motion

Neuroscientist Michael Gazzaniga describes the challenge of understanding how neural cells lead to felt conscious states in the human mind as "the toughest problem in all of science" (LeDoux, 2015, p. ii).

Much of the function and structure of our neural networks implies that, of all emotions, fear poses the greatest threat to one's sense of self-efficacy and self-control (Hope, 1996) – with the limbic brain working as an ever-vigilant system striving to keep its owner safe.

At the base of each medial temporal lobe, above the brain stem, the amygdala act as the brain's emotion-processing centre (Cozolino, 2010), cyclically receiving environmental, internal and social stimuli that it is continuously assessing for their emotional significance. To imagine where your amygdala are, an area in each half of the brain, visualize a line going inwards from your left ear to meet a line going inwards from your left eye: and then the same for the right ear and eye. Those two areas are almond-shaped (the Greek word for almond is 'amygdalon'). An intensely sensitive radar that is a key part of the system for assessing and managing all emotions, the amygdala network appears to have a particular preoccupation with sorting stimuli for fear significance. Attending to potential threats and seeking to first establish who and what is safe, and who and what is threatening, it is the gateway to our fear reaction–response circuitry.

My flight companion's story suggests that the state of 'caring' is a potential answer to managing this strong primordial emotion in pursuit of solutions to anxiety and other insecurity-driven neuropsychological conditions that assail the post-modern human. Conditions such as depression, eating disorders, gambling, pain addiction and compulsive behaviour disorders are all disorders of the 'self' (LeDoux, 1996). What if their cure lies in each 'other'? Furthermore, could the practice of empathy arrest emotional responses that lever more intrinsic patterns of self-destructive thought that fall outside the realm of diagnosed conditions but are common to human struggle?

While Joseph LeDoux, a pioneer in the neurobiological analysis of fear, warns that, "we should not mix findings about different emotions all together independent of the emotion that they are findings about" (1996, p. 16), he draws attention to the wider importance of fear studies: "Fear conditioning became one of the most popular areas of research in neuroscience, and one known for having made great strides in relating brain to behaviour" (LeDoux, 2015, p. 11).

In the struggle to understand the complex interplay between our neural circuitry, conscious and non-conscious thought, and felt emotional states, let's explore the idea that 'others thinking' – shifting the mind's attention from 'self' to 'other' – shrinks the threat response and generates an affective trust response to counter the most powerful of our escape/avoidance emotions and generate attachment emotions.

The limits of 'I' thinking

In the grip of fear, the prospect of forming new neural pathways for attachment emotions fully tests the promises of neuroplasticity (Hope, 1996). As the limbic brain picks up threatening stimuli (for example, a room in which we've received a hurtful insult, the face of a person who mocked us, the memory of receiving alarming news), the amygdala will attach a fear emotion to the signal and on to neurons. The neurons fire along our cortical pathways, travelling along axons and reaching each synapse. Neurotransmitters are released into the synapse and attach to the post-synaptic receptor, releasing chemicals – in particular, the stress hormone cortisol – that respond to and create our emotions of stress and anxiety.

Simultaneously, chemical responses course through the sympathetic nervous system, while right-side frontal regions such as the right ventro-lateral prefrontal cortex receive the fear emotion, shrinking the brain's glucose and oxygen supply and, along with it, the best of our rational thinking. We attach a fear-based language, now in conscious receipt of this information, ("I can't do this"; "I need to get out", "I feel stupid", "I am totally out of my depth" ...) and the pattern repeats (Panksepp, 2008).

Identifying a synaptic force strong enough to disrupt this deeply established cortical response requires us to first understand the source of the fear emotion: 'self', 'I'. LeDoux proposes that 'I' thinking continues the preoccupation with 'self' and does not offer the potential to ignite neurological pathways to shrink the threat response:

> Fear and anxiety, as I will argue later, both involve the self. To experience fear is to know that YOU are in a dangerous situation, and to experience anxiety is to worry about

whether future threats may harm YOU. This involvement of the self in fear and anxiety is a defining feature of these and other human emotions. (LeDoux, 2015, p. 11)

Illuminating the neurobiology behind this premise, David Franks observes the significance of the strength of the cortical pathways between the parts of our limbic system that involve emotions, such as the amygdala, and our conscious brain:

> The ... neuronal channels going up from the emotional centers of the brain to the more cognitive centers are denser and more robust than the cognitive centers going down to inhibit and control the emotional structures. Self-conscious efforts to avoid prejudice, fear, hatred, and depression are often rendered unsuccessful by this imbalance (Franks, 2006, p. 39).

Affective neuroscience researchers Richard Davidson and Sharon Begley identify that the awareness of self in the brain heavily involves the insula, located in the cerebral cortex between the temporal and frontal lobes (Davidson and Begley, 2012). The insula, especially the insula in the right hemisphere, is also highly activated in the experience of emotional as well as physical pain.

Davidson and Begley found that greater awareness of both physical sensations and the emotions of self are associated with higher insula activation. Few would argue the importance of self-awareness – that is, the awareness of an individual's own emotions, thoughts and actions, and their impacts. However, self-awareness and self-preoccupation are two very different neurobiological constructs. Just as LeDoux proposed, a fixation with one's own thoughts, feelings and senses, spotlighted by Davidson's findings of associated heightened insula activity, can keep us bound by deleterious emotion/thought patterns and narratives. Indeed, Davidson found that over-activation of the insula can produce hypochondria and panic attacks (Davidson and Begley, 2012).

The power of 'others thinking'

Expanding neuroscientific knowledge about the function of a system of mirror neurons in the human brain is reshaping ideas of 'I' in relationship to 'us' and deepening our understanding of the nature of the social brain (Siegel, 2010a). Found in the premotor cortex, supplementary motor cortex, primary somatosensory cortex and inferior parietal cortex, mirror neurons fire when one person communicates with another, helping us understand, empathize and connect. Accordingly, in developing the field of interpersonal neurobiology, Daniel Siegel and others propose 'the mind' as something shared between people, rather than owned.

Communication neuroscientists, Andrew Newberg and Mark Waldman, describe the mirror neuron system as key to understanding how our brains know what is going on in the brains of others: "These unique neurons are located in areas directly affected by meditation and appear to be intimately involved in the processes of facial recognition, compassion, communication and self/other consciousness" (Newberg and Waldman, 2009, p. 45).

These findings indicate that mirror neurons play a crucial role in enabling a shift in our attention from 'self' to 'other' thinking, allowing us to create emotion/thought-pattern pathways out of self-awareness-driven 'I' thinking and to transfer attention to the needs of the 'other': an emotion/thought-pattern shift that, when repeated, may have powerful potential to change our brain chemistry. The operating of mirror neurons would of course be subject to cultural experiences of all kinds, Western cultures being perhaps much more intrigued by delineations such as 'I' and 'other' than Eastern cultures.

Indeed, Siegel proposes that we can only understand 'me' in relationship to 'we', and that our mirror neuron system is the key to attending to 'other': "Right hemisphere signals are those the mirror neuron system uses to simulate the 'other' within ourselves and so construct a neural map of our *interdependent* sense of 'self'" (Siegel, 2011).

A study by Davidson in which he recorded *magnetic resonance imaging (MRI)* scans of Tibetan monks in states of prayer and meditation demonstrated that, through meditation, single-focus concentration and generating compassion, the pathways of the brain can be changed (Davidson and Begley, 2012).

Davidson and Begley, who also note the involvement of the left ventro-lateral prefrontal cortex, the nucleus accumbens and the anterior cingulate cortex in positive attention towards others, say that the brain can be changed by compassion meditation so that, "Rather than becoming depressed by suffering, people who are trained in compassion meditation develop a strong disposition to alleviate suffering and to wish others to be happy" (2012, p. 223).

Newberg and Waldman expound this theme in their model of 'compassionate communication', which proposes that, if we can speak from "the depth of our beings" and not from a place of defensiveness and self-protection, we can communicate with less anger and more honesty, and to greater result. Moreover, we can access the truths in the exchange not with fear but through trust:

> Contemplative practices stimulate activity in the anterior cingulate cortex, thus helping a person to become more sensitive to the feelings of others. Meditating on any form of love ... appears to strengthen the same neurological circuits that allow us to feel compassion towards others ... We believe that meditation is particularly important for the brain because it counteracts our biological propensity to react to dangerous situations with animosity or fear (Newberg and Waldman, 2009, p. 53).

Newberg, Waldman, Davidson, Begley and Siegel all propose, in their own various research-based narratives, that an individual's 'mind' comes from interpersonal processes as well as from brain structure or neurobiology. Siegel proposes that we can liberate ourselves from harmful, debilitating thought patterns by concentrating the mind on others-focused exchanges in our interpersonal relationships, creating new forms of mental flow and new neural connections that shape the locus of our attention.

Even in the face of conditioned chemical, neurological and physiological threat responses, the mental processes of imagination and attention can change the firing in the brain to produce love, trust, excitement and joy – and return our sense of safety.

The transfer – making the shift

Jeffrey Schwartz and Sharon Begley at the University of California are among numbers of leading scientists to provide firm evidence that the mind can control the brain's chemistry (Schwartz and Begley, 2002b).

Neuroscientists continue to test and prove the power of patterned thoughts to change our brain chemistry, but note that it must be a change in emotion that comes first, before the change in perception. Then, attaching a new perception can change the emotion (Brown, Kingsley and Paterson, 2015). In this almost symbiotic relationship between thought and emotion lies the nexus of neuroplasticity.

Schwartz and Begley, through an extensive study involving patients with obsessive-compulsive disorder, concluded that people could change the way they "thought about their thoughts" through deliberate, regular refocusing to shift them out of automatic thought patterns to intentional thought patterns (Schwartz and Begley, 2002a).

Where, as LeDoux (2015) and Davidson and Begley (2012) propose, overly heightened 'self' thoughts bind individuals in states of stress, fear and anxiety, mindfulness and cognitive-behaviour therapy techniques can help settle down the activity of the insula and make required cognitive shifts. Among them, Davidson suggests that attaching a lesser perceived significance to stimuli and their consequent emotions is a valuable technique, choosing the emotional significance of an experience to which we have attached distress. However, as LeDoux proposes, fear and anxiety are by necessity preoccupations with how 'I' feel, directing our needful attention to the potential of strategies that focus on 'other'.

A region that may be especially important to us in this shift is the ventromedial prefrontal cortex (vmPFC). Several studies strongly associate the vmPFC with two very important functions – the practice of cognitive empathy (Shamay-Tsoory, Aharon-Peretz and Perry, 2009) and the extinction of fear (LeDoux, 2003). Drawn together, these exciting findings on the vmPFC suggest that fear regulation and empathy are interrelated. More specifically, they suggest that this region is a centre capable of creating patterns in pathways activated when we learn how to *override* a fear response and then consolidate that learning. It seems that what we are in fact 'learning' here is how to stimulate, sustain and repeat a state of empathy – and, in so doing, while not paying cognitive attention to self, extinguish fear emotions. Indeed, cognitive empathy, as described by Simone Shamay-Tsoory, is 'learned' empathy, able to be consciously summoned and practised. So let's explore a little further how we might give effect to that learning ...

Newberg and Waldman assert that "Activities involving meditation and intensive prayer permanently strengthen neural functioning in specific parts of the brain that are involved with lowering anxiety and depression, enhancing social awareness and empathy, and improving cognitive and intellectual functioning" (2009, p. 49).

Similarly, Siegel exhorts mindfulness as a means of helping people regulate their emotions, attention and personal interactions, stimulating the growth of integrative fibres in the brain. He also proposes that interpersonal relationships are attuned to promote the growth of these integrative fibres – drawing us again to a focus on others as key to our mental health:

It is these regulatory fibres that enable the embodied brain to function well and for the mind to have a deep sense of coherence and wellbeing. Such a state also creates the possibility of a sense of being connected to a larger world. The natural outcome of integration is compassion, kindness, and resilience (Siegel, 2011).

In shifting the mind's attention to others to promote empathy, Manning et al. draw attention to the importance of consciously relaxing, staying present, cultivating inner silence, increasing positive thoughts, reflecting on deepest values, accessing pleasant memories, observing non-verbal cues, expressing appreciation, listening, and speaking warmly and slowly (2012, p. 44).

In allowing for the effect of non-verbal cues to create changes in thought pathways in the context of interpersonal exchanges, the human brain's fundamental attraction to faces is paramount. Our sensitivity to the small differences between facial expressions and characteristics in others is higher than for any other object category (O'Toole, 2005).

Above all other stimuli, our amygdala scan faces, then body language, tone of voice, early words and their intonation to assess the presence of a threat or the potential to trust (Franks, 2006). Focusing in on the need indicated in the face of another and shifting attention to their vulnerability or insecurity, with questions such as "What do they need?", "What can I do for them?", "How can I meet their insecurity?" may be a vital ingredient in facilitating a 'self' to 'other' transfer. The findings of Katharina Henke et al. into the powerful subliminal effect of words and faces demonstrate that subliminally presented stimuli – in particular, facial expressions – influence subjects' choices and so must have been perceived, and that the role of the cerebral cortex seems to play a dominant role in subliminal perception (Henke, Landis and Markowitsch, 1994).

Siegel describes the prefrontal cortex as "the portal through which interpersonal relations are established": "The brain is exquisitely social, and emotions are its fundamental language: Through them we become integrated and develop an emergent resonance with the internal state of the *other*" (2011).

Could it be that contemporary neuroscience is puzzling together an ancient truth? Is the emotional system in the prefrontal cortex inviting us on a journey from self to other and pointing us towards a defining feature of human purpose and prosperity?

Thus, because he loves to pacify the pains of others, he whose mind is attuned in this way, would enter even the deepest hell, just as a wild goose plunges into a lotus pond.

Arya Shantideva, A guide to the Bodhisattva's way of life

Perfect love casteth out fear.
John the Evangelist, 1 John 4:18

References

Brown, P., Kingsley J. and Paterson, S. (2015) *The fear free organization: Vital insights from neuroscience to transform your business culture.* London: Kogan Page.

Cozolino, L. (2010) *The neuroscience of psychotherapy: Healing the social brain.* 2nd edn. Norton Series on Interpersonal Neurobiology. New York: W. W. Norton & Company.

Davidson, R.J. and Begley, S. (2012) *The emotional life of your brain: How its unique patterns affect the way you think, feel and live – and how you can change them.* New York: Plume.

Franks, D.D. (2006) 'The neuroscience of emotions', in Stets, J.E. and Turner, J.H. (eds) *Handbook of the sociology of emotions.* Boston, MA: Springer.

Henke K., Landis T. and Markowitsch H.J. (1994) 'Subliminal perception of words and faces', *International Journal of Neuroscience*, 75(3–4), pp. 181–7.

Hope, D.A. (ed.) (1996) *Nebraska Symposium on Motivation, 1995: Perspectives on anxiety, panic and fear.* Lincoln, NE: University of Nebraska Press.

LeDoux, J. (1996) *The emotional brain: The mysterious underpinnings of emotional life.* New York: Simon and Schuster.

LeDoux J. (2003) 'The emotional brain, fear, and the amygdala', *Cellular and Molecular Neurobiology*, October, 23(4–5), pp. 727–738.

LeDoux, J. (2015) *Anxious: Using the brain to understand and treat fear and anxiety.* Baltimore, MD: Penguin Books.

Manning, C. et al. (2012) 'Personal inner values – A key to effective face-to-face business communication', *Journal of Executive Education*, 11(1), pp. 37–65.

Newberg, A. and Waldman, M. (2009) *How God changes your brain.* New York: Ballantine Books.

O'Toole, A.J. (2005) 'Psychological and neural perspectives on human face recognition', in Li, S.Z. and Jain, A.K (eds). *Handbook of face recognition.* New York: Springer.

Panksepp, J. (2008) 'The affective brain and core-consciousness: How does neural activity generate emotional feelings?', in Lewis M., Haviland, J.M. and Barrett, L.F. (eds) *Handbook of emotions*. New York: Guilford Press.

Schwartz, J. and Begley, S. (2002a) *Neuroplasticity and the power of mental thought*. New York: HarperCollins.

Schwartz, J. and Begley, S. (2002b) *The mind and the brain*. New York: HarperCollins.

Shamay-Tsoory, S.G., Aharon-Peretz, J. and Perry D. (2009) 'Two systems for empathy: A double dissociation between emotional and cognitive empathy in inferior frontal gyrus versus ventromedial prefrontal lesions', in *Brain*, March, 132(Pt 3), pp. 617–627, Haifa, Israel.

Siegel, D. (2010a) *Mindsight*. New York: Bantam Press.

Siegel, D. (2010b) *The mindful therapist*. New York: W. W. Norton & Company.

Siegel, D. (2011) 'The neurobiology of "We"', in *Parabola Magazine*, Patty de Llosa (ed.), New York.

Biography

Leanne Drew-McKain is re-shaping the way we understand and harness the neuroscience of communication behaviour in organizations.

CEO and Founder of Australian company Coach Pty Ltd, Leanne is highly regarded for her unique ability to build organizational communication culture and improve communication capabilities in leaders and staff – creating her own coaching brand and suite of culture-change programs that have forged a new and needed place in the business marketplace.

Leanne's innovative doctoral research into the neuroscience of workplace communication behaviour is contributing to a world-first applied neuroscience-based conceptual framework to help people prevent, eliminate and recover from workplace bullying and psychosocial safety risks. Her highly regarded Class Act Conduct programme has brought relief to tens of thousands of leaders and staff suffering the stressors of workplace incivility.

Leanne and her team are at the frontline of fostering cultures of respect in sectors such as education, health, higher education and business.

CHAPTER 11

Biology, Brains and Bias in Business

Emma Russell

> "I was mortified!" groans Emma. "There was this bloody mess in the bottom of the boat – and my coach had seen it. It was one of those awful moments where I wanted the ground to swallow me up."

Emma Wiggs and I are having a Zoom conversation. She's inspirational – a double Paralympic Gold Medal winner and a ten-time world champion paracanoeist. She's effervescent and joyful, full of energy and purpose. We've only just met and we're having a pretty intimate conversation. We're talking about periods. In fact, we're talking about all aspects of female physiology, and how surprising it is that research and funding have been focused for years on the male body at the expense of the female.

Emma's face lights up as a thought comes to her mind. Her excitement is visible:

> "If I was the coach of a female athlete," she says, "I would be so excited about the potential she could offer! With our deeper understanding and change in approach, we could take her performance from here (she motions with her hand) to here (she indicates a much higher level). That's the real difference we could be making."

Physiology impacts performance

What Emma's referring to is so obvious and simple it seems strange that it took us until 2019 to get there. It's about understanding that female physiology (how the body works) has an impact on performance. It's about working with female physiology – instead of against it – which was the default. And it's about recognizing the distinct differences between male and female physiologies. In the past, medicine and the whole biological research community made assumptions that the physiology doesn't differ too much between the sexes. It turns out that it does.

Emma believes that this change in approach has helped her to tap into a whole new level of performance and health as an Olympic athlete. Enthusiastically, she explains:

> "For years, the menstrual cycle was completely taboo in sport. Men don't want to talk about it and women don't want it to be seen as an excuse or something that could hamper their performance. For me, this is about catering for the female body that I've got and maximizing it, and unleashing all its potential. To do that, we need to look at all the factors that affect me, including my menstrual cycle. Actually, with the knowledge I now have, it feels like a secret weapon, to be maximized and unleashed, rather than something to be fearful, or ashamed, of. Knowledge of my individual cycle completely changed my thinking about my own performance and training and has led to huge gains. That's empowering as well as exciting!"

A source of untapped potential

The opportunity to tap into a whole new level of health and performance, as Emma Wiggs has done, exists for any woman, and not only in her career. But the path to get there is messy, for historical reasons. Although roughly half the population is female, we don't really understand women's bodies. It's controversial but, for centuries, we've chosen to study the male at the expense of the female. This has led to an under-representation of women in clinical trials, and systemic bias within the medical system and beyond. The bias is so significant that there is a considerable gap in our understanding of the female body. And, as a result, *we don't yet know enough about women.* Rachel Gross highlights this elegantly in her beautifully written *Vagina Obscura*. There are parts of the female body "less known than the bottom of the ocean, or the surface of Mars," she writes (Gross, 2022, p. xii).

What about those who are transgender, non-binary, intersex or who don't identify as either sex?

In this chapter, I talk about female bodies, and I use the terms male and female, woman and man. I appreciate that these terms are not applicable to everyone: my aim is not to be exclusive. If we don't know enough about female bodies, imagine how much less we know about the bodies of those who are transgender, intersex, non-binary or who don't identify as either sex. The bias is enormous and further research is very much needed for all under-represented groups.

Blinkered by bias

The challenge of the past and the bias that exists have made us blinkered. We see what we expect to see and we miss things we aren't looking for. In *Bitch: A revolutionary guide to sex, evolution and the female animal* (2022), biologist Lucy Cooke tells many stories of the complications of sex and gender in the animal kingdom. She also refers to the blinkers and the 'accidental sexism' in science that have led us to a distorted view of how we perceive female animals, including the human variety. She writes: "Males were the main event and became the model organism –

the default from which the female deviated, the standard by which the species was judged" (Cooke, 2022, p. xvii). Perhaps Darwin set us off to a bad start when he stated that there was a difference in intellectual powers between men and women – namely, that men could attain 'higher eminence' than women. He concluded: "thus man has ultimately become superior to woman" (Darwin, 1871).

Even in a group of women, women of colour have been studied far less than white women and experience considerably more bias. Black women in both the US and the UK experience higher rates of preventable pregnancy or childbirth-related deaths than white women (Knight et al., 2021), (Petersen et al., 2019). For centuries, it was mistakenly assumed that people of colour experience less pain than white people do. Shockingly, it's very common, even today, for black patients not to receive adequate pain relief (Hoffman et al., 2016).

Hysterical women or real medical issues?

It's a beautiful sunny day in London and I'm excited to meet Lottie Patterson, a Strategic Account Manager at Amazon. Lottie is young, gregarious, ambitious and smart. Some of her stories of her experiences at work make me laugh out loud but, as I ask her about her menstrual cycle, our conversation takes on a more serious note. Lottie tells me that she suffered terribly with debilitating pain and heavy periods:

> "It was getting so bad," she explained. "I was passing out. It happened twice. Once on the street in London and once at home. I hit my head on the sink. I was really worried, not just about my health, but also about my physical safety."

Lottie went to see her doctor who told her that she was hysterical and that there was absolutely nothing wrong with her – painful periods were simply part of being a woman. It shook her confidence and it made her doubt herself, even though she knew something was very wrong. She struggled on, before finally receiving a diagnosis of endometriosis and having a surgical procedure. Following her operation, Lottie has recovered well and now receives excellent medical care. This is important because endometriosis is a long-term condition and she may need further operations in the future.

Endometriosis is a condition where tissue similar to that of the uterus lining begins to grow outside the uterus, perhaps in the ovaries or fallopian tubes, or even in the intestines, bladder and other organs. It causes severe pain and discomfort. It is commonly misdiagnosed, with a worrying mean time delay from symptom onset until diagnosis of over eight years (Bontempo and Mikesell, 2020). Although it affects roughly 10% of women of reproductive age (As-Sanie et al., 2019), endometriosis experts state that there are fundamental gaps in knowledge and misconceptions regarding the disease. Many women receive a diagnosis of a mental health problem or are dismissed by their GPs (as in Lottie's case) rather than being taken seriously. In fact, some endometriosis experts argue that hysteria (from the Greek word for uterus – *hystera*) could have been endometriosis all along. In 2012, three brothers – all endometriosis experts, published a report in which they stated:

> "We were able to uncover substantial, if not irrefutable, evidence that hysteria, the now discredited mystery disorder presumed for centuries to be psychological in origin, was

most likely endometriosis in the majority of cases. If so, then this would constitute one of the most colossal mass misdiagnoses in human history, one that over the centuries has subjected women to murder, madhouses, and lives of unremitting physical, social, and psychological pain" (Nezhat et al., 2012).

Endometriosis, despite not being a rare condition, receives very little funding or research. We still don't know or fully understand what causes it.

There are many other conditions like endometriosis that affect only women that we don't know very much about. Historic preference has been towards studying the male, even though women's bodies are different from men's bodies. Women respond differently from men to disease and they also respond differently to the drugs that are used to treat disease.

Male and female bodies respond differently to drugs

Zolpidem Tartrate is a sleeping tablet used to treat insomnia. In 2013, the US Food and Drug Administration (FDA) announced that it was cutting the recommended dose of the drug in half, but only for women (FDA, 2013). Why? Women, more commonly than men, had been reporting serious side effects such as hallucinations. Women and men metabolize the drug in different ways so that women had higher concentrations of the drug in their blood plasma the morning after taking it. This increased their risk of impaired driving (Verster and Roth, 2012). Zolpidem was the first drug in the US to have a different suggested dose for men and women. Interestingly, the differing effect in blood plasma concentrations was known before the drug was released to market in 1992. It was still approved because, at the time, there was no awareness that female–male differences mattered. The European Medicines Agency (2014) did not follow the US's lead, finding that the data was not sufficiently conclusive.

Women experience adverse drug reactions nearly twice as often as men

The Zolpidem example is just the tip of the iceberg in the challenge of understanding the important differences in reactions to drugs between men and women. Between 1997 and 2000, 80% of the drugs withdrawn from the market were removed because of their harmful side effects on women (Llamas, 2015) (Heinrich et al., 2001). Today, in every single one of the top ten selling drugs in the US, there are more side effects reported – some serious, some minor – in women than in men. And women experience adverse drug reactions nearly twice as often as men (Zucker and Prendergast, 2020). Even today, women are at still at risk from unsafe medication (Carey et al., 2017). The easy conclusion to assume here is that women complain more than men, but the real reason is that women's bodies are physiologically different from men's bodies. The systemic bias that has existed in medicine for years has prevented us from seeing and understanding sex differences. Medical research has traditionally been performed on men and the results then applied to women. We have assumed that we can understand everyone by studying men. But why?

One size fits all? Unfortunately not ...

The logic was that men are easier to study than women because they don't have the complexity of menstrual cycles and hormonal fluctuations. Studying men also removes the complexity of ethical complications that might arise should a woman fall pregnant during any scientific research. The thalidomide disaster in the 1960s showed that drugs taken in pregnancy can have serious effects on unborn children. In 1977, the FDA issued guidelines that effectively excluded women of child-bearing age from early stage clinical trials (FDA, 1977; Merkatz, 1998).

So, males became the 'model organism' and men and women were thought to be pretty much the same, with the exception of 'bikini medicine'. This derogatory term refers to the areas of a woman's body that would be underneath a bikini – namely, her breasts and genitals – and relates to reproductive health, as well as to diseases such as breast and ovarian cancer. But the differences are much wider and more complex than the term would suggest. Men and women have different metabolic chemistry, immune system differences, different combinations of muscle fibres, brain differences and differences in normal cardiovascular function. These cardiovascular differences are also not well understood, meaning that women suffering from heart disease are often misdiagnosed (Wu et al., 2018).

Things are improving though, and, today, legislation exists to ensure that men and women are equally represented in clinical trials. But many researchers don't take the next step of analyzing the results by sex. More male animals than female are still used in medical research, even for diseases that affect more women than they do men. For diseases that affect only women, a meta-review of the research between 2011 and 2012 demonstrated that female animals were only used 12% of the time (Yoon et al., 2014). Often those doing the research don't even question it – it has always been done this way.

Surprising sex differences

Dr Doris Taylor, now the CEO of a medical consulting group and a bioengineering company, and formerly the Director of Regenerative Medicine at the Texas Heart Institute, is a pioneer in cardiovascular regenerative medicine. She accidentally came across a significant sex difference in her animal research. She was investigating whether injections of stem cells could reduce plaque build-up in arteries. She discovered that female stem cells reduced the plaque build-up, but male stem cells did not. She subsequently found that the same differences exist in human male and female stem cells.

Speaking on the American TV documentary programme, *60 Minutes*, back in 2014, Dr Taylor said:

> "As a woman, I am embarrassed to admit that it had never really occurred to me that doing the experiment in male versus female animals would give completely different results" ('Sex matters', *60 Minutes*, 2014).

Why do we know so much more about the penis than the vagina or the clitoris?

Surprisingly, the knowledge gaps go beyond physiology into areas as fundamental as anatomy. It wasn't until 1998 that we first began to fully understand the detailed anatomy of the clitoris, thanks to urologist Helen O'Connell, who led the first comprehensive study of it (O'Connell et al., 1998, O'Connell et al., 2005). She revealed that in the literature – and especially the medical education literature – there were major shortcomings of the understanding and description of clitoral anatomy, particularly regarding size and neurovascular supply. The clitoris is a beautiful structure when viewed in 3D, consisting of an external glans and hood and an internal body, root, crura and bulbs (Pauls, 2015). It is intimately connected with the urethra and vagina, and longer than the average flaccid penis – being 9–11cm long in its non-aroused state (Pauls, 2015). The full anatomy of the clitoris is still not properly shown in many medical textbooks, even those published as recently as 2020, yet the penis typically receives several dedicated pages.

In 2017, a study examined 17 major anatomy textbooks published between 2008 and 2013. The authors found that the female was under-represented compared to the male: "The biased construction of gender in anatomy textbooks designed for medical education provides future healthcare providers with inadequate and unrealistic information about patients" (Parker, Larkin and Cockburn, 2017).

Push-up bras and crash test dummies

Sadly, it's not just a lack of knowledge about the female body. The way women are depicted is also a problem. In 2019, Cambridge University Press withdrew its 2014 edition of *Examination techniques in orthopaedics* after neurologist Kate Ahmad called out some of the photographs depicting women dressed inappropriately in underwear for medical examinations of their shoulders and elbows. In one image, a female model posed seductively for the camera wearing a push-up bra for a pectoral examination. The 2002 edition of the same text featured a woman in a white see-through bra and red hot pants having her *heel* examined by a male doctor (Harris and Stanley, 2002). Cambridge University Press has since released a more appropriate 2022 version (Ali and Harris, 2022).

The biases extend yet further still when we consider the data gap that results from the study of the male at the expense of the female. In her wonderful book, *Invisible Women*, Caroline Criado Perez (2019) exposes how dangerous this gap can be for women – for example, the risk of dying or being badly injured in a car accident because the safety tests are not designed around the female body. In fact, it took us until 2022 for the first crash test dummy designed on the body of the average female to be released (McCallum, 2022).

What about brains?

The most controversial area regarding sex differences is the human brain. It's so controversial, in fact, that those who study such differences are often labelled 'neurosexist'. Two schools of thought exist: one that the brain is essentially unisex and the other that sex differences exist. Larry Cahill, Professor of Neurobiology and Behaviour at the University of California, Irvine, has been labelled as one of the neurosexists. He has dedicated 20 years of his career to studying brain sex differences. His opposers are feminists, concerned that studying difference might lead to the view that one group is somehow better than the other. On a cold and wintry evening, he offers me his professional opinion:

> "There are sex influences of all sizes, of all kinds, at all levels of mammalian brain function. It's abundantly clear from a neuroscience perspective that men and women are both the same, or similar, in many respects, and different a little to a lot, in many respects. It's the different part that has not been well studied, even believed by neuroscience. Assuming men and women are identical actually does a disservice to both men and women."

Professor Cahill was also part of a CBS News episode on sex differences ('Sex matters', 60 Minutes, 2014) and shares with me that after the programme was aired the then Director for the Institute of Health, Francis Collins, was called in front of Congress where he was questioned as to why diseases that almost exclusively affected women were being studied almost exclusively on men (Cahill, 2022). Collins didn't have a good answer. Shortly afterwards, in May 2014, he unveiled policies to ensure that pre-clinical research funded by the US National Institutes of Health considered both males and females (Clayton and Collins, 2014). Formal policy 'sex as a biological variable' went into effect in the US in January 2016.

Professor Cahill is used to being called a neurosexist, but nothing could be further from the truth. He feels strongly that the male bias in medical research is harmful to everybody. He tells the story of the pharmaceutical company, Upjohn, now part of Viatris, which discovered a class of drugs called Lazaroids, so named because it was believed that they had Lazarus-like capabilities in limiting brain damage after traumatic brain injuries or strokes. The drug class was withdrawn at clinical trial stage when it did not give the expected results in patients who had experienced traumatic brain injuries or strokes. However, a later analysis revealed that sex differences had been largely ignored. Because of this, a drug that had the potential to significantly improve the lives of men who suffered stokes was not released to market (Cahill and Hall, 2017).

Professor Cahill shares with me that he feels as if we are standing on the edge of something big when it comes to finally accepting neurobiological differences and at long last being able to study and understand them. "There's so much smoke, there's got to be a huge fire, but we haven't quite got there yet," he tells me, "The bias is so profound."

And we talk about the work of Cordelia Fine, Gina Rippon and Daphna Joel – all of whom argue that there are no differences between male and female brains (Fine, 2010; Rippon, 2019; Joel and Vikhanski, 2019). But, in 2018, the Journal of Neuroscience was the first international peer-reviewed journal in its field to establish a policy stating that sex differences must be considered, acknowledging thereby the importance of studying brain sex differences.

In 2021, the UK government acknowledged the significant male bias in the medical system. It called for public views to help inform the development of the Women's Health Strategy. Part of the Ministerial foreword states:

> For generations, women have lived with a health and care system that is mostly designed by men, for men. This has meant that not enough is known about conditions that affect only women or about how conditions that affect both men and women impact women in different ways. Pregnant women and women of child-bearing age are also under-represented in clinical trials, which can create troubling gaps in data and understanding (UK Department of Health and Social Care, 2021).

Designed 'by men for men' in business too?

Does the statement 'by men for men' apply to the world of business too? Self-evident though it seems, even to say that women have lived with systems in organizations that were mostly designed by men, for men, and have largely stood the test of time, is controversial. But it makes sense. The first organizations contained only men, so they naturally evolved rules based on what worked well for the group. Arguably, these rules don't work for anyone anymore because so much has changed. Coming into the corporate world in their own right, women have had to prove themselves against men, rather than being celebrated because of their differences. And, even though we've been making record progress, today just 10.6% of the Fortune 500 have female CEOs (Hinchcliffe, 2023).

I am incredibly honoured to meet Steve, now 90 years old, who did something quite remarkable back in the 1960s. Starting out in a cottage in Buckinghamshire in the UK with just £6, Steve created an IT company called Freelance Programmers and grew it into a business valued at over USD 3 billion. When the company floated in 1996, it made 70 of its employees into millionaires. What makes this truly ground-breaking is that, when Freelance Programmers was established, every employee, including Steve, was a woman.

Steve is Dame Stephanie Shirley CH, but the affectionate family nickname Steve became her hook for generating business. She found that no one would take her seriously as a woman and it frustrated her. She discovered that writing to potential clients using the name Steve got responses. After an initial surprise, clients learned that behind the name Steve lay a highly intelligent and capable woman. They began to trust her. Contracts were signed and the work came in. Dame Stephanie describes how driven, qualified women were kept out of the workforce because they had recently married or had their first child. Her frustration at the way women were treated inspired to establish her own company:

"I was always incredibly frustrated by the blatant sexism that was everywhere I looked. In my first job, there was one pay scale for men, and another, much lower, pay scale for women – and that infuriated me. As a young married woman, I couldn't even set up a bank account without my husband's permission. I decided to set up a company of women, for women, driven by women – a family friendly company."

Dame Stephanie had no trouble attracting talent. A simple newspaper reference would give her access to hundreds of interested applicants. Her policies were flexible. Her staff simply needed access to a telephone. They could work from home if they chose, and work the hours that suited them, because they were compensated based on output. It was a similar set-up to the gig economy, 50 years before the gig economy was established. Her company offered fixed prices for contracts to disguise the fact that the contract obligations were being fulfilled by women working part-time from their dining-room tables. When taking telephone calls, the women would often play tape recordings of people typing in the background to give the impression that they were working in a busy office environment.

It was only in 1975, when the Sex Discrimination Act came into force in the UK, protecting men and women from discrimination on the grounds of sex or marital status, that Freelance Programmers started to recruit men. Dame Stephanie reflects that when she left the organization back in 1993, unfortunately, and to her chagrin, the majority of the most senior positions had become occupied by men.

I ask Dame Stephanie about the values upon which she set up her organization. She tells me that she designed it based on her own principles, creating something that was reflective of herself. The culture was very relationship driven, and the relationships were long-term and collaborative:

> "I thought it was important to listen to people rather than just trying to show how clever I was," says Dame Stephanie. "I learned to build up relationships long before I opened my mouth. I recruited on the basis of values. The business was all about doing the right thing as well as doing things right. Sometimes that meant not making the most commercially savvy decision but making the right decision. We gave more than we were paid for."

As I listen to Dame Stephanie, something that comes across very clearly is that her company valued lasting relationships, collaboration and long-term thinking. She created a high-trust, flexible environment where employees were autonomous but supported. Hierarchy was unimportant and the company was competitive externally but not internally. It was a place where people were free to be themselves. It is a design that matches many new start-ups today, now that we recognize the importance of long-term sustainability, both for the organization and for those within it.

Dame Stephanie was a Jewish refugee and decided when she came to the UK in 1939, at the age of 5, escaping the barbarities that were to come, that she had better make her life count. Now retired, she is a venture philanthropist and has donated millions of pounds to charity. She is a trailblazer, one of the first to demonstrate the value that women bring to the workplace. She describes how, when she first started her company and it became successful, her male critics commented that it was only a success because it was small. Later, as she began to grow the organization, her critics agreed that it was sizeable but of no strategic interest. Finally, when the company was valued at USD 3 billion, her critics simply commented, "Well done, Steve!"

Downplaying difference

In having had to prove themselves in a world where masculine rules still dominate, women have often had to downplay their natural strengths, or make adaptations in order to succeed.

Annerie Vreugdenhil, Chief Commercial Officer and member of the Executive Board at ABN AMRO Bank, tells me of the adjustments she made in her career and the advice she offers younger women:

> "Women say to me – we have to be able to be ourselves. I say to them, well ... you have to be able to be effective. I'm Dutch. I can be outspoken and blunt. But, if I have to do business in Japan, I will get nowhere by being myself. I have to change my behaviour in order be effective. Being a woman in a man's world is like being an expat in another culture. It doesn't mean you have to change yourself: you just need to change your behaviour in order to be effective."

Annerie's experiences are like those of many other women. Eléonore Dachicourt is Head of Sustainable and Responsible Investment, Asia, at BNP Paribas. She shares with me the surprising feedback that she received from a former employer in her 2021 performance review:

> "My female boss told me that I was over-collaborative. She advised me that I needed

to suppress that part of my personality. According to her, I needed to make people more afraid of me. I'd learned over years how to adapt in a corporate environment. For me, it was about being irreproachable when it came to competence. Whatever I was asked to deliver, I was achieving. I was making sure that I was being excellent. That feeling of excellence and being competent allowed me to grow in confidence. The change I was asked to make was too much. I love collaboration, and it's one of my strengths. And I don't want my team to be afraid of me. Ultimately, I decided I would be better off leaving the organization."

I wonder if younger women, or women in industries that are more female focused, have similar challenges of having to change their natural styles or their behaviour in order to be successful? I have a fascinating conversation with Kerry Randall, Global Head of Site Activation at IQVIA, the health information technology company, who shares with me that her industry is heavily female weighted except at the most senior positions, where the balance shifts:

"I never felt that I had to change who I am," she tells me. "I was lucky enough to have lots of positive female role models. My first boss was very interested in female leadership, and supported and mentored me. Now I'm much more senior though, I recognize I have to adapt in order to represent my team in the best way when I meet with the top executives. I'm very driven but in a quieter and more reserved way. I don't want to talk for the sake of talking, but I will speak up if I have something to say. I

> recognize the need to be more assertive, vocal and louder. There is an element of male/female difference but there's also a cultural element too."

Sylvia Yin has appeared in the Asia Forbes Top 30 Under 30. Her credentials are impressive. She is the youngest and first female entrepreneur in technology to make the Forbes list in Malaysia. She is inspiring but also humble and down to earth. Her eyes sparkle as she tells me about the company that she co-founded with two of her university friends. Omnilytics provides retail brands such as Adidas, Puma and Zalora with insights into the market allowing its customers to make informed decisions for production, merchandising, strategy and marketing. Sylvia and her co-founders created and designed the culture of the organization and she has never felt she has to compete in a man's world. However, there are times when she still senses a bias against women:

> "I'm lucky enough to have had the opportunity to create an environment in which I want to work," she explains. "We hire on values. I've learned though that even though you can come from a blank slate and have the best of intentions, bias against women is still very ingrained in our society. We have a great engineering manager, but he blurted out one day that he was afraid of giving feedback to one of the female engineers because she might cry. The people we hire are not corporate misogynists; they are open to listening, but they still think that female developers will eventually drop out because they have to take care of their families. It will take time to undo that bias."

In all my conversations with women, there is a theme of having to adapt, or make choices they didn't feel comfortable with in order to preserve credibility. Something else that comes up is a sense of guilt about either not having sufficient time to spend with their families or sometimes feeling stressed and distracted with work matters when with their children. Some wanted more maternity leave but came back to work for fear that their careers wouldn't progress if they weren't seen as committed. All the women had stories. Being expected to be back at work the day after having a miscarriage; the embarrassment of hot flushes in the middle of meetings; worries about period leaks; struggling on despite crippling pain; sexual harassment; having to bind a pregnant belly because of fears of negative consequences. And many had chosen to lie rather than to admit to a physical problem related to women's health because of a fear of being viewed as less competent or capable.

These are real issues faced by real women in today's world. But does an opportunity exist here? For years in the business world, we've been assuming that people are the same. We've done this with good intent because we want people to be equal. But actually, we're not all the same: there's such beauty and power in difference.

Something women do, all the time, is to ignore, downplay or try to control (through taking hormones or drugs) – their feminine biology. Nobody really wants to talk about periods or the menopause. These natural biological events are often viewed negatively by society. And a woman who's trying to be a top performer in the workplace certainly doesn't want to highlight these issues. She doesn't want to appear as weak. She doesn't want her biology to be seen as an excuse, or something that could hamper her performance. So she's silent about it.

But there's a unique opportunity here. An opportunity for women to tap into something that we haven't fully understood or appreciated, largely because we just don't know enough about women. Let's go back full circle to the bloody mess in Emma's boat.

The power of the menstrual cycle

In the past ten years, professional athletes and sportswomen like Emma have been starting to work with their physiology instead of ignoring it or trying to control it with hormones or drugs. As a result, they have discovered a whole new level of health and performance. Now, of course, the corporate world is very different from the world of sport, but the same opportunity is directly applicable to the business world. It involves women tracking, being aware of and understanding the changes that take place in their cycles. Having a menstrual cycle creates important hormonal changes. The levels of hormones are fluctuating day by day and, in some cases, hour by hour. There's an optimal time in the cycle for public speaking, an optimal time for strategic thinking and an optimal time for reflection, deep inward focus and creative solutions. Menstrual cycles are intelligent and come with the possibility of creating new life. They are an important indicator of health, affected by the complex interplay of all the systems within the human female body. Many women suffer terribly with their menstrual cycles, but tuning into the natural intelligence of the body, instead of being a passive bystander, gives a completely different experience of the cycle, and in many cases significantly reduces symptoms. If we understood this better, women could not only increase their performance but also improve their health and well-being.

Julia Söderqvist, a 30-year-old entrepreneur and one of my coaching clients, explains her own experience of learning to embrace her menstrual cycle:

> "I remember being age 11 and thinking – ugh! It's so disgusting! What am I going to do when I get my period? I felt shame. I was taught that having my period is not something I should want in life. I could take tablets to stop it. Girls were even encouraged to do so. But now my experience has completely changed. After working with my cycle for the last six months and understanding it, my relationship with power has completely changed. There is power and wisdom in the cycle, but we've been taught otherwise. The more I become aware of what it is to be a woman, the more I feel true to myself and the more incredible I realize it is to be a woman."

The rollercoaster of perimenopause

Women not only have to manage their menstrual cycles. Another important physiological aspect of a woman's life is the menopause. Women often experience symptoms without knowing and understanding that they are related to perimenopause. Many people don't even know what perimenopause is! This reverse puberty can start as early as ten years before women officially go through the menopause and stop having periods. Symptoms might start as early as the late 30s or early 40s, when women might be reaching senior leadership positions.

Perimenopause can present a rollercoaster of confusing changes including difficulty sleeping – especially early waking and being unable to get back to sleep; hot flushes, shivers and night sweats; migraines, heart palpitations; anxiety; weight gain; increased risk of osteoporosis and mild cognitive impairment – particularly forgetting things. The symptoms are often frightening and can have a significant impact on women's lives – especially the sleep deprivation and hot flushes that are poorly understood physiologically.

HSBC was the first organization in the UK to put in place an official menopause policy and to run an internal campaign to raise awareness of the menopause. Rabia Jones is a Senior Producer within HSBC who worked on the campaign. She shared with me that she was inundated with women wanting to share their stories and who were happy that this complex and challenging time in women's lives was now being talked about.

In a 2020 British Medical Association (BMA) survey of over 2,000 female doctors, 90% responded that their working lives had been affected by menopause symptoms and 38% had been unable to make the changes to their work life that they needed in order to cope with symptoms. Almost 50% of the women had wanted to discuss and seek support but didn't feel comfortable doing so and were concerned at being laughed at or ridiculed (BMA, 2020).

Why is it that, nearly a quarter of the way into the 21st century, women are still having to hide aspects of themselves and downplay who they are, instead of being valued because of who they are? Even though we are starting to understand the power of the menstrual cycle, as well as how better to support women as they go through perimenopause and beyond, the knowledge and the information available to women is still terribly lacking.

Jerilynn Prior is an endocrinologist and Professor of Medicine at the University of British Columbia, Canada, and the founder of the Centre of Menstrual Cycle and Ovulation Research. Professor Prior has dedicated her entire career to understanding the menstrual cycle and to promoting a better understanding of the hormone, progesterone, which, together with oestrogen, is essential to female health. Despite the positives that contraception can bring, Professor Prior points out that, sadly, when young women and girls are prescribed the contraceptive pill, very rarely are they warned of the long-term risks to their health. The pill prevents ovulation, and ovulation and the subsequent production of progesterone are essential for healthy bone development and the prevention of spinal bone loss. It can take up to ten years for a young woman to ovulate regularly and going on the pill at a young age may have an impact on a woman's fertility in later life (Prior, 2015).

Prior has also shown through meta-analysis that prescribed oral progesterone can assist with symptoms in perimenopause, although this too is not largely understood (Prior et al., 2020). In fact, hormone therapy, which can be of real benefit to women in perimenopause and menopause, has attracted a bad press (Cagnacci and Venier, 2019). After the first analysis of the Women's Health Initiative was published in 2002, the press widely reported that HRT (or Hormone Replacement Therapy) had more risks than benefits for women. However, the full findings showed a different story, revealing that HRT in women under 60 is safe and beneficial (Cagnacci and Venier, 2019; British Menopause Society, 2022). The term 'hormone therapy' is the modern term for HRT – it's a better term because the changing sex hormones are not a deficiency.

It's time for a re-think

Our knowledge and understanding of the female body is years behind our understanding of the male body. We don't yet know enough about women, but the time feels right for a re-think about how women can be free to be themselves, and to get to know the parts of themselves that they've collectively silenced over the years. This is already starting, in pockets. It feels like we're on the edge of a scientific understanding of differences and a realization that all under-represented groups have been subjected to bias. The 'one-size-fits-all' approach to medical research and treatment has brought serious consequences for women's health. Likewise, the one-size-fits-all approach to business has had disappointing consequences for women's progression in the workplace.

There are only 14 countries in the world that offer full legal protection to women. This data comes from a 2023 report by the World Bank, which states: "on average (across the world), women have just three quarters of the rights of men". The US and the UK don't make the grade – neither offer full legal protection to women. From a business perspective globally, we know that there is both a gender participation and a gender pay gap – more men work than women, and men get paid, on average, more than women for the same work. The proportion of men in senior executive positions is higher than the proportion of women. Even though the numbers have been steadily climbing to record proportions, as mentioned earlier, just 53 women are at the top of the world's largest 500 companies, making 10.6% of the total in 2023.

There's no future in the idea that is still implicit in the corporate world that what's needed is to 'fix' women. Michelle King showed this elegantly in her 2020 book, *The*

Fix. There's no need to fix any under-represented group. At the heart of the problem is the design of the system and the way everyone operates within the system. The first step is to recognize the flaws in the system, even if we don't know how to change it yet. Concurrently, we can celebrate difference, not just of women but of all under-represented groups. The urgent task is to raise perceptions, knowledge and consciousness of the untapped value that exists in the feminine, especially in a world that's going to require more and more collaboration and regard for established and long-term relationships.

It seems fitting to end with the words of Alexis Fosler, Chief Operating Officer at Como Shambala Lifestyle. A highly experienced COO and Chief Executive Officer, Alexis offers her own view:

> "I think women are often forced to mould the way they enact or engage or deliver. Quite often, we are forced to constrain our thinking or to formulate our thinking in a vessel that is not necessarily our own. But we learn this way of being and we get used to it, and we wear the shirt that fits."

What if we could choose our own shirts?

References

Ali, F. and Harris, N. (eds) (2022) *Orthopaedic examination techniques: A practical guide*, 3rd edition. Cambridge: Cambridge University Press

As-Sanie, S. et al. (2019) 'Assessing research gaps and unmet needs in endometriosis', *American Journal of Obstetrics and Gynecology*, 221(2), 86–94. Available at: https://doi.org/10.1016/j.ajog.2019.02.033 (Accessed: 11 February 2023).

BMA (2020) 'Challenging the culture on menopause for working doctors'. Available at: https://www.bma.org.uk/media/2913/bma-challenging-the-culture-on-menopause-for-working-doctors-report-aug-2020.pdf (Accessed: 11 February 2023).

Bontempo, A.C. and Mikesell, L. (2020) 'Patient perceptions of misdiagnosis of endometriosis: Results from an online national survey', *Diagnosis* (Berlin, Germany), 7(2), 97–106. Available at: https://doi.org/10.1515/dx-2019-0020 (Accessed: 11 February 2023).

British Menopause Society (2022) 'HRT: The history'. Available at: https://www.womens-health-concern.org/wp-content/uploads/2022/11/10-WHC-FACTSHEET-HRT-The-history-NOV22-A.pdf (Accessed: 11 February 2023).

Cagnacci, A. and Venier, M. (2019) 'The controversial history of hormone replacement therapy', *Medicina* (Kaunas, Lithuania), 55(9), 602. Available at: https://doi.org/10.3390/medicina55090602 (Accessed: 11 February 2023).

Cahill, L. (2022, January). Interview by the author.

Cahill, L. and Hall, E.D. (2017) 'Is it time to resurrect lazaroids?', *Journal of Neuroscience Research*, 95 (1–2), 17–20. Available at: https://dx.doi.org/10.1002/jnr.23842 (Accessed: 11 February 2023).

Carey, J.L. et al. (2017). 'Drugs and medical devices: Adverse events and the impact on women's health', *Clinical Therapeutics*, 39(1), 10–22. Available at: https://www.clinicaltherapeutics.com/article/S0149-2918(16)30922-5/fulltext (Accessed: 11 February 2023).

Clayton, J. and Collins, F. (2014) 'Policy: NIH to balance sex in cell and animal studies' *Nature*, 509, 282–283. Available at: https://doi.org/10.1038/509282a (Accessed: 11 February 2023).

Cooke, L. (2022) *Bitch: A revolutionary guide to sex, evolution and the female animal.* London: Transworld.

Criado Perez, C. (2019) *Invisible women – Exposing data bias in a world designed for men.* New York: Penguin Random House.

Dachicourt, E. (2022, March). Interview by the author.

Darwin, C. (1871) *The descent of man, and selection in relation to sex.* London: John Murray.

European Medicines Agency (2014) *Zolpidem-containing medicines.* EMA/427574/2014. Available at: https://www.ema.europa.eu/en/medicines/human/referrals/zolpidem-containing-medicines (Accessed: 11 February 2023).

FDA (1977) *General considerations for the clinical evaluation of drugs.* (Publication no. HEW [FDA] 77-3040). Washington, DC: FDA.

FDA (2013) *Risk of next-morning impairment after use of insomnia drugs; FDA requires lower recommended doses for certain drugs containing zolpidem (Ambien, Ambien CR, Edluar, and Zolpimist).* Washington, DC: FDA. Available at: https://www.fda.gov/drugs/drug-safety-and-availability/questions-and-answers-risk-next-morning-impairment-after-use-insomnia-drugs-fda-requires-lower (Accessed: 11 February 2023).

Fine, C. (2010). *Delusions of gender: How our minds, society, and neurosexism create difference.* New York: W.W. Norton and Company.

Fosler, A. (2021, December). Interview by the author.

Gross, R. (2022) *Vagina obscura.* New York: W.W. Norton and Company.

Harris, N. and Stanley, D. (eds) (2002) *Advanced examination techniques in orthopaedics.* New York: Cambridge University Press.

Heinrich, J. et al. (2001) *Drug safety: Most drugs withdrawn in recent years had greater health risks for women*. Washington, DC: United States General Accounting Office.

Hinchcliffe, E. (2023) 'Women CEOs run more than 10% of Fortune 500 companies for the first time in history', *Fortune*, 12 January.

Hoffman, K.M. et al. (2016) 'Racial bias in pain assessment and treatment recommendations, and false beliefs about biological differences between blacks and whites', *Proceedings of the National Academy of Sciences of the United States of America*, 113(16), 4296–4301. Available at: https://doi.org/10.1073/pnas.1516047113 (Accessed: 11 February 2023).

Joel, D. and Vikhanski, L. (2019) *Gender mosaic: Beyond the myth of the male and female brain*. London: Endeavour Press.

Jones, R. (2022, January). Interview by the author.

King, M.P. (2020) *The fix – How to overcome the invisible barriers that are holding women back at work*. New York: Simon and Schuster.

Knight, M. et al. (eds) (2021) 'Saving lives, improving mothers' care – Lessons learned to inform maternity care from the UK and Ireland confidential enquiries into maternal deaths and morbidity 2018–2020', MBRRACE-UK: Mothers and babies: Reducing risk through audits and confidential enquiries across the UK. Available at: https://www.npeu.ox.ac.uk/mbrrace-uk (Accessed: 11 February 2023).

Llamas, M. (2015) 'How the FDA let women down', *Drugwatch*. Available at: https://www.drugwatch.com/featured/fda-let-women-down (Accessed: 11 February 2023).

McCallum, S. (2022) 'The crash test dummy aimed at protecting women drivers', BBC News. Available at: https://www.bbc.co.uk/news/technology-62877930 (Accessed: 11 February 2023).

Merkatz R.B. (1998) 'Inclusion of women in clinical trials: A historical overview of scientific, ethical, and legal issues', *Journal of Obstetric, Gynecologic & Neonatal Nursing*. Jan-Feb; 27(1), 78–84. Available at: https://onlinelibrary.wiley.com/

doi/abs/10.1111/j.1552-6909.1998.tb02594.x (Accessed: 11 February 2023).

Nezhat, C., Nezhat, F. and Nezhat, C. (2012) 'Endometriosis: Ancient disease, ancient treatments', *Fertility and Sterility*, 98(6 Suppl.), S1–S62. Available at: https://doi.org/10.1016/j.fertnstert.2012.08.001 (Accessed: 11 February 2023).

O'Connell, H.E. et al. (1998) 'Anatomical relationship between urethra and clitoris', *Journal of Urology*, 159(6), 1892–1897.

O'Connell, H.E., Sanjeevan, K.V. and Hutson, J.M. (2005) 'Anatomy of the clitoris', *Journal of Urology*, 174(4 Pt 1), 1189–1195. Available at: https://doi.org/10.1097/01.ju.0000173639.3889 (Accessed: 11 February 2023).

Parker, R., Larkin, T. and Cockburn, J. (2017) 'A visual analysis of gender bias in contemporary anatomy textbooks', *Social Science & Medicine*, 180, 106–113. Available at: https://doi.org/10.1016/j.socscimed.2017.03.032 (Accessed: 11 February 2023).

Patterson, L. (2022, January). Interview by the author.

Pauls R.N. (2015) 'Anatomy of the clitoris and the female sexual response', *Clinical Anatomy*, 28(3), 376–384. Available at: https://doi.org/10.1002/ca.22524 (Accessed: 11 February 2023).

Petersen, E.E. et al. (2019) 'Racial/ethnic disparities in pregnancy-related deaths – United States, 2007–2016' *MMWR. Morbidity and Mortality Weekly Report*, 68(35), 762–765. Available at: https://doi.org/10.15585/mmwr.mm6835a3 (Accessed: 11 February 2023).

Prior, J.C. (2015) *Contraceptive choices – Seeking effective, convenient, safe and ovulation-friendly birth control.* CeMCOR: The Centre for Menstrual Cycle and Ovulation Research. Available at: https://www.cemcor.ca/resources/contraceptive-choices_effective-convenient-safe (Accessed: 11 February 2023).

Prior, J.C. et al. (2020) 'Oral micronized progesterone for perimenopausal night sweats and hot flushes: A 12-week randomized phase III Canada-wide clinical trial', *The Lancet*

Preprints. Available at: http://dx.doi.org/10.2139/ssrn.3517407 (Accessed: 11 February 2023).

Randall, K. (2022, January). Interview by the author.

Rippon, G. (2019) *The gendered brain: The new neuroscience that shatters the myth of the female brain*. London: Bodley Head.

Sex Matters: *60 Minutes* (2014) investigates men, women and drug dosage. Presenter: Lesley Stahl. Contributors: Professor Larry Cahill, Dr Doris Taylor. New York: CBS News. Preview available at: https://www.cbsnews.com/video/sex-matters-60-minutes-investigates-men-women-and-drug-dosage (Accessed: 11 February 2023).

Shirley (Companion's Honour), Dame S. (2022, January). Interview by the author.

Söderqvist, J. (2022, April). Interview by the author.

UK Department of Health and Social Care (2021) *Consultation outcome. Women's health strategy: Call for evidence*. Available at: https://www.gov.uk/government/consultations/womens-health-strategy-call-for-evidence/womens-health-strategy-call-for-evidence (Accessed: 11 February 2023).

Verster, J.C. and Roth, T. (2012) 'Gender differences in highway driving performance after administration of sleep medication: A review of the literature', *Traffic injury prevention*, 13(3), 286–292. Available at: https://doi.org/10.1080/15389588.2011.652751 (Accessed: 11 February 2023).

Vreugdenhil, A. (2021, October). Interview by the author.

Wiggs, E. (2022, February). Interview by the author.

World Bank (2023) *Women, Business and the Law 2023*. Washington, DC: World Bank. Available at: https://openknowledge.worldbank.org/server/api/core/bitstreams/105265e8-311a-4b39-a71b-e455a86dd0ba/content (Accessed: 16 March 2023).

Wu, J. et al. (2018) Editor's choice – 'Impact of initial hospital diagnosis on mortality for acute myocardial infarction: A national cohort study', *European Heart Journal. Acute Cardiovascular Care*, 7(2), 139–148. Available at: https://doi.

org/10.1177/2048872616661693 (Accessed: 11 February 2023).

Yin, S. (2022, March). Interview by the author.

Yoon, D.Y. et al. (2014) 'Sex bias exists in basic science and translational surgical research', *Surgery*, 156(3), 508–516. Available at: https://doi.org/10.1016/j.surg.2014.07.001 (Accessed: 11 February 2023).

Zucker, I. and Prendergast, B.J. (2020) 'Sex differences in pharmacokinetics predict adverse drug reactions in women', *Biology of Sex Differences*, 11(1), 32. Available at: https://doi.org/10.1186/s13293-020-00308-5 (Accessed: 11 February 2023).

Biography

Emma Russell is an executive coach, consultant and speaker with a special interest in how biology influences human behaviour. Prior to coaching, Emma spent 17 years in the corporate environment and held senior leadership roles across Europe and Asia. Emma is a biologist by degree and has returned to her interest in the subject through applied research, teaching, writing and coaching. She holds an Executive MBA (Dean's List) from INSEAD and is a founding member of the ION Partnership. Emma lives in the UK with her husband and two children. When she's not buried deep in academic papers or scientific books, you can find her in the kitchen cooking up a storm or playing games and exploring nature with her children.

CHAPTER 12

Play Your Way to Resilience

Imogen Maresch

I have always been passionate about play.

As a drama student at university, many of the skills we learned were acquired through games. We learned to step into the shoes of different characters through role play, explored how to convey emotion through movement and voice exercises, and learned to think on our feet using improvisation (which was both invigorating and terrifying in equal measure).

While at the time I could not have imagined the long-term benefits of play, I now cannot imagine my work without it.

In my roles leading change programmes, I saw how cold introductions quickly melted into warm connection through using (suitably titled) icebreakers. In my years as a leadership development trainer, much of which was working with culturally diverse groups, experiential activities were a key way of sharing concepts and embedding learning. And, as an executive coach, playful exploration (including using objects, images and creative tools) has helped clients tap into alternate ways of both seeing and being. More recently, as a researcher in the field of resilience and well-being, I have become increasingly convinced that play offers a route to weathering the constantly changing climate we all exist in, wherever we might be in the world.

Leveraging play, therefore, has proven to be essential.

Playfulness, defined as the propensity to frame a situation as humorous, amusing or entertaining (Barnett, 2007), is often considered a personality trait, which some people might be more predisposed to than others. However, play as an activity or behaviour is available to us all, in some shape or form. Indeed, as humans, we have a predisposition for play.

I invite you to cast your mind back and think about what and how you used to play as a child and, particularly, the feelings this evoked in you. Perhaps you spent hours playing a particular game or with a special toy. Maybe you loved to build with bricks, or set up tea parties for your beloved teddies. Or, perhaps, like my children, nothing brought you more joy than scrambling up the tallest tree in sight – competing to occupy the highest branches and see the world from a different vantage point.

Whatever type of play brought you joy as a child, what we know is that it is critical to childhood learning and development. When children play, they learn about the world around them and develop the skills needed to survive, and to thrive, in it. It is now widely accepted that play helps children develop the physical, cognitive, emotional and social skills needed for childhood and beyond. More recently, the American Academy of Pediatrics has suggested that play also has the potential to change brain structure and function (Yogman et al., 2018). While recognizing that most research has been done with animals other than humans, they suggest that play builds executive function and promotes prosocial behaviour – areas of development that can be disrupted by experiencing adversity. Play, in these circumstances, therefore becomes even more crucial.

The 2018 *Play Well Report* released by Lego® found that 95% of parents believe that play is essential to their child's well-being. In a follow-up study in 2020, 40% of parents said resilience is one of the most important skills for their child's future success. Play is clearly a necessary activity for the holistic development of children.

And I would argue that it is not that different for adults either. However, for many of us, as we age, play declines.

Perhaps we see playtime as futile or wasteful, particularly in the back-to-back nature of our 'always on' lives. Maybe we deem ourselves, or the tasks we do, too serious for play. Or, perhaps, we think we are too old for what we may perceive as a childish pastime. George Bernard Shaw reflects that perhaps "we don't stop playing because we grow old; we grow old because we stop playing".

It turns out that, at least from a brain-based perspective, Shaw was on to something. Recent research suggests aerobic movement (which might include physical play such as a game of tennis or skipping) can improve focus and mood (Basso and Suzuki, 2017). When sustained, this can promote growth in areas of the brain particularly associated with memory and executive functioning (Suzuki, 2017). Because these areas are susceptible to neurodegenerative diseases like Alzheimer's and dementia, this means that, while play-based activity may not prevent the natural processes of aging, strengthening these critical areas may delay the decline. Indeed, several recent studies show that ongoing puzzle play in later years leads to better brain function on a range of tests, including those assessing memory, attention and reasoning (Brooker et al., 2019; Wesnes et al., 2019). So, it appears that both physical and cognitive play have the potential to slow down the effects of aging.

And there's a growing evidence base showing that it pays to play at work too.

Play at work

While play at work is a relatively under-researched area, studies have shown that it can have a number of positive benefits, including boosting creativity, improving problem solving, reducing stress, reducing fatigue and boredom, increasing job satisfaction and enhancing learning (see Petelczyc, Capezio and Wang, 2018).

Also, on an interpersonal level, studies suggest that play can help strengthen relationships and enhance trust between team members (Hunter, Jemielniak and Postula, 2010; Sørensen and Spoelestra, 2012), and, on an organizational level, has the potential to support creative, flexible work cultures (Pors and Andersen, 2015; West, Hoff and Carlsson, 2016).

And, right now, developing flexibility is anything but futile, because our ability to flex and adapt to constantly changing environments, like those of the past few years, is at the heart of resilience.

By April 2020, over 2.5 billion people had gone into lockdown and, those of us lucky enough to do so had moved out of our offices and online. After a while, the effect on our collective well-being started to show. A study conducted in 2020 reported that 89% of respondents said that their work life was getting worse and 85% of people felt that their well-being had declined (Moss, 2021).

While the pandemic has been a collective challenge, it has, nonetheless, been an individualized experience. We might all have been in the same storm, but we were often in different boats.

For many people, there have certainly been some adverse psychological affects, with reports showing increases in stress, anxiety and depression (Cao et al., 2020; Galea, Merchant and Lurie, 2020; Ganesan et al., 2021; Ivbijaro et al., 2020; Yıldırım and Solmaz, 2022) with the expectation that the effects will outlast the enforced isolations.

However, many of us, as the waves of lockdowns hit, may not have felt unwell as such but, perhaps, we were left feeling as though we were just keeping our head above the waterline. Or perhaps we felt knocked off course by challenges or change. Or at least, at times, we may have felt as if we were swimming against the tide.

And that's where resilience comes in.

The route to resilience

When the pandemic hit, I was midway through a Master's in Positive Psychology and Coaching Psychology. Often mistaken as a field that is exclusively focused on, as the Monty Pythons might say, 'the bright side of life', positive psychology is in fact better conceptualized as the science of well-being. The field emerged in response to an almost exclusive prior focus on psychopathology. Rather than a goal of removing 'ill-being' (i.e. moving from negative to neutral), positive psychology aims to research and support people to feel well, do well and be well (i.e. moving from neutral to positive). Gable and Haidt define it as "the study of the conditions and processes that contribute to the flourishing or optimal functioning of people" (2005, p. 104) and this includes the good and the bad times. One area of increasing focus within the field, especially over the past few years, is that of resilience.

There exists an enormous array of definitions of resilience: one study identified 122 (Meredith et al., 2011). Sisto et al.'s (2019) review highlights some common themes in these definitions, including adapting to and 'bouncing back' from adversity. A common misconception, however, is that adapting means keeping going, whatever the conditions. Resilience, on the other hand, sometimes means choosing to steer a different course, or even knowing that you need to shore up and do some maintenance for a while.

Also, 'bounce back' implies that we rebound quickly

from setbacks. However, sometimes we may not return to the same state as before we experienced adversity (or at least, perhaps, not quickly). Indeed, sometimes (possibly often) we actually change and grow as a result of the challenges we face.

While resilience has previously been viewed as an outcome or a trait, increasingly it is conceptualized as a dynamic process that is contextual (we may find it easier to activate resilience in some settings rather than others). Resilience isn't, therefore, something we are or aren't – in fact, we are all resilient in our own way and we show it day to day, moment by moment. Ann Masten (2001) encapsulates this, rather beautifully, by describing resilience as "ordinary magic".

At the risk of adding definition 123 to the ocean of descriptors, in my research I define resilience as "the practice of positively utilising multi-dimensional resources to ready for, respond to and recover from challenge and adversity" (Maresch and Kampman, 2022). At the core of resilience, therefore, is identifying the range of resources you can use to support you through your journey, whatever stage you're at.

Practising resilience is a personal, ongoing journey and our individual 'practice' looks different for all of us. The key is to identify resources, both internal and external, that work well for you. The more we recognize and use our available resources, the more flexible and adaptable we become – whatever the climate.

Playing for resilience

So, how does resilience relate to play? Because play helps us to unlock resources.

It can feel strange to talk about play in times of difficulty. But, what the science shows is that we naturally reach for play when the going gets tough. When finding themselves in immediate danger, animals cease to play. However, under moderate levels of stress and anxiety, studies have shown that animals actually engage in more play (Pellis and Pellis, 2013). This may well reflect our core human need to both survive and thrive.

Dr Paul Brown's *London Protocol of the Emotions* (2023) (a model that maps primary emotions to the autonomic nervous system, and the ensuing neurochemicals and hormones that are released)[1], suggests that emotions such as fear, anger, sadness, shame and disgust mobilize an avoidance, or escape, response – leading, logically, to survival. This usually means activating one of the core stress responses, such as fight, flight or freeze. However, he notes that emotions such as excitement, joy, love and trust (which can result from play) also have important functions in creating attachment and, perhaps therefore, support thriving (Brown and Dzendrowskyj, 2018).

Dr Stuart Brown, a scientist, founder of the National Institute for Play, and author of *Play: How it shapes the brain, opens the imagination and invigorates the soul* (2010) suggests that play might be a key mechanism through which adaptability is enhanced. Play, he asserts, provides an opportunity to practise skills safely, experiment to

---

[1] Source: Lanz, K. and Brown, P. [2020] *All the brains in the business: The engendered brain in the 21st century organization.* Switzerland: Palgrave Macmillan.

make sense of the world and, crucially, encode learning to help weather future storms.

Play clearly serves a purpose or animals would not engage in it, given its potential to consume resources that could be put to other use. While play in the animal kingdom might provide the opportunity for skills development and rehearsal for real-life risks, the bonds created between play partners also, perhaps, promote survival in other ways. Certainly, the collective strength of a pack can be protective, meaning that attachment might be advantageous to survival too.

Stuart Brown asserts that play is "one of the most advanced methods nature has invented to allow a complex brain to create itself" (2010, p. 40). Creating itself in this case means the forming (and then reducing or reinforcing) of new neural connections gained through novel experiences. Through the relative safety of play, the brain is open to new possibilities, and therefore new neural pathways, which might be strengthened by repetition. John Byers, a zoologist who has researched the development of the brain at play, posits that during play the brain is "making sense of itself" (cited in Brown, 2010, p. 34). Given Paul Brown's conceptualization of the brain as the primary organ in the body for sense-making, energy management and relationship forming, it appears therefore that play might create the perfect conditions for optimising the brain's capability to support us in all these areas.

During the pandemic, as we stopped going out, many of us, instead, got our games out. Quizzes and Zoom games became a source of welcome distraction and connection for many people, and this phenomenon formed the basis of my own research.

Based on positive psychology and coaching theory, I created an online board game, *Not All Plain Sailing*™, to help people identify resources they could use to ready for, respond to and recover from the adversity of the pandemic – and beyond it. Groups of three to four participants, from multiple countries across the world, played the game in a live, facilitated environment via Zoom. Based on the narrative of a boat journey from a desert island to the shores of home, participants were presented with a range of challenges and invited to gain treasure for their collective 'resilience treasure chest' by completing tasks. These included locating objects, drawing pictures, movement, and sharing stories and jokes, among others, all of which were designed to elicit surprise and enjoyment. The tasks themselves related to scientifically supported interventions drawn from positive psychology (e.g. character strengths, meaning, movement, relationships, gratitude, optimism and savouring).

I was curious about whether, by exploring a range of possible resources through play (especially in an online environment), people might learn or develop new approaches they could draw on in real life.

The building blocks of play

While a game is one means of play, in practice, the definition of play is broad and varied, particularly in adulthood. Drawing on the range of definitions that exist (see, e.g. Van Vleet and Feeney, 2015, and Yogman et al., 2018), I propose that there are three building blocks to play. Play is:
- **Enjoyable** – It stimulates feelings of enjoyment, entertainment or amusement. If it doesn't feel good, it probably isn't play.

- **Engaging** – It is interactive and absorbing (we often lose sense of time and become deeply immersed in it), and intrinsically motivating (it is voluntarily undertaken: the act of play *is* the purpose).
- **Exploratory** – It has elements of experimentation and improvisation in it that promote discovery (while rules may exist to frame it, there is space for flexibility and spontaneity).

As with resilience, my belief is that we all have the capacity to engage in the activity of play. However, *how* we like to play differs. Indeed, like resilience, play is a personal thing – hence the notion to play *your* way. Having gathered examples from groups and individuals across the years of how they prefer to play, activities range from physical play (including fort-building and model-making) to word and idea play – whereby concepts and language are manipulated in innovative combinations to produce structures of equal beauty. Creating and building have the potential to happen, therefore, with both our hands and our minds.

As a means of illustrating the 'many ways to play', I offer the following model (Figure 12.1) that uses the axes of physical play to cognitive play, and structured play to free play. Examples have been given to illustrate what might be placed in each quadrant, with the recognition that these are neither absolute nor exhaustive. As the wife of a drummer and a trained singer myself, I would be inclined to place musical play towards the centre, depending on the type of music being played.

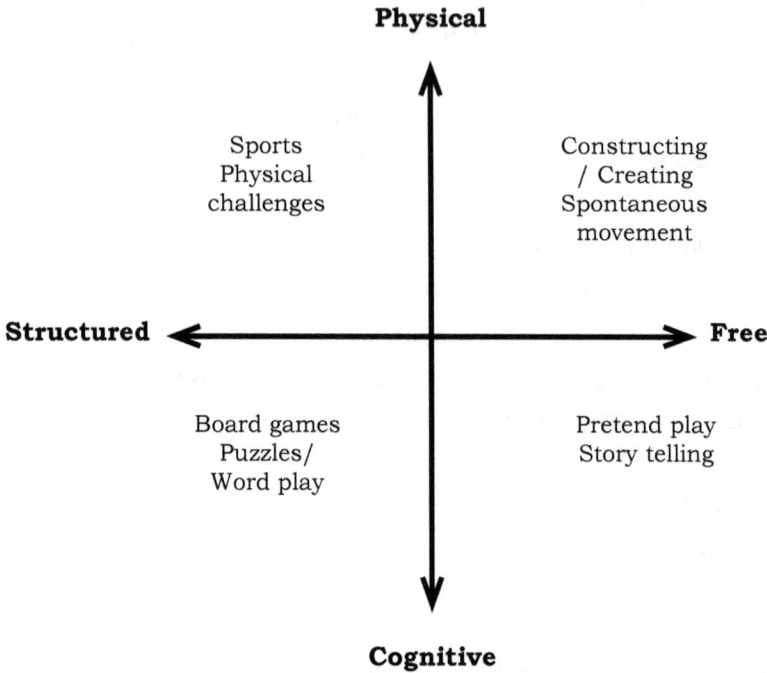

Figure 12.1 Many ways to play

While play can be individual, often it involves others. In one play-at-work study where people were offered a range of ways to play, overwhelmingly most chose options that allowed them to play with others (Fourie, Els and De Beer, 2020).

Sometimes play might involve just bringing a playful approach to a situation and allowing yourself to be silly for a while. One organization I work with has a dressing-up box for those days when a feather boa or top hat is just what you need to shift your state – and perhaps bring a smile to those around you. I describe this as putting the 'sili' in resilience.

Making play work

In a work context, there may be times when our playtime is separate from our worktime. There is little research on the 'dark side of play', so it is unclear how much is too much play. However, like anything, my sense is that it is a balance. Not having a pure task focus at times probably ends up negating the benefits that play can offer.

However, I think there is a cross-over place where we can effectively bring play into our work. Richard Branson (2019) stated, "I don't think of work and play as separate, it's all living." As both a researcher and a passionate play practitioner, I am fascinated by this place of living, where play and work effectively combine. Based on the many stories I have heard from leaders and teams over the past few years, I am increasingly convinced that integrating play at work has the potential to support both well-being and performance, particularly during challenging times.

The 2020 World Economic Forum's *The Future of Jobs Report* identified the top job skills employers believed would be needed for 2025. These included critical thinking and analysis as well as problem solving but also skills in self-management such as active learning, stress tolerance, flexibility – and resilience.

Play offers a novel, yet natural, route to developing these skills. In particular, I propose that play has an impact on three distinct, yet interconnected, areas that collectively support resilience (see Figure 12.2):

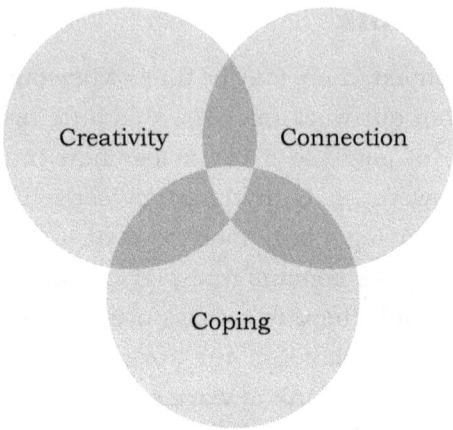

Figure 12.2 Playful Resilience model

Creativity

When we use play as an approach to encouraging creativity, we can stretch the boundaries of what is possible. As previously mentioned, in the animal kingdom, play is a crucial way of developing pathways, both neural and literal, giving a broader range of responses with which to navigate challenges and respond to possible threats. As humans, we can also use that approach to plan for our future.

In coaching, for instance, we often invite people to imagine the future, let ourselves dream that the problem is fixed, or role play responses from someone else's shoes. Coaching, therefore, offers a rich playground for exploration. I, like many coaches, often play with metaphors and language, invite clients to create pictures or other creative means of processing and capturing thoughts, and integrate movement (be it breathing, postural change or changing a vantage point in the room). All of this can help clients learn new perspectives and possibilities which, I believe, is what makes coaching effective.

Some research shows that explicitly integrating play into coaching can aid thinking. A study exploring the use of a LEGO® Serious Play® approach in one-to-one coaching (Quinn, Trinh and Passmore, 2022) found that building models gave people time to think and facilitated a feeling of safety. Ultimately, this allowed people to gain new awareness and insights that they reported might not otherwise have been reached.

When we play, we activate multiple areas of our brain. Emotions like joy and excitement stimulate the secretion of endorphins (our 'feel good' hormones), and pump oxygen and glucose to the brain, which fuels creative thinking.

Also, when our attention is focused (i.e. the engagement building block of play), the emotional and memory centres in our brain are particularly activated – which is one reason why we might remember learning more when it's linked to playful experiences.

In my years in learning and development, I have often seen ideas resonate through play (whether it be a team-building activity or role playing a response to a challenging situation). One classic activity I have played with hundreds of learners over the years is the marshmallow challenge.[2] Participants are given 20 sticks of spaghetti, some tape, string and a marshmallow. The challenge is to build, in 18 minutes, the tallest freestanding structure that is strong enough to balance the marshmallow on top.

Research collated by the creators of the challenge shows that MBA graduates do worst at this overall. As an MBA graduate, I find that both embarrassing and understandable. We waste time coming up with the one

---

[2] See www.marshmallowchallenge.com for full instructions.

winning idea (often shooting down the creative, wild ones). The people who do the best at this activity are children. They don't fall into the traps of perfection or pride – they are not looking for one brilliant solution. Instead, they prototype and play. They explore, test, tinker and generally have fun. While discovering innovative, effective solutions to the challenge, they also build the most exciting structures.

One experience, out of the hundreds of towers I've seen people make, stands out. One team began by playing with ideas and started animatedly brainstorming possible approaches. They settled on a plan to test it out and turned to get started, only to find that one of their team members (who was convinced that triangles was the way forward) was busy cutting up the spaghetti into small sections and preparing to stick them together with the tape. Not a bad idea, but not one that the group wanted to try out. So, they requested more spaghetti, which the rules of the game didn't allow. They had to stick to the one idea, which sadly didn't win them the challenge.

At the end of the day, when we ran through learnings, more than one person had the same takeaway: "Don't cut the spaghetti too soon."

My belief is that the concept of not moving too quickly to action (particularly without making sure that others are on board) is a lesson that will have stayed with that group for a long time. This anchoring of learning is facilitated, I believe, through the emotional charge of the experience, which helps tag it as important and so bank it for the future.

In a team context, stimulating creativity through play might involve creating spaces or opportunities for people to generate, capture or share their ideas in novel ways, and giving people time, and license, to play without fear of reprisal. And the results of this can be powerful. For example, a tech company I recently worked with encouraged their teams to play with how meeting updates were given, encouraging them to explore creative ways of sharing complex information. The teams produced newscasts and mock adverts, and generally had fun. One of the leaders recounted how they left the session 'buzzing' and, perhaps most importantly, told me how they remembered more of the information they heard compared with previous meetings because of the playful way it was presented.

Leadership increasingly requires the ability to find creative ways to navigate around unforeseen and novel challenges – and this in turn demands an ability to be flexible, take risks and 'think on our feet'. Several leaders I know have explored improvised theatre practices as a means to develop these critical skills, and some studies have explored how these approaches can support leaders to develop resilience (Dennis, 2014). While improvisation certainly requires quick thinking and creativity, it also relies on connection between players. Anticipating and building on the opportunities presented, while also creating chances for others to do the same, is key to maintaining the flow of any improvised piece. Perhaps, therefore, the seemingly trivial games I experienced during my own drama training may well have been teaching fundamental skills of empathy and trust (which I would argue are the foundations for high-performing teams).

Play provides an environment where ideas can emerge and develop without incurring risk. Indeed, play helps us to feel safe to experiment and explore – after all, as Stuart Brown notes, "we are safe because we are just playing" (2010, p. 34). However, to enable this, we must encourage a culture that advocates toying, tinkering and testing, without fear of being rushed or ridiculed. In doing so, we have the potential to find innovative solutions we might not have discovered before – and ultimately to find ways to be more flexible and adaptable in responding to the unforeseen challenges of the future.

Connection

The second area play supports in terms of resilience is connection.

Humans are inherently social creatures and we know that positive relationships are central to well-being and predictors of resilience following adversity (Saltzman, Hansel and Bordnick, 2020). When we can reach out to others for help when and how we need it, it can make all the difference to how we feel and how we perform.

Play has been shown to increase trust and bonds between players (Hunter, Jemielniak and Postula, 2010; Uy, 2019). Some research even suggests that it can help reduce the hierarchical boundaries that might exist between people at different levels in an organization (Locke, 1989). And this is particularly useful for diverse teams.

One of my clients, Anna Mascolo, is an Executive Vice President at Shell. Finding herself in a new role in Asia, with cultural barriers to cross and a new team to form, she describes how she consciously used play to bridge culture and create connection across the team because, as she puts it, "play is a universal language". She encouraged the team to create videos to celebrate key achievements. Sub-teams worked together to create photo montages and stop motion animation clips, movie trailers and videos set to music. Crucially, each sub-team did this in their own way, and the result was uplifting and inspiring. This, she says, was the start of creating a strong team culture of achievements, with bonds forged across international boundaries and the ability to effectively weather business storms together.

While we may be emerging from the immediate crisis of the past few years, and the lockdowns are lifting across the globe, the need for connection is critical. For many people, working remotely has led to them feeling isolated (indeed, it is noteworthy that the 2022 theme for Mental Health Awareness Week in the UK was loneliness). Some people who changed roles in the past two years may not yet have even met their colleagues in person.

I believe we have a need to rethink how our workplaces can be a place for connection and joy. The It pays to play study, produced by BrightHR, reports that millennials, in particular, expect fun and play to be integral parts of their lives at work. But I think we all crave it. While, at least in the short term, we can manage without play, we often feel a stronger desire to engage in it when we've gone a long time without it. Brown describes how animals deprived of play will engage in "rebound play" (2010, p. 43) whereby they try and catch up on missed play once they are able to.

All this means that we're probably craving play even more now and need to work harder to create spaces, both planned and spontaneous, for playful connections to happen. As many organizations move to hybrid working, with fewer opportunities for in-person meet ups and the prospect of relentless online schedules continuing, it becomes even more imperative to rethink our 'ways to play' to make them fit for modern ways of working.

This might mean recrafting team meetings by, perhaps, playing with the format, location or content to include playful moments that promote connection, such as inviting people to share successes or moments of joy. Or, maybe, inviting people to collaborate to solve problems or take on team challenges. Or simply creating spaces where people can take a break and play together – in person or online.

Coping

The final area that I believe play enables in terms of resilience is coping.

Coping relates to the strategies we use to respond to the demands of our environment. Sometimes these strategies can be helpful, sometimes not – particularly in the long run. Working through the evenings to attend meetings in different time zones, or drinking coffee to keep awake and make a deadline, might work in the short term but are rarely effective longer-term.

Play can help us to learn positive means of coping – partly because, by playing, we activate the systems in our bodies that counter anxiety and stress. When we start to feel stressed, we mobilize internal resources to respond accordingly. We pump more oxygen and glucose around the body to fuel muscles, and release hormones and neurochemicals such as adrenalin (which gives us increased energy) and cortisol (which increases alertness). Our non-essential functions are suppressed – who needs to eat, sleep or procreate when we are under threat? Without our discharging these chemicals and hormones by, for instance, exhibiting a stress response, they stay in our system. Over prolonged periods, this can have a range of detrimental physical and physiological effects.

Play, however – and especially any type of spontaneous movement (e.g. dancing, jumping on a trampoline, throwing a ball in the air) – can help discharge this excess energy and encourage the body's systems to reset more rapidly. Indeed, even other forms of play have been shown to help us recover (Eschleman et al., 2014): for example, one study found that 45 minutes of visual art making led to a reduction in cortisol levels (Kaimal, Ray and Muniz, 2016).

Because playing makes us feel good, we release hormones and neurochemicals including serotonin and oxytocin. These help to counter the potentially harmful effects of stress hormones such as cortisol. Also, when we experience emotions like excitement and joy (which we know can come from play), rather than narrowing our focus to counter potential risks, our attention is broadened. This helps us to spot extra resources that could potentially help us. Barbara Fredrickson (2001) conceptualizes this process as the 'broaden and build theory', asserting that the benefits of this tend to build in an upwards spiral. Through broadening awareness of, and subsequently accessing, resources, we also equip ourselves to better respond to future challenges – thereby building our ongoing capacity for resilience.

I have seen this upwards spiral in action through my own research. Participants described how the game mechanisms (both the imaginary setting and the elements of chance, choice and challenge) helped them to both enjoy the experience and feel safe to engage. In particular, they reported that the online setting enhanced this by providing a familiar and secure space in which to participate. Also, the turn taking of the game helped people feel safe to speak without interruption. Many of us have learned from experience that overtalking results in both voices being lost, so it seemed the benefit was mutually reinforcing – the turn taking supported the online setting and the online setting supported the turn taking. Rather than learning new resources, however, the findings suggested that the play setting gave the participants the conditions within which to reflect meaningfully on their prior experiences, and so to remember what they already had to help them to cope. Ordinary magic in action!

Finally, in terms of coping, sometimes we just need to cut loose and have a break. Because resilience isn't keeping going until you break: sometimes, it's taking a break so you can keep going.

Presenteeism and 'leaveism' (working when unwell, or through weekends or leave) is one of the biggest drains on productivity (Deloitte, 2020), and has been shown to lead to burnout and significant cost in both human and financial terms.

Taking a break to play can help buffer against potential burnout. In one play-at-work study (Fourie, Els and De Beer, 2020), telemarketers at a company in South Africa were given the opportunity to play a range of games in their lunch hour over several weeks. What they found was that, when people played in their breaks, they experienced greater psychological detachment from work (i.e. it gave them a proper break). And what we know from previous studies is that detaching from work supports people to recover and replenish resources (Sonnentag and Fritz, 2015; Sonnentag and Kühnel, 2016).

But, interestingly, team performance also increased in the teams who played. These teams achieved a higher number of sales compared with both the same period one month before the intervention and also the same period a year before – another example of how play at work, even if it's not *in* the work itself, can have a positive impact on both well-being and performance.

Prioritizing play

So, what can leaders do to bring the power of play into work? I offer three steps to realizing the benefits of play at work:

1. **Explore it** – find *your* way to play. Reflect on what you loved doing as a child and notice what brings you joy now (there is a reason why adult colouring books and experience games have risen in popularity: we all crave play and need to carve out space for it in our lives).
2. **Embed it** – once you know your 'way to play', prioritize it, both inside and outside work. It doesn't have to be lengthy: even five minutes between meetings to do a puzzle or play tug with the dog can refresh and rejuvenate you.
3. **Encourage it** – find ways to facilitate playful interactions in your teams and build the benefits of play into their days at work. Remember the variety of ways we play and create opportunities for people to play *their* way. Involve them in rethinking how tasks or spaces might be more playful (especially in a hybrid world) and make it legitimate for people to take a break to play. While you can't force fun, you can promote play.

Play is critical to life-long learning and, in particular, learning how to live and lead in the complex, changing and challenging times we are in now.

I encourage *you* to find ways to bring more play into your days – so that you create the conditions for you, and those around you, to enjoy the journey of work – even when it's not all plain sailing.

References

Barnett, L.A. (2007) 'The nature of playfulness in young adults', Personality and Individual Differences, 43(4), 949–958. Available at: https://doi.org/10.1016/j.paid.2007.02.018 (Accessed 6 October 2022).

Basso, J.C. and Suzuki, W.A. (2017) 'The effects of acute exercise on mood, cognition, neurophysiology, and neurochemical pathways: A review', Brain Plasticity, 2(2), 127–152. Available at: https://doi.org/10.3233/BPL-160040 (Accessed 6 October 2022).

Branson, R. (2019) Feeling burned out. Available at: https://www.virgin.com/branson-family/richard-branson-blog/feeling-burned-out (Accessed 6 October 2022).

Bright HR (n.d.) It pays to play. Available at: https://pages.brighthr.com/it-pays-to-play-report.html (Accessed 6 October 2022).

Brooker, H. et al. (2019) 'The relationship between the frequency of number puzzle use and baseline cognitive function in a large online sample of adults aged 50 and over', International Journal of Geriatric Psychiatry, 34(7), 932–940. Available at: https://pubmed.ncbi.nlm.nih.gov/30746778/ (Accessed 6 October 2022)

Brown, P. (2022) 'Refining the solution to an emotional muddle', Developing Leaders, 39, 133–142.

Brown, P. and Dzendrowskyj, T. (2018) 'Sorting out an emotional muddle: Insights from neuroscience on the organizational value of emotions', Developing Leaders, 29, 26–31.

Brown, S. (2010) *Play: How it shapes the brain, opens the imagination, and invigorates the soul.* New York: Penguin.

Cao, W. et al. (2020) 'The psychological impact of the COVID-19 epidemic on college students in China'. *Psychiatry Research*, 287. Available at: https://doi.org/10.1016/j.psychres.2020.112934 (Accessed 6 October 2022).

Deloitte (2020) 'Mental health and employers. Refreshing the case for investment'. January. Available at: https://www2.deloitte.com/uk/en/pages/consulting/articles/mental-health-and-employers-refreshing-the-case-for-investment.html (Accessed 6 October 2022).

Dennis, R. (2014) 'Improvised performance: Nurturing natural leadership', *Journal of Organizational Transformation & Social Change*, 11(2), 108–124. Available at: http://dx.doi.org/10.1179/1477963313Z.00000000016 (Accessed 6 October 2022).

Eschleman, K.J. et al. (2014) 'Benefiting from creative activity: The positive relationships between creative activity, recovery experiences, and performance-related outcomes', *Journal of Occupational and Organizational Psychology*, 87(3), 579–598. Available at: https://doi.org/10.1111/joop.12064 (Accessed 6 October 2022).

Fourie, L., Els, C., and De Beer, L.T. (2020) A play-at-work intervention: What are the benefits? *South African Journal of Economic and Management Sciences*, 23(1). Available at: https://doi.org/10.4102/sajems.v23il.2815 (Accessed 6 October 2022).

Fredrickson, B.L. (2001) The role of positive emotions in positive psychology: The broaden-and-build theory of positive emotions. *American Psychologist*, 56(3), 218–226. Available at: https://doi.org/10.1037/0003-066x.56.3.218 (Accessed 6 October 2022).

Gable, S.L. and Haidt, J. (2005) 'What (and why) is positive psychology?' *Review of General Psychology*, 9(2), 103–110. Available at: https://doi.org/10.1037/1089-2680.9.2.103 (Accessed 6 October 2022).

Galea, S., Merchant, R. and Lurie, N. (2020) 'The mental health consequences of Covid-19 and physical distancing: The need for prevention and early intervention', *JAMA Internal Medicine*, 180(6), 817–818. Available at: https://jamanetwork.com/journals/jamainternalmedicine/fullarticle/2764404 (Accessed 6 October 2022).

Ganesan, B. et al. (2021) 'Impact of coronavirus disease 2019 (COVID-19) outbreak quarantine, isolation, and lockdown policies on mental health and suicide. *Frontiers in*

Psychiatry, 12. Available at: https://doi.org/doi: 10.3389/fpsyt.2021.565190 (Accessed 6 October 2022).

Hunter, C., Jemielniak, D. and Postula, A. (2010) 'Temporal and spatial shifts within playful work.' *Journal of Organizational Change Management*, 23(1), 87–102. Available at: https://doi.org/10.1108/09534811011017225 (Accessed 6 October 2022).

Ivbijaro, G. et al. (2020) 'Psychological impact and psychosocial consequences of the COVID 19 pandemic. Resilience, mental well-being, and the coronavirus pandemic'. *Indian Journal of Psychiatry*, 62(3), 395–404. Available at: https://doi.org/10.4103/psychiatry.IndianJPsychiatry_1031_20 (Accessed 6 October 2022).

Kaimal, G., Ray, K. and Muniz, J. (2016) 'Reduction of cortisol levels and participants' responses following art making', *Art Therapy*, 33(2), 74–80. Available at: https://doi.org/10.1080/07421656.2016.1166832 (Accessed 6 October 2022).

LEGO® (2018) *Play well report*: 'Families that play more are happier, but even children say they are too busy for fun and games'. Available at: https://www.lego.com/en-sg/aboutus/news/2018/august/lego-play-well-report (Accessed 6 October 2022).

Locke, K.D. (1989) 'Social play in daily interactions at a workplace: An ethnographic description of social play and its relationship to social solidarity in a medical setting'. Unpublished doctoral dissertation, Case Western Reserve University, Cleveland, Ohio.

Maresch, I. and Kampman, H. (2022) 'Playing for resilience in a pandemic: Exploring the role of an online board game in recognising resources', *International Journal of Applied Positive Psychology*. Available at: https://doi.org/10.1007/s41042-022-00069-z (Accessed 6 October 2022).

Masten, A.S. (2001) 'Ordinary magic: Resilience processes in development', *American Psychologist*, 56(3), 227–238. Available at: https://doi.org/10.1037/0003-066X.56.3.227 (Accessed 6 October 2022).

Meredith, L.S. et al. (2011) 'Promoting psychological resilience in the U.S. Military', *Rand Health Quarterly*. Available at: https://www.rand.org/pubs/monographs/MG996.html (Accessed 6 October 2022).

Moss, J, (2021) 'Beyond burned out', *Harvard Business Review*, 10 February. Available at: https://hbr.org/2021/02/beyond-burned-out (Accessed 6 October 2022).

Pellis, S. and Pellis, V. (2013) *The playful brain: Venturing to the limits of neuroscience*. Iran: Oneworld Publications.

Petelczyc, C.A., Capezio, A. and Wang, L. (2017) 'Play at work: An integrative review and agenda for future research', *Journal of Management*, 44(1), 161–190. Available at: https://doi.org/10.1177/0149206317731519 (Accessed 6 October 2022).

Pors, J.G. and Andersen, N.Å. (2015). 'Playful organizations: Undecidability as a scarce resource', *Culture and Organization*, 21(4), 338–354. Available at: https://doi.org/10.1080/14759551.2014.924936 (Accessed 6 October 2022).

Quinn, T., Trinh, S.H. and Passmore, J. (2022) 'An exploration into using LEGO® SERIOUS PLAY® (LSP) within a positive psychology framework in individual coaching: An interpretative phenomenological analysis (IPA)'. *Coaching: An International Journal of Theory Research and Practice*, 15(1), 102–116. Available at: https://doi.org/10.1080/17521882.2021.1898427 (Accessed 6 October 2022).

Saltzman, L., Hansel, T. and Bordnick, P. (2020) 'Loneliness, isolation, and social support factors in post COVID-19 mental health', *Psychological Trauma: Theory, Research, Practice, and Policy*, 12(S1), S55–S57. Available at: https://doi.org/10.1037/tra0000703 (Accessed 6 October 2022).

Sisto, A. et al. (2019) 'Towards a transversal definition of psychological resilience: A literature review', *Medicina*, 55(11), 745. Available at: https://doi.org/10.3390/medicina55110745 (Accessed 6 October 2022).

Sonnentag, S. and Fritz, C. (2015) 'Recovery from job stress: The stressor-detachment model as an integrative framework', *Journal of Organizational Behaviour*, 36(1), 72–103. Available at: https://doi.org/10.1002/job.1924 (Accessed 6 October 2022).

Sonnentag, S. and Kühnel, J. (2016) 'Coming back to work in the morning: Psychological detachment and reattachment as predictors of work engagement', *Journal of Occupational Health Psychology*, 21(4), 379–390. Available at: https://doi.org/10.1037/ocp0000020 (Accessed 6 October 2022).

Sørensen, B.M. and Spoelstra, S. (2012) 'Play at work: Continuation, intervention and usurpation', *Organization*, 19(1), 81–97. Available at: https://doi.org/10.1177/1350508411407369 (Accessed 6 October 2022).

Suzuki, W. (2017) *The brain-changing benefits of exercise.* Available at: https://ed.ted.com/best_of_web/X93aZK9s (Accessed 6 October 2022).

Uy, D.J. (2019) 'Career SUPERDRIVE : A qualitative evaluation of serious play in the career exploration process', *Asia Pacific Career Development Journal*, 2(2), 63–81.

Van Vleet, M. and Feeney, B.C. (2015) 'Play behavior and playfulness in adulthood', *Social and Personality Psychology Compass*, 9(11), 630–643. Available at: https://doi.org/10.1111/spc3.12205 (Accessed 6 October 2022).

Wesnes, K.A. et al. (2019) 'An online investigation of the relationship between the frequency of word puzzle use and cognitive function in a large sample of older adults', *International Journal of Geriatric Psychiatry*, 34(7), 921–931. Available at: https://doi.org/10.1002/gps.5033 (Accessed 6 October 2022).

West, S.E., Hoff, E. and Carlsson, I. (2016) 'Play and productivity: Enhancing the creative climate at workplace meetings with play cues', *American Journal of Play*, 9(1), 71–86.

World Economic Forum (2020) *The future of jobs report.* Available at: https://www.weforum.org/reports/the-future-of-jobs-report-2020 - report-nav (Accessed 6 October 2022).

Yıldırım, M. and Solmaz, F. (2022) 'COVID-19 burnout, COVID-19 stress and resilience: Initial psychometric properties of COVID-19 Burnout Scale', *Death Studies*, 46(3), 524–532. Available at: https://doi.org/10.1080/07481187.2020.1818885 (Accessed 6 October 2022).

Yogman, M. et al. (2018) 'The power of play: A pediatric role in enhancing development in young children', *Pediatrics*, 142(3). AAP Committee on psychosocial aspects of child and family health; Council on communications and media. Available at: https://doi.org/10.1542/peds.2018-2058 (Accessed 6 October 2022).

Biography

Imogen Maresch is an executive coach, facilitator and researcher in the field of applied positive psychology and coaching psychology. With a background in drama, 15 years' experience in learning and development, and a track record of leadership roles in both the private and public sectors, Imogen brings a unique perspective to the world of work. She holds an MBA from the University of Leicester and an MSc in Applied Positive Psychology and Coaching Psychology (MAPPCP) from the University of East London, both with distinction. Imogen is creator of *Not all Plain Sailing*™, an innovative board game that supports individuals and teams to boost resilience and wellbeing. Her research study, *Playing for Resilience in a Pandemic* (which piloted an online version of the game with people in lockdown), was recently published in a leading academic journal. Imogen is a founding member of the ION Partnership and, in her spare time, volunteers as a coach for a number of UK charities and hosts legendary games nights. For more information, contact imogen@presenceofmind.uk

CHAPTER 13

Getting to Know How the Brain Works – A historical review

Compiled by Dr Sue Paterson MBE

Introduction

These days, we generally understand that the brain is the organ that defines who we are and how we interact with the world. Without it, we wouldn't be able to see, hear, smell, taste, or appreciate touch and we wouldn't be able to distinguish textures. We would be unable to make memories, take decisions or register feelings. Parts of our bodies might still be able to move but not in a coordinated way. We wouldn't recognize loved ones and we wouldn't be able to learn. We wouldn't even know how to keep ourselves safe.

This understanding has not always been the case: our ideas about what the brain does have changed significantly over the years. The study of the brain has had a long and chequered past, with ideas and models influenced by the science and culture of the day. As knowledge expanded, and scientific methods and cultural beliefs shifted, so theoretical models to explain what the brain does and how it works reached their useful limits and new ideas took over.

Furthermore, while we think we now understand what the brain does, we are still in the early days of understanding exactly how it works – how it does what it does.

Many neuroscientists believe it's important that our understanding of how the brain works is grounded in science. The word 'science' is derived from the Latin '*scientia*', which is knowledge based on demonstrable and reproducible data and observation. Science aims for measurable results through testing and analysis. Scientific methods usually involve testing hypotheses of theories or models by collecting measurable evidence in experiments to confirm or refute them.

The science of the nervous system, including the brain, has only recently become formalized and is called 'neuroscience'. It only began to be recognized as a distinct academic discipline in the late 19th century. The Society of Neuroscience was founded in 1969 with just 500 affiliates – today, it has over 40,000 members. It is generally accepted that neuroscience covers a wide range of disciplines including, for example, anatomy and physiology, psychology, neurology and cognitive neuroscience.

This chapter explores how our understanding of how the brain works is dependent on the scientific context we work in, and it looks to the future – how might our comprehension be shaped by new ideas?

Source material for this chapter comes from Wickens (2015) and Cobb (2020), supplemented by internet searches and personal discussions with fellow scientists.

From Ancient Egypt to the Renaissance and the 16th century

"The centre of thought is the heart, not the brain"

Records of humans' knowledge of how our brain works covering the past 5,000 years show that, until relatively recently, the brain was not considered to be important. Mummies from Ancient Egypt around 3,000 BC illustrate that the brain was not prized at all: after death, it was likely pulled through the nose and discarded (see Figure 13.1), while the heart was carefully preserved and buried with its owner in a bid to provide a safe haven for the soul as it waited for Judgement Day. Egyptians regarded the heart as the source of thoughts, desires and actions: they believed that it was the heart that represented the person's self and held the key to eternity. The brain, on the other hand, was thought to be a container for passing wet mucus or snot to the nose.

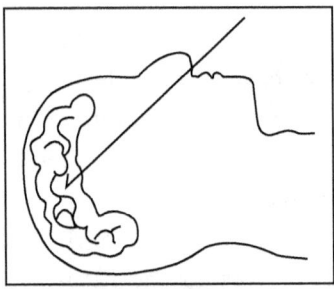

Figure 13.1 During mummification, Ancient Egyptians got rid of the brain by pulling it out through the nose

Ancient Greeks generally followed that tradition: they believed that mental and emotional characteristics were related to the soul, and that this was based in the chest, not the head. In Homer's stories of the Iliad and the Odyssey, for example, written down more than 2,500 years ago, the self is described as composed of many different "spiritual agents and forces", all based in the chest.

The first person on record to have recognized that the brain may have important powers was the Greek philosopher Alcmaeon in the 4th century BC. Although none of his original writing has survived, other contemporary philosophers described how he studied anatomy by dissecting animals, discovering that the eyes were connected to the brain by two 'channels', which today we recognize as the optic nerves. He went on to hypothesize that similar passages existed for the ears, nose and tongue, and concluded that "all senses are connected to the brain" and, furthermore, that "the governing facility of intelligence is the brain".

In the 3rd century BC, heated debates continued as to where the sources of sensations and intelligence were located. Important philosophers took opposing views. Hippocrates (460–370 BC) asserted that the brain was responsible for all our mental activity, including intelligence and emotions. In *On the Sacred Disease*, a book about epilepsy in which he described it as a disease of the brain in contrast to the prevailing belief that it was a disease of the spirit, he said:

> It ought to be generally known that the source of our pleasure, merriment, laughter, and amusement, as of our grief, pain, anxiety and tears is none other than the brain. It is specially that organ which enables us to think, see, hear and to distinguish the ugly, and the beautiful, the bad and good, pleasant the unpleasant... it is the brain too which is the source of madness and delirium, of the fears and frights which assail us... it is the thing where lies the cause of insomnia and sleep walking, of thoughts that will not come, forgotten duties and eccentricities... so long as the brain is still, a man is in his right mind.

Aristotle (384–322 BC), however, continued to believe that it was the heart that was the most important organ, arguing that "The brain is not responsible for any sensations at all. The correct view is that the seat and source of sensation is the region of the heart."

This opinion was based on the belief that warmth was essential for life, and Aristotle considered the heart to be "the furnace of the body". He regarded the brain as the coldest and wettest part of the body, which led him to see it as little more than a cooling organ.

Aristotle's views prevailed.

The importance of the heart was maintained during Biblical times. The translation of the Old Testament into Greek, mainly completed in the 2nd century BC, has very few mentions of the brain but hundreds of references to the heart, which continued to be viewed as the source of people's intelligence and emotion.

It wasn't until around 300 BC that a breakthrough in understanding the importance of the brain occurred, at a time when human dissection was first sanctioned in Alexandria, Egypt, then an outpost of the Greek empire. Allowing humans to be cut up was remarkable at a time when it went against the prevailing reverence of the dead in both Egyptian and Greek cultures. This practice of human dissections lasted only about 20–30 years and it wasn't until the 14th century that human dissections restarted in northern Italy. Even then, they weren't performed more widely in Europe until the 16th century.

The best-known early Egyptian anatomists were Herophilus (335–280 BC) and Erasistratus (310–250 BC). Herophilus was the first person to describe the anatomy of the human brain and to discover the nervous system. He described thin thread-like pathways that originated from the brain and spinal cord, and recognized that the brain was the main control centre. Erasistratus used a mechanistic approach to explain physiological processes, rejecting the idea that hidden "spirits or forces" in the body were in charge. He focused some effort on trying to understand the brain, for the first time relating the convoluted shape of the cerebral hemispheres to intelligence. Despite their accurate descriptions, the work of Herophilus and

Erasistratus did not settle the issue of whether the heart or the brain was the centre of thought and feeling – it just showed that the brain was complex.

Aristotle's view of a heart-centred body persisted for the next 1,500 years.

The Roman Claudius Galen (AD 129–200) was a revered doctor as well as a prolific writer, and it is to him that we owe the synthesis of previous works of anatomy and physiology from writers like Herophilus and Erasistratus, whose original works were lost. Galen supplemented what was already known with his own observations and theories from experiments on live animals, not humans, and his influence remained important in medicine for almost 1,500 years after his death. He gave the first detailed description of the brain structure and the nervous system, which left no doubt that the source of all nerves, sensations and voluntary motion was the brain. His theory, elaborated from the original Greek idea that the nerves and brain functioned because of a 'fluid', would not be overthrown until the 18th century, when it was replaced by ideas about electricity. Galen's writings survived for centuries and were translated from Greek into Syriac and Arabic, forming the basis of medicine throughout the Islamic world for centuries after the fall of the Roman Empire in the 4th century.

After the fall of Rome, practically all ancient Greek and Roman knowledge was lost, leading to a time of intellectual stagnation in Europe that some call 'the Dark Ages'.

However, studies of the brain continued to thrive in the Middle East and Northern Africa during these times. One particularly important theory, developed by scholars such as Nemesius in present-day Syria in the 4th century and St Augustine in present-day Algeria in the

5th century, postulated that different parts of the brain were responsible for different mental functions such as sensations, movement and memory.

Later studies focused on how the mind and body interacted: Islamic scholars like Al-Zahrawi, for example, who lived in Iberia around the year 1000, were known to successfully perform surgical treatment of head injuries, and Avicenna (980–1037), who was based in Persia, did early work on the diagnosis and treatment of psychological disorders. His book, *The Book of Healing*, became a standard medical text at many universities and remained in use as late as 1650. However, while Avicenna accepted Galen's observations of nerves running from the brain to the body, he continued to believe Aristotle's view that the main source of sensation was the heart.

When the Dark Ages began to lift in Western Europe during the 12th and 13th centuries, Galen was among the first of the classical authors to be translated into Latin from texts preserved in the East. The return of the expanded classical texts was one of many first steps in the 'rebirth of knowledge' or 'Renaissance' that began in universities in Italy. The works had been significantly extended by Eastern scholars, incorporating their own observations and theories. They were aware of the difference between the heart-centred view of Aristotle and Avicenna and Galen's brain-centred arguments, and there were many attempts to reconcile the two.

Dissection of human corpses restarted after a long hiatus, most notably in the 14th century in northern Italy by the anatomist Mondino de Luzzi (1275–1326). It's likely that the taboo about dissecting human bodies was lifted because Crusaders began the custom of returning the bodies of killed warriors – or sometimes just their hearts

– back to their homes. It may also have been related to efforts to understand the causes of the plague, which was rampant at the time.

Mondino wrote his dissection manual (*Anatomia Mundini*) in 1316. It wasn't published until 1478 – over a hundred years after his death. Although the original version lacked illustrations, this was rectified in 1345 by one of Mondino's pupils and these pictures form the first-ever modern anatomical drawings of the nervous system (Figure 13.2 is an illustration from a publication in 1541). Mondino's book showed that dissection and observation were the basis for understanding, thereby challenging the prevailing culture that knowledge was founded on faith, not fact. Modern scientific methods were born.

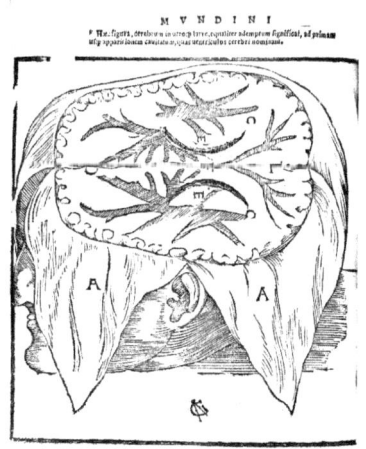

Figure 13.2 Section of brain in dissected skull, from Mondino Dei Luzzi's 'Anatomia Mundini', 1541 (https://en.wikipedia.org/wiki/Mondino_de_Luzzi)

Leonardo Da Vinci (1452–1519) was also a great illustrator of human anatomy, but his drawings were never published during his lifetime and became 'lost' until the late 18th century (see Figure 13.3). He made models of structures within the brain – for example, by injecting hot wax into the brain of an ox, which helped to define the shape and size of the brain in situ for the first time.

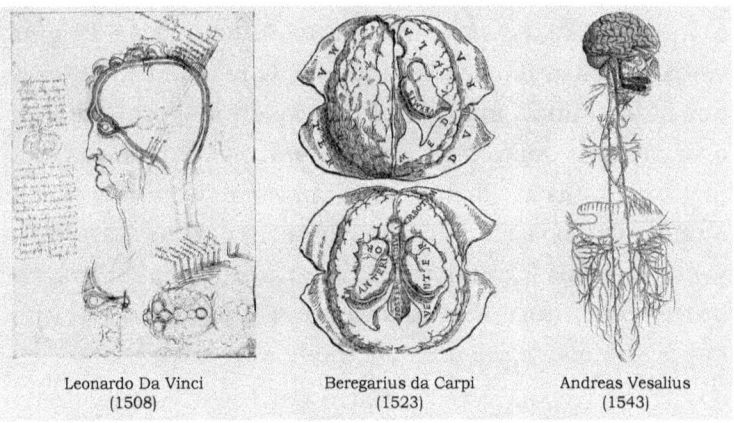

Leonardo Da Vinci (1508)   Beregarius da Carpi (1523)   Andreas Vesalius (1543)

Figure 13.3 Illustrations of the brain and nervous system from Leonardo Da Vinci and others in the 16th century

From the 15th century onwards, the pace of cultural and scientific change accelerated as the Renaissance took hold and old ideas started to be challenged.

By the 16th century, the first clear errors in Galen's anatomical and physiological writings began to be discovered, and Aristotle's heart-centred ideas to be systematically challenged. Beregarius da Carpi, appointed a Lecturer in Surgery in Bologna in 1502, was the first to provide the original thinking about the brain since antiquity. His publication in 1521 showed that some of the structures described by Galen did not exist in humans because they had been identified from his work on animals (see Figure 13.3).

In 1543, that publication was followed by another book on anatomy and physiology by Vesalius (known as the

'*Fabrica*'), which led to a decisive break from the old ideas and offered new concepts about how the body and brain worked. Scholars at the time were shocked to discover from this book that Galen had made as many as over two hundred errors in his work.

Vesalius's book used the new printing technology to the full and included over 200 illustrations, which was revolutionary at the time (Figure 13.3). His study of the brain was based on the idea that it was the brain, not the heart, that was the origin of thought, although his evidence was limited. His ideas of how the brain worked were linked to the 'fluid' beliefs of the day, and he admitted that he was unable to form any opinion as to how the brain carried out such activities as imagination, reasoning and memory.

While this book challenged ancient dogmas, it was not widely accepted and there was considerable opposition from those unwilling to relinquish Galen's views.

The 17th and 18th centuries
"The brain is a mechanical machine"

Gradually, the idea that the brain was the centre of thought and feeling became accepted during the 16th century, and by the 17th century this was the norm. The French philosopher, mathematician and scientist Rene Descartes (1596–1650) was influential in this respect, carrying out brain dissections in the 1620s and 1630s. He provided a new foundation for scientific thought called 'rationalism', which was based on the belief of innate ideas, reason and deduction, and is the basis for scientific thinking today. 'Science' as we now understand it began to consolidate itself after the establishing of what has become the world's oldest scientific society, The Royal

Society of London, which emerged in 1660. 'Experimental philosophy' began to become physics.

Descartes applied this theory to living things as well, claiming that all life could be explained through material processes belonging to the physical world and not to mysterious vague spiritual forces.

However, Descartes believed that the mind and body were separate and distinct (the 'dualism' theory). He thought that the body worked like a hydraulic-powered machine, but that the mind (or soul) was separate, non-material and free from the laws of nature. This continues to be debated today with some neuroscientists arguing that the mind is an integral part of the brain and others asserting that it is separate, although without any specific form or location.

Descartes was the first person to explain the functioning of the brain and nervous system as a mechanical machine – "automated responses carried by a fluid", possibly contained in the blood. These automated reflexes included processes like movement of the body, digestion of food, circulation of blood, respiration, sleeping, sensory processes, imagination, memory and emotion. He based these ideas on the moving statues that were fashionable in French circles at the time. The debate about the nature of the 'fluid' that connected brain and body would last for at least another hundred years.

Descartes' hydraulic model was surpassed by the idea that the brain's working was based on clockwork mechanisms because intricate clockwork machines were built that enabled statues to move realistically.

Thomas Willis (1621–75) was an English doctor who studied the brain and nerves using extensive autopsies, clinical observation and experimentation. His book *Cerebri Anatome*, published in 1664, was the most comprehensive and detailed description of the brain structure and nervous system up to that date. He was the first to recognize that blood circulated to the brain and he proposed that mental functions (for example, intelligence, memory and senses) could be attributed to different parts of the brain.

Around the time that Willis published his book, other scientists were investigating the brain using early microscopes. Marcelo Malpighi (1628–94) was able to observe nerve cells for the first time and he called these "glands with long fine channels".

In 1662, the first experiment that showed the connection between nerves and muscles was carried out by a young Dutchman called Jan Swammerdam (1637–80). In a series of experiments on frogs' legs, he showed that muscular contraction could occur without any connection between muscle and brain. He also demonstrated that the theory about fluids being the source of movement was incorrect – he found no evidence of the physical presence of any such fluid. Ideas continued to abound about how nerves move muscles, ranging from intrinsic 'irritability' to non-material forces – for example, the 'sentient principle'.

The 18th and 19th centuries
"The brain works on electrical stimulation"

Electrical phenomena began to be experimented with in the 18th century, but it wasn't until the end of that century that the concept of electricity was incorporated into the understanding of the brain and nervous system. During experiments with frogs' legs in the 1780s, Luigi Galvani (1737–98) believed that he had discovered a form of electricity intrinsic to all living organisms. He published his ideas in 1791, but they weren't confirmed until 30 years later by Carlo Matteucci (1811–68) using a newly invented galvanometer that could measure the small current flows in biological tissue. Refinements of instrumentation in the 1840s made it possible to measure and confirm nerve impulses as electrical signals.

So, after more than 2,000 years, the idea of 'spiritual forces' and 'fluids' governing the body's processes was replaced by one involving electrical signals. This was a step change in understanding how the brain works.

The 18th and 19th centuries
"The brain's functions are localized"

Breakthroughs continued with detailed mapping of the brain structures but, increasingly, interest was focused on identifying where specific functions in the brain resided. Interest in structure expanded to interest in function – two determining foci of interest that today have been expanded to the new science of 'connectomics': how is it all connected?

In the late 18th century, phrenology, the practice of measuring bumps on the skull to predict mental traits, became very popular. It was developed by the German Franz Joseph Gall (1758–1828), who proposed that the human mind had a set of mental faculties with each one represented in a different area of the brain, the strength of which could be determined by the bumps, indentations and shape of the skull. While the idea that faculties were in different parts of the brain is still considered sound, the theory that these were related to indentations in the skull has been completely discredited.

The French physiologist Marie Jean Pierre Flourens

(1794–1867) carried out a series of experiments surgically removing different parts of animals' brains and observing their subsequent behaviour. His intention was to investigate localization: whether different parts of the brain had different functions, as proposed by phrenology. For the first time, he was able to demonstrate convincingly that the main divisions of the brain were indeed responsible for different functions. He concluded that, while higher behavioural functions – for example, thought – appear to be broadly distributed in the cortex and are not highly localized, the simple physiological and motor behaviours show strong localization.

In the 19th century, mapping of human brain functions onto different brain areas was done mainly by correlating changes in behaviour and capacity that occurred in people who had brain injuries or had undergone surgery. Invasive brain studies on humans became more possible with the widespread adoption of anaesthetics in the mid-19th century.

In the 1820s, Frenchman Jean-Baptiste Bouilland (1796–1881) noticed that people with damaged frontal lobes frequently had language disturbances. At the time, his conclusion that this part of the brain was associated with speech was received with much scepticism. In 1861, however, an eminent French brain scientist, Paul Broca (1824–80), showed, by correlating results of autopsies on patients who had lost the ability to speak, that a localized area in the brain was indeed likely to be related to speech production.

In 1870, by using electrical stimulations of dogs' brains, the Germans Eduard Hitzig (1838–1907) and Gustave Fritsch (1837–1927) identified a small region in the brain that initiated movement. The Scottish neurologist and psychologist David Ferrier (1843–1928) confirmed these findings by using similar techniques on a wide variety of animals. Published in 1873, he found that each animal's movements were produced from slightly different areas of their brains, indicating that each type of animal had evolved its own type of motor specialization. He also discovered localized areas for hearing, vision and even intelligence. He was the first to draw a diagram of localized cerebral motor functions in humans based on his experiments with monkeys. In 1881, he also became the first scientist to be tried under the Cruelty to Animals Act, 1876, following public outcries against vivisection.

Ferrier noted that, in all his experiments, the frontal part of the brain had failed to produce specific responses to his electrical probing. He was struck by a detail in an 1868 report on Phineas Gage, who had his frontal lobe pierced in a blasting accident in 1848. While working on a railway line in New England, Gage accidentally dropped a tamping iron that created a spark as it struck rock, thereby igniting the blasting powder in the hole that was being prepared for an explosion to shatter the rock, and sending the steel rod through his left cheek and out of the top of his head (see Figure 13.4). The blast was so powerful that the rod, which weighed around 13 pounds, landed about 30 metres away. Despite the injury, Gage remained conscious, his mind seemed to be unaffected, and he walked away from first-aid treatment without any help. Surviving a penetrating head injury was extremely rare at the time and it soon became apparent that, while physically capable of work, Gage's personality had undergone a dramatic change. Before the accident, he had been known as responsible, hard-working and considerate but, after it, he became impulsive and lacked inhibition, using foul language and being aggressive. About 12 years after his accident, he started to have seizures and died in 1860 at the age of 38. His physician John Harlow later examined his skull and reported that the accident had destroyed most of his anterior frontal lobe. Building on his work done on monkeys, Ferrier proposed that the frontal lobe injury could produce personality change without loss of sensory or motor function. He concluded that various aspects of attention and behaviour were localized in the frontal parts of the brain.

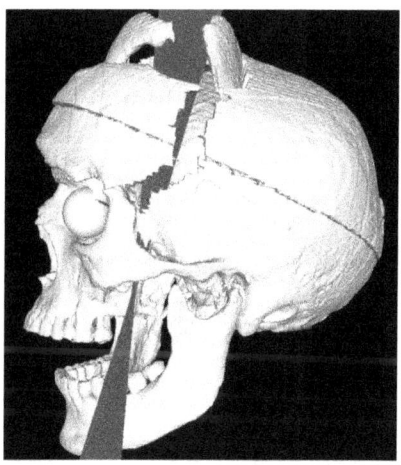

Figure 13.4 Phineas Gage's skull showing location of tampering iron after his accident (https://en.wikipedia.org/wiki/Phineas_Gage)

However, when it came to the more complex aspect of brain function – thought – the evidence continued to argue against localization. Damage on one side of the human brain was observed to lead to loss of function on the opposite side of the body, but the ability to think was apparently unaffected.

The 19th century
"The brain has evolved"

Charles Darwin (1809–82) was interested in how his theory of natural selection shaped organisms, and he explored the implications of this for the link between brain and mind. He thought that, if the brain makes a thought, then there must be a link between the brain structure and the type of thought it produces. Natural selection could therefore alter mind and behaviour by altering brain structure. This could explain instinctive behaviours as well as – possibly – the human mind, he thought. Many scientists at the time disagreed, suggesting that human evolution required a supernatural explanation, a theory that was called 'vitalism' and was similar to Descartes' ideas of 'dualism'.

Darwin's book, *The Descent of Man*, published in 1871, argued that humans and apes had common ancestors, and that there was no "fundamental difference between man and higher animals in their mental faculties". Thomas Huxley (1825–95), known as 'Darwin's bulldog', supported this idea and showed that the brain structures of humans and apes were very similar. Although not supportive of the slave trade, his claims in 1865 that white people had, by volume, bigger brains than black people meant that this produced differences in mental ability were not helpful. He also believed that differences in brain sizes between men and women led to differences in ability. The argument about size and power is still work in progress, although now with regard to male and female brains. It seems that, while the male brain is larger by volume than the female, the female brain contains more neurons than the male.

Darwin proposed that the brains of different animals

had different shapes because they had evolved to produce different behaviours. He also considered that in more developed brains there should be less function localization, so that 'free intercommunication' would account for more complex intellectual processes.

"The brain can switch activity on and off"

In the mid-1800s, it became clear that nerves were able to make activities happen (for example, a muscle contract) but that they could also stop activities. Brothers Ernst and Edward Weber, working in 1845, discovered that continuous electrical stimulation of the vagus nerve seemed to inhibit the heart beating and that sufficient stimulation stopped it altogether. In 1863, the Russian physiologist Ivan Sechenov (1829–1905) proposed that the brain could either intensify actions or inhibit them and he summarized this with the reflex pathway theory of how the brain works:

Stimulus -> Central intensification/inhibition -> Muscular response

Ferrier knew of Sechenov's work and agreed: he argued that inhibition was "the essential factor of attention". The organism must inhibit responses to extraneous events in order to focus on one particular stimulus, and inhibition could be viewed as a key factor in intelligence. However, it wasn't at all clear how inhibition worked, despite experiments based on the absence of inhibition due to the application of narcotics and anaesthetics.

In 1865, Francis Anstie (1833–74) suggested that the overall function of the brain was to control the body, with ideas of inhibition and control being tightly linked. The British neurologist John Hughlings Jackson (1835–1911) argued that epilepsy could be understood as a loss of control in the brain and the psychologist Conwy Lloyd Morgan (1852–1936) suggested that inhibition was an essential factor in learning to control behaviour.

For Sigmund Freud (1856–1939), inhibition could be a part of behaviour but he was not really interested in how the brain worked. He believed that brain function could not explain psychology and insisted that his psychological theories were "not concerned with anatomical locations but with regions in the mental apparatus irrespective of their possible situation in the body".

After inhibition and control, a third unexpected aspect of brain function was discovered in the 1860s. In his book, *Handbook of Physiological Optics* published in 1867, the German physicist and physician Herman von Helmholtz (1821–94) realized that the nervous system, and in particular the brain, played an active part in constructing humans' perception of even quite straightforward things. His observations about how humans see, despite a 'blind spot' in the centre of the eye, and construct 3D images from slightly different images from two eyes, led him to propose that the brain does not simply register a stimulus but "draws a conclusion" about the nature of the stimulation it is receiving. He also argued that perception is a kind of filter – the brain does not pay equal attention to all the stimuli it is presented with. This view of the brain as an active organ, and of perception as an imperfect and selective process leading to a view of the world, was a major breakthrough in understanding and still dominates today.

Scientists were beginning to realize that, in order to understand brain activity better, they needed to understand what the brain was made of.

The 19th and 20th centuries
"The brain is made of individual neurons"

Microscopes had helped to identify small individual structures in the body since the 17th century and, in the late 1830s, this led Theodor Schwann (1810–82) to publish the theory that animal and plant tissue was composed of independent, self-governing 'cells'. But the detailed structure of the brain remained hidden until 1873 when the Italian Camillo Golgi (1843–1926) discovered silver impregnation staining, which allowed individual cells to be highlighted and studied in detail. The Spaniard Santiago Ramón y Cajal (1852–1934) perfected this technique for the brain and was able to produce the most exquisitely detailed drawings of nerve cells in the brain, called 'neurons'. His neuron doctrine proposed that neurons were the basic structural and functioning units of the nervous system, and that they were discrete cells not connected in a meshwork.

Ramón y Cajal used a telegraph network model to describe the basics of how the brain worked, with the nerve cell (soma) comprising a receptor for electrical currents collected by highly branched dendrites, long tube-like axons that act as a transmitting apparatus, and a distribution centre occurring at nerve endings (see Figure 13.5). He deduced the direction of information flow through neural networks (from dendrite to axon terminals) and recognized that neurons were separated by tiny gaps.

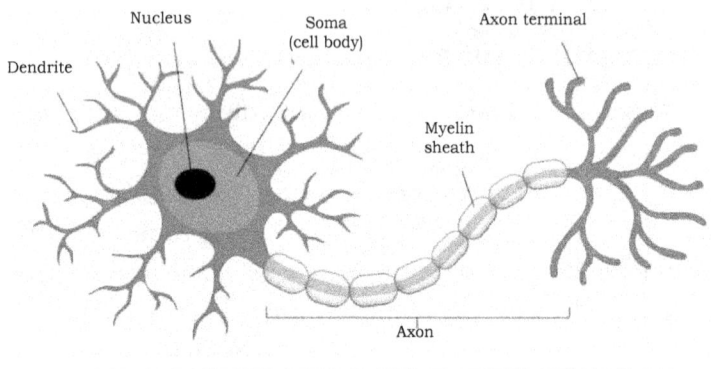

Figure 13.5 Simple diagram of a neuron
(https://owlcation.com/stem/Neuroscience-Basics-The-Neuron)

He realized, however, that this model couldn't take into account the complexity of the nervous system with its numerous connections and that the connections changed with experience. Learning, Ramón y Cajal claimed, led to increased connectivity.

Although they had never met before, Golgi and Ramón y Cajal won a joint Nobel prize in 1906 for their work on the structure of the nervous system.

Other workers also used similar technological analogues of the time to explain how the brain could work: the French philosopher Henri Bergson (1859–1941) postulated that the brain was no more than a central telephonic exchange, allowing or delaying communications, whereas the French anatomist Matthias-Marie Duval (1844–1907) explained in 1893 that the independence of nerve cells implied that "nerve pathways ... appear to be endowed with an infinite number of switches".

While theories abounded about what happened along the nerves themselves, it wasn't clear what happened next

– somehow the nerve impulse passed from one nerve cell to another, even though they were separate. In 1897, Charles Sherrington (1857–1952) introduced a term to describe the place where two cells interact: the 'synapsis', now known as the 'synapse'. It would take years to establish what happened at synapses, with theories broadly falling into two camps: 'soups' relying on the idea that chemicals transmitted the signals between nerve cells, and 'sparks' preferring the idea of electrical transmission.

The 20th century
"The brain communicates with chemicals and electricity"

Cambridge physiologist John Langley (1852–1925) studied the effects of adrenaline on the nervous system as it inhibited the action of the intestines and bladder, dilated pupils and increased blood pressure. While recognizing the effects, he dismissed the idea that adrenaline could act at synapses because he didn't believe that it was possible for nerve endings to secrete the substance. In the early 1930s, however, Henry Dale (1875–1968) was able to show that a wide variety of nerves did indeed secrete chemicals into synapses. The idea that chemicals, or 'neurotransmitters', were important in nervous function was gradually accepted.

During the 1960s, a bewildering array of neurotransmitters was discovered. One of the key factors that convinced scientists of the existence of these substances was the use of fluorescence or radioactivity to create images that revealed their presence. Neurotransmitters could be seen being released from synapses using electron microscopes.

It also became apparent that some neurons did not use neurotransmitters at all but instead functioned as electrical synapses, or gap junctions (see Figure 13.6). Both the 'soup' and 'spark' theories turned out to be correct.

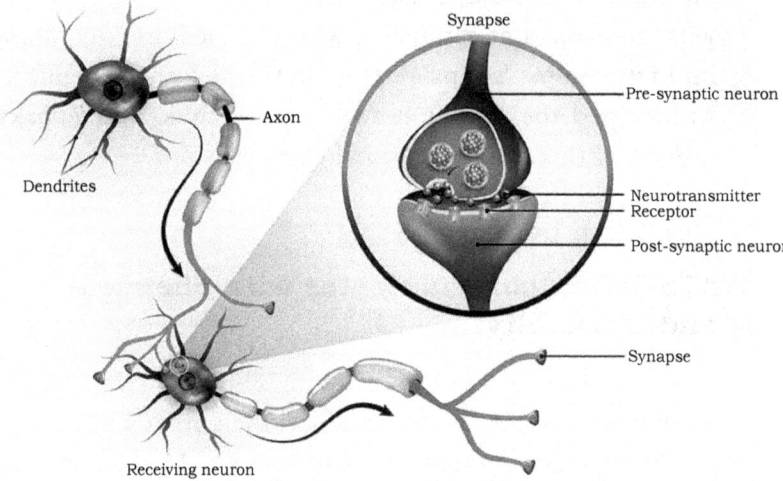

Figure 13.6 Diagram showing how neurons communicate across synapses
(https://www.genetex.com/Research/Overview/neuroscience/neurites_synapses)

1900–30

"The brain transmits information"

Nerve impulses had already been described as messages that were being transmitted, but no one had yet considered what those messages might be. English electrophysiologist Edgar Adrian (1889–1972) worked with Swedish researcher Yngve Zotterman (1898–1982) and they were able to record the amplified activity of sensory nerve fibres attached to stretch receptors in a frog's leg. They showed that sensory neurons respond in an 'all-or-none' way: if the stimulus is above a threshold, then the neuron fires; otherwise, it does not. They also showed that, if the neuron is continuously stimulated, the cell stops responding. Furthermore, when the neuron fires, the amplitude and shape (spike) of the response is constant, but the frequency of the firing changes with stimulus intensity.

The conclusions from this work, and other experiments that Adrian carried out with others, were that a neuron tells the nervous system how intense a stimulus is by changing its firing rate, although each of the responses from any given cell is identical. He described this as being similar to the way the Morse code operates – information is being encoded. Adrian believed that the whole point of the nervous system was to transmit encoded information about the world along neuronal pathways.

1930–50
"The brain can change – it is plastic"

In 1949, the Canadian psychologist Donald Hebb (1904–85) published *The Organization of Behaviour*, which started out by assuming that the mind was simply a product of activity in the brain. One of his major insights was how learning occurs at a cellular level. He suggested that synapses can develop and grow stronger when neurons are activated together. The phrase "cells that fire together wire together" sums up what became known as 'Hebb's Law'. He thought that the fine structure of the nervous system was formed through experience and that the same cell assembly could function in different ways in different circumstances.

Hebb's Law implies that the brain's structure and function can change through experience and learning, giving the brain the characteristic of 'plasticity'. Many subsequent experiments and observations have confirmed the validity of this theory.

In the 1930s, the development of advanced anaesthetics allowed the localization of brain functions to be mapped. The American Canadian neurosurgeon Wilder Penfield (1891–1976) was able to stimulate the brains of conscious patients with electric currents carried by delicate electrodes. Penfield's technique allowed him to create maps of where in the brain the sensory and motor responses were located in the cortex (the cortical homunculus, see Figure 13.7).

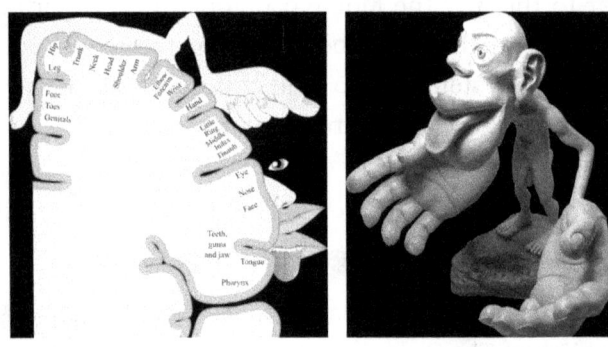

Figure 13.7 The cortical humunculus (https://www.liveconsciouslyconnected.com/the-cortical-homunculus-reshaping-the-brain-through-movement/)

The maps indicate how the brain sees the body from an inside perspective, showing the proportions of the brain dedicated to processing different motor and sensory functions for different parts of the body. It is still in use today. Because of the brain's plasticity, what these maps look like varies from person to person. An artist, for example, will have a large hand representation whereas a chef's sense of taste will be more significant.

1930–50

"The brain is a computer"

After the end of the First World War, scientists started to apply terms like 'feedback', 'circuit' and 'input and output' to biological phenomena, including the nervous system.

In 1941, the logician Walter Pitts (1923–69) and cybernetician Warren McCulloch (1898–1969) applied logic to understand biological processes and used the computer as a metaphor for the brain for the first time. McCulloch realized that the 'all-or-none' nature of nerve signals was the equivalent of a logic proposition: a statement was either true or false. Basic logical functions (on or off), combined with gates representing AND, OR and NOT could be shown to model complex biological phenomena. The breakthrough in this work was that it focused attention on processes rather than anatomical regions. Explaining the brain appeared to involve describing algorithms embedded in networks of neurons, or interactions between organs, although it was recognized that this was a huge oversimplification. Life is more complex than logic!

Mexican physiologist Arturo Rosenbleuth (1900–70), American mathematician Norberto Wiener (1894–1964) and the computer engineer Julian Bigelow (1913–2003) co-authored one of the founding papers on cybernetics called 'Behaviour, purpose and teleology' in 1943, and paved the way for the future of artificial intelligence (AI). They described how, using positive and negative feedback, nervous systems could apparently show purposeful behaviour. For example, once a certain activity produced a given state, negative feedback could stop the behaviour in future, giving the impression of purpose.

Wiener also highlighted the difference between brains and computers: the possibility that chemicals act as messengers in the body and can affect the brain and behaviour. These chemicals may not be hardwired and may circulate freely in the body, which is very different from how a computer works.

With the development of computers, scientists including Alan Turing (1912–54) explored the analogy of the brain as a computer. Based on his code work, he developed an understanding that the decisions we make every day are based on simple statistical analyse to find the most convenient outcomes. Turing was fascinated by the question 'Can machines think?' and developed the 'Turing test' in his 1950 paper *Computing machinery and intelligence*. This postulated that, if a device can answer a question, and a human can have a conversation with it and not be able to detect that it was a machine, then it could think. Turing believed this was possible and that it would simply be a matter of programming the machine.

Early researchers tried to model the functions of the brain by exploring the rules governing the interconnections between neurons. In 1958, Oliver Selfridge (1926–2008) introduced a hierarchical processing system called 'Pandemonium'. Cobb (2020) describes it well: the starting point was the creation of simple units that would recognize elements of their environment by comparing a feature (for example, a line) with some predetermined internal template. These 'computational' elements would then tell the next layer up, the 'cognitive elements', what they had detected, which would then weigh the evidence. Each 'cognitive element' computed a sort of 'shriek', and from all the shrieks the next and highest layer up, the 'decision element', would make the decision by simply selecting the loudest shriek. The end result was that a complex feature – for example, a letter – would be recognized by the decision element. The system could learn as it went along and the programme noticed how accurate it was in classifying objects. By running the programme repeatedly, the system became increasingly accurate over time and could even start to recognize things for which it had not been designed. If provided with appropriate feedback about its success, the programme's functions could change over time.

The key insight from Pandemonium was that any effective description of perception – in humans or computers – had to include substantial elements of feedback and plasticity. Hebb's Law was crucial to learning. These ideas were completely different from the old models about the brain based on mechanical or pressure metaphors.

In the mid-1980s, a new computational approach called 'parallel distributed processing' (PDP) led to a better understanding of neural networks that transformed computational neurobiology and AI. PDP networks share the same basic three-layer structure of the original Pandemonium machine: an input layer that responds when some feature triggers a given unit and an output layer that informs the outside world once all the work has been done. The intermediate layer uses various systems of interconnections and algorithms that follow Hebb's Law: connections that are simultaneously activated are favoured. PDP networks perform tasks so effectively because of the ability of information to go both ways between layers to form a feedback loop. This allows the programme to refine behaviour, leading to more accurate output. These days, 'deep learning' using PDP networks has developed to the extent that face recognition, scene analysis, driverless cars, instant language translations and chess playing are now possible. Deep learning systems can identify the content of huge datasets and have recently become even more effective because of the introduction of modules that can remember things.

Just because computers and brains generate similar behaviours doesn't necessarily mean that the two systems share the same structure or function. Numerous experiments have highlighted how machines make very different errors compared with those made by humans and animals, suggesting that the computer programmes are processing things in a different way. Animals learn very quickly – often based on a single example – whereas programmes require extended training and large learning sets.

The ten-year Human Brain Project began in Lausanne in 2013, funded by the European Union with over €1 billion, with the aim of producing "cellular-level simulations of the complete human brain" if suitably powerful computers were available. A major part of the project was devoted to developing new computing approaches and database management systems that might give insights into how the brain works.

Nowadays, few scientists would argue that the computer analogy for the brain is completely valid, but it is useful to think of it as a computational organ that can manipulate symbolic representations of the outside world to explore and predict what will happen and to produce behaviours. It's not like a machine because it bathes in a complex system of chemical and electrical communication, and its activities are partly determined by its own internal states. It is a wetware rather than a hardware system.

The 20th and 21st centuries
"The brain is a network"

At the beginning of the 1980s, a molecular revolution was transforming biology, making it possible to describe complex molecules within cells and to identify the genes that produced the components of them. New tools made it possible to visualize neurons and their organization in ways not possible before. New maps of the brain and nervous system were made, some based on the genes the cells express rather than their physical structure. New ways of manipulating neurons became available, allowing genes to be deleted or added. Optogenetics allowed the introduction of genes that encoded a light-detecting molecule into a cell of interest. This molecule could then be activated using light and make the cell respond – it provided a way of very precisely identifying and stimulating neurons, and it transformed the ability to study the brain.

It was thought that describing the wiring diagram of a particular organism or one part of the brain would enable new insights about how behaviour and sensations emerge from neural circuit activity. Even in a simple circuit, however, each neuron is connected to many others both by chemical synapses and gap junctions that allow electrical signals to pass. Each neuron can secrete several different types of neurotransmitters into the synapse, which can be either inhibitory or excitatory, so even a simple system very quickly becomes very complicated.

New techniques for recording electrophysiological activity, using tools like the electroencephalogram (EEG) and computerized tomography (CT) scans, transformed the way the brain was viewed. They were, however, too slow and imprecise for researchers to be able to establish clear links between structures and functions. Magnetic resonance imaging (MRI), which uses strong magnetic fields and radio waves to generate images of the body, provided better contrast in images of soft tissues like the brain compared with CT scans. MRI was invented by the American chemist Paul Lauterbur (1929–2007) in 1971. The first full body clinical MRI scans were produced in 1980 at the University of Aberdeen by a team led by John Mallard (1927–2021). The pictures were in black and white, and rather grainy.

A further breakthrough came about with the development of functional magnetic resonance imaging (fMRI), which was able to measure brain activity by detecting changes in blood flow. The first brain fMRI pictures published were by Jack Belliveau (1959–2014) in 1991 in *Science*, showing changes to blood flow in the visual cortex during visual stimulation (see Figure 13.8).

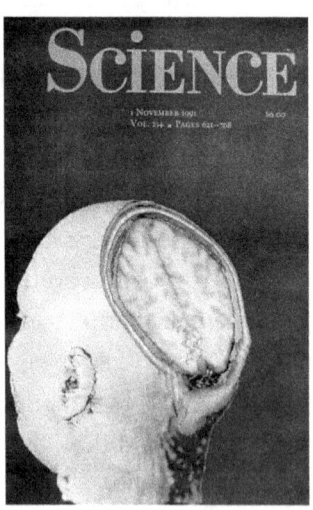

Figure 13.8 *The first brain images using functional magnetic resonance imaging were published by Jack Belliveau in the 1991 edition of Science magazine*

In 2001, Nikos Logothetis (1950–) showed experimentally that fMRI is tightly linked to neuronal activity. However, the images are not straightforward to interpret: the brain is highly active and researchers must pick out the changes that they are interested in. Calculating these, often small, anomalies involves complex software packages that can produce errors. Furthermore, fMRI has an inherent lack of resolution and can only measure the activity of large bundles of neurons in a relatively slow timescale compared with neuron-level activity. Logothetis calculated that each pixel of an fMRI image probably contains between 22 and 55 billion synapses, or 22 km of nerves endings (dendrites) and 220 km of nerve tubing (axons)! Although fMRI has allowed a step change in interpretation of how the brain works, more precise imaging methods are needed to allow a detailed understanding.

These imaging studies have done much to emphasize the dynamic role of the brain and to highlight significant connections between regions during mental activity. The latest models all describe the brain as a network. They also challenge the rigid view of functions as being strictly localized: even when direct stimulation of a particular neuron or network alters or restores a given function, it doesn't necessarily mean that the function is solely located in that structure. It just shows that the structure is required for the function: it cannot be ruled out that cells in other locations in the brain may also be involved. Increasingly, when a function has been claimed to be localized in a particular structure, it is discovered to be more complex and to involve other parts of the brain too. Function is both localized and distributed – for the function to operate well, it needs to be integrated into the whole brain. Furthermore, the brain's plasticity is key to moving functional locations within it, as demonstrated, for example, in cases where the brain recovers from injury. The attempt to show all the connectivity in a brain requires enormous computing power and the dilemma that all brains are different.

In 2005, two separate research groups came up with a term to describe a comprehensive network of elements and connections forming the human brain: the 'connectome'. This is the relatively new science of connectomics, which represents a shift in attempts to understand the brain from asking: 'What does it look like?' (structure) to: 'What does it do?' (function) to: 'How is it all connected? (connectomics).

In 2009, the US Human Connectome Project was declared to be "mapping the wiring diagram of the entire human brain" but, in reality, it uses the rather imprecise tool of brain scans to look at large bundles of neurons that connect different regions in the brain.

The study claimed to show stronger connectivity within the brains of people with more "positive variables" such as education, endurance and good memory performance compared with those with more "negative variables" like aggression, smoking or alcohol problems, as well as differences between the brains of men and women (see Figure 13.9). Are these observations real and, if so, are the differences causes or consequences of the suggested behavioural differences?

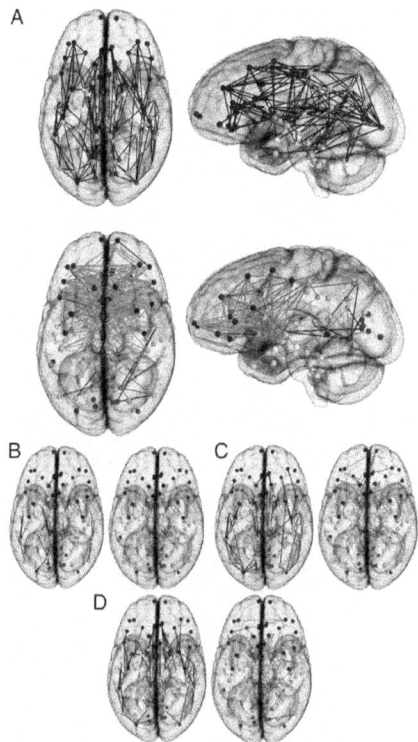

Figure 13.9 Connection-wise analysis of male and female connectomes (Ingalhalikar, M. et al. [2014] Proceedings of the National Academy of Sciences USA, 111, pp. 823–828). (A) Brain networks show increased connectivity in males (upper) and females (lower). analysis on the child (B), adolescent (C) and young adult (D) groups is shown. Intra-hemispheric connections are shown in dark lines and inter-hemispheric connections in lighter lines. https://www.pnas.org/doi/full/10.1073/pnas.1316909110

Recently, neuroscientists have started to think that the concept of neurons is not adequate for understanding the complexity of the brain and that unknown collective properties emerging from the activities of groups of neurons may turn out to be significant. In 2015, the Spanish neurobiologist Rafael Yuste (1963–) argued that many parts of the brain appear to be organized in networks – for example, inhibitory neurons that are often linked to each other by gap junctions as though they are designed to work as a unit. He is one of the initiators of the Brain Research through Advancing Innovative Neurotechnologies (BRAIN)® Initiative, launched by President Obama in 2015, that funds neuroscience research in over 500 labs with over $110 million.

There is no theoretical framework or experimental evidence yet that links molecules, single cells and networks to behavioural output, but one idea that is popular at present and proposed by Hungarian neuroscientist Gyorgy Buzsaki (1949–) is that the activity of cell assemblies should be seen in terms of their outputs rather than how they represent the outside world. Another increasingly popular framework uses complex mathematics to explore network-wide changes in activities of a given network to see how the system shifts from one state to another after stimulation. Although the activity of individual neurons may vary over time, the activity of the synchronously active network can be very stable.

Eve Marder's (1948-)[1] work on the small network of 30 neurons in the crustacean's stomach, summarized in Nassim (2018), suggested that circuits are not 'hard-wired' to produce a single output or behaviour but can be reconfigured by 'neuromodulators' to produce many outputs and behaviours while maintaining the integrity of the circuit. So, the activity of each neuron is affected not only by its identity (the genes that determine its position and function) but also by the previous activity of the neuron. This could explain the long-term individual differences in behaviour between animals with identical wiring diagrams

---

[1] https://www.kavliprize.org/eve-marder-autobiography

– their 'personality' in a way. The work also implies that the same behaviour need not involve the same structure or pattern of neuron activity: the function of a given network can switch from one mode to another as the multiple connections between the same pair of neurons are altered by the activity of the cells in the circuit. The same network can produce radically different behaviours and the same behaviours can be produced by very different networks.

It was realized that the rich chemical world of the brain was even more complex when it was observed that cerebral activity involves not only the action of neurotransmitters and neuromodulators but also the effects of slower-acting neurohormones that release chemical messengers like adrenalin directly into the bloodstream while also acting within the central nervous system. They are involved in the long-term control of essential physiological processes, many of which have a behavioural component (for example, stress responses, reproduction, looking after young, and feeding behaviours). Neurohormones can be released in very large numbers in pulses that can go on for days. Each of these systems, influenced by internal and external conditions, has its own feedback loops controlling how it changes brain activity.

A connectome is therefore not enough to explain how the brain works: the chemical and electrical connections between the cells also need to be understood to assess how many alternative functional outputs are possible. The complexity is mind-boggling!

Despite all these advances, there is still no clear understanding of the detail of how the brain works except in the simplest of organisms. What can be said, however, is that the brain is a complicated parallel processing organ that uses feedback loops to adapt and learn: it can do many things at any one time, using an astonishingly diverse and complex mixture of chemicals and electrical signals.

The future?

In his book *The Idea of The Brain*, zoologist Matthew Cobb (1957–) suggests that the computational and network metaphors for the brain are reaching the end of their usefulness – we should think of the brain not as representing information but as constructing it.

Coming up with new metaphors is of course challenging – as we have seen, many of those used in the past rely heavily on the technology and cultural ideas of the day. Nevertheless, Cobb does attempt to predict possible new concepts that may enhance our understanding of how the brain works. These include the brain as:

- a distributed computer system, like the internet or cloud computing, with each brain cell acting as a minicomputer;
- an organ with emergent properties – one in which properties cannot be predicted from an analysis of individual components, but which emerge as the system functions (e.g., a property of deep learning programmes);
- a 'wetware' system: what is happening (mind) and where it is happening (brain) are completely intertwined. (This is in contrast to the software/hardware model where software (mind) and hardware (brain) are separate, i.e., Descartes' dualism theory); and
- integrated with the body and environment (i.e., animals' behaviour is not just their brains' behaviour: every brain has a body and lives in its environment). It is known, for example, that the brain interacts with

the gut microbiome and that fundamental aspects of brain biochemistry can be affected by microbes that live in the gut. This is especially true when it comes to studying emotions.

There is no shortage of data to test any of these hypotheses, but the experimental methods neuroscientists currently use may be limiting the type of data that needs to be collected.

It may well be that theories may emerge from the huge amounts of imaging data being generated, or that an overall theory will come out of various separate but satisfactory explanations. Integrating other disciplines like physiology with biochemistry and anatomy, or the application of evolutionary studies, may shed new light on how the brain works. New, as yet undiscovered, technologies – or a new framework from other disciplines like cybernetics or complexity theory – could also radically alter how we think about the brain. Or maybe we will just have to accept that there is no overarching theory to be found because brains have no overall logic and each part works as it does.

References

Cobb, M. (2020) *The idea of the brain – A history*. London: Profile Books.

Nassim, C. (2018) *Lessons from the lobster: Eve Marder's work in neuroscience*. Cambridge, MA: MIT Press.

Rosenbleuth, A., Wiener, N. and Bigelow, J. (1943) 'Behaviour, purpose and theology', in *Philosophy of Science*, 10(1).

Sormaz, M., Murphy, C., Wang, H-T et al. (2018) 'Default mode network can support the level of detail in experience during active task states', *Proceedings of the National Academy of Sciences*, 115(37), 9318–9323, PMC 6140531, PMID 30150393.
Turing, A.M. (1950) 'Computing machinery and intelligence', *Mind*, New series, 59(236), pp. 433–460.

Wickens, A.P. (2015) *A history of the brain: From Stone Age to modern neuroscience*. London and New York: Psychology Press.

Biography

Dr Sue Paterson MBE is an oil and gas professional with both FTSE-100 UK and international executive experience.

She has non-executive director experience in the private, public and voluntary sectors, including as board chair. Among others, she is currently serving on the Board of Scottish Enterprise as well as the community-led North East Scotland Climate Action Network (NESCAN). She received an MBE in the 2020 New Year Honours for services to the community in North East Scotland.

Sue holds a degree in Physics from Imperial College, London, and a PhD in Marine Geophysics from Cambridge University, as well as a Post-Graduate Certificate in Sustainability in Business from the Cambridge Institute for Sustainability Leadership.

She is the co-author of *The Fear Free Organization: Vital insights from neuroscience to transform your business culture*, which was published by Kogan Page in 2015.

Sue is currently involved in helping deliver the transition to a low carbon economy in Scotland, as well as working with her local community to get to net zero, reduce biodiversity loss and eliminate waste.

She has two sons and currently lives in rural Aberdeenshire with her husband. She enjoys travelling, walking and cycling.

Index

A

acceptance, 53, 172, 201, 218
Adrenaline, 47, 235, 363
Adversity, 71, 313, 316–17, 320, 328
Ageing, 214
Agile, 70, 73, 77, 88, 194–95
Agility, 72, 120
Amygdala, 56–57, 117, 183, 185, 212, 216, 234–35, 263, 265–66, 272, 274
 hijack, 57, 183
Anxiety, 44, 47–48, 50, 56–57, 75, 77, 203–4, 206, 213–14, 219–20, 261–75, 315, 318
Appreciation, 13, 30, 232–34, 240, 246, 272
Attachment, 22, 45, 164, 167, 169, 179, 217, 225, 234, 264–65, 318–19
Attention, 79, 122–23, 146, 190, 198–99, 201–2, 205–7, 211–14, 232, 234–35, 238–39, 246–47, 252–53, 264, 267–72, 359–60
Authentic, 32, 115, 176, 208, 251, 256
Autonomy, 82, 218

B

BANI, 242
Beliefs, 43, 46, 48, 56, 60, 78, 85, 111, 115, 117, 119
Belonging, 131–32, 167, 172, 228, 241, 246, 352
Biological, 45, 167, 169, 171, 174, 269, 279, 289, 297, 306, 367
Boredom, 314
bounce-back, 98, 317
Brain, 10–13, 15–16, 27–67, 74–78, 80–83, 89–91, 93–103, 110–13, 128–31, 133–36, 144–48, 160–64, 172–75, 177–79, 212–17, 220–22, 263–75, 288–90, 318–19, 341–79
 Entrepreneurial, 93, 97–98, 101
 mammalian, 76, 288
 plasticity, 80, 334, 366, 369, 373
 snake, 33
Brainstorming, 116, 144, 326
Breathing, 33, 42, 57, 162, 198, 217, 222, 324
Bullying, 35, 276
Burnout, 36, 47, 57, 63, 70–71, 247, 332, 338

C

Career transition, 251
Caring, 264
Challenge, 41, 54, 57, 115, 117, 120, 137, 140–41, 144–45, 262–63, 315, 317, 325–26
Change, 49–51, 58, 82, 91–93, 95–96, 110, 124, 130, 137, 142, 144, 163–64, 193–94, 268–70, 278–79, 294–95, 312–13, 316–17, 356–57, 365
chemistry in coaching, 108
Chi, 105–19

Index

choice, 13, 50, 121–51, 165, 194, 218, 238, 308, 331
Clitoris, 286–87, 307
collaboration, 74, 232, 236, 241, 293, 303
Compassion, 50, 56–57, 63, 176, 267–69, 272
Competency models, 30
Competition, male, 39, 233
Connectome, 38, 374, 377
Connectomics, 354, 374
Conversations, 18, 50, 82, 116, 127, 130, 139–41, 144, 175, 187, 193
  honest, 82
Coping, 86, 324, 330, 332
Cortex, 33, 76, 129, 214–15, 217, 234–35, 265–69, 271, 273, 366, 372
  pre-frontal, 33
Cortisol, 47, 75–77, 79, 117, 130, 213, 220, 235, 265, 330–31, 336
Courage, 58, 218, 233, 262
Creativity, 50, 78, 107, 110, 120, 159, 169, 257, 314, 324, 326–27
Culture, 16, 77, 228, 231, 234–36, 242, 247–48, 274, 276, 293–94, 296, 304, 327–28
curiosity, 74, 125, 135, 141–42, 144, 149, 208, 218
  professional, 114
cybernetics, 367, 379

D

Deconstruction, 217
Default Mode Network (DMN), 52, 217, 221
Depression, 206, 214, 264, 266, 271, 315
Design, 14, 28, 74, 77, 82, 106–8, 128, 293, 303
detection, 75, 128
Difference, 63, 113–14, 195, 232–33, 246–47, 278, 281, 286, 288, 294, 296–97, 303, 305
Discomfort, 99, 198, 208–9, 282
Disconnect(ion), 235
disorder, 270, 282
diversity, 35, 65, 67, 74, 83, 233, 240, 246–47
  neurologically-based, 35
Doomscrolling, 78
Drugs, 283–85, 289, 297–98, 304–6
Dualism, 352, 358, 378

E

Ease, 106, 108, 141, 207–9, 232–34, 242, 246–47
Electric, 366
electricity, 15, 347, 353, 363
emotions
  attachment, 169, 264–65
  basic, 22, 166, 169
  consequent, 270
  escape/avoidance, 264
  exacerbated, 75
  human, 266

morbid, 219
positive, 86, 335
primary, 318
strong primordial, 264
Empowerment, 253–54
Encourage, 137, 139, 239, 327, 330, 333
energy/ energy flow, 14–17, 21–22, 33, 44–45, 73–74, 76–77, 99, 110, 115, 159, 167–69, 173–74, 184, 187–88, 190–92, 229–30, 242, 246, 248–49, 330
Engagement, 118, 125, 127, 142, 146, 148, 158, 160, 164, 169, 189–90, 220, 225
Entrepreneur, 90, 92, 94–95, 98–100, 103, 222, 296, 299
Equality, 59, 232, 234, 243, 246–47
Equanimity, 210, 220
Evolutionary purpose, 226
Exhaustion, 36, 70, 82, 85, 148, 189

F
facial expression, 169, 272
Faint, 33, 45, 168, 175
Fatigue, 57, 63, 314
Fear, 34, 36, 41, 44, 46–50, 57–58, 134–36, 145, 166–67, 169–70, 177–78, 224, 255–56, 261–75, 297
 of failure, 31, 48
fear-free, 145, 161, 169, 178, 224, 256
Fear-free, 145, 161, 169, 178, 224, 256
Feelings, 12–13, 166, 175, 177, 199, 201, 226, 232–35, 247, 249, 253, 267, 269
Flourish, 83
Freedom, 53, 218, 224, 226, 228, 236–37, 254–55
Freeze, 33, 45, 48, 50, 167–68, 175, 318

G
gastrointestinal, 99
Gender, 37, 39, 59–60, 64, 280, 287, 302, 305–8
 balance, 37
 equality, 59
 mosaic, 306
generosity, 201, 218, 259
gratitude, 201, 218, 220, 320
guilt, 219, 297

H
Habits, 49, 58, 63, 135, 145–46, 160, 163
Health, 65, 70–77, 79–81, 85–86, 99, 102, 171–72, 178, 203–4, 213–14, 279, 281–82, 289–90, 297–99, 301–2, 304, 308, 335, 337–39
Helplessness, 143
Hierarchy, 126, 130, 248, 293
Hope, 24, 81, 96, 119, 176, 228, 263, 265, 274
Hormones, 234–35, 297–98, 301, 318, 325, 330–31

Humancentric, 78
Hysterical, 281–82

I
Identity, 48, 114–15, 150, 193, 240, 248, 251, 376
Imagination, 71, 92, 107, 127, 269, 318, 334, 351–52
Imposter syndrome, 46–48, 64
Improvisation, 312, 321, 327
Incisive questions, 233–34, 238, 240
Industrial revolution, 72
information, 42–43, 97, 173–74, 229–30, 232–34, 238, 242, 246–48,
    251, 327, 361, 364–65, 369
Inner critic, 46–47, 56
Innovation, 31, 77–78, 91, 117–18, 128, 159, 169, 245
Insomnia, 283, 305, 345
Inspiration, 186
inspiring, 10–378
Intelligent Emotions, 21
interdependent, 184, 237, 268
Interpersonal neurobiology , 161, 173
Intuition, 41, 97
Irrational, 159
Irritable bowel syndrome, 99
Isolation, 83, 172, 335, 337

J
job design, 82
Job satisfaction, 315

K
Kindness, 53, 201, 218, 272

L
Laws of nature, 155–56, 352
Leadership quality, 158
Letting go, 32, 54, 111–12, 201
Limbic system, 76, 117, 266
Loneliness, 172, 329, 337
Loving-kindness, 201

M
Magnetic resonance imaging , 38, 212, 268, 372
management, 17, 40, 50, 122–23, 125, 155, 157–58, 187–88, 190–93,
    226–27, 230, 319, 335–37
Meditation, 56, 199–206, 208–12, 214–22, 267–69, 271
Memory, 56, 64, 76, 79–80, 97, 206, 212, 214–15, 314, 348, 351–53
Menopause, 297, 299–301, 304
Menstrual cycle, 279, 281, 298–301, 307
Mental Health, 72, 75–76, 81, 83, 85, 99, 102, 171, 203–4, 329, 335
Mentor, 236, 238–39

Mentoring, 103, 238–39, 245, 258
mind, 20–21, 29, 44, 70, 90–95, 173–75, 177–78, 199–204, 206–9, 213, 217, 221–22, 229–30, 257–58, 269–70, 272–73, 352, 358, 378
conscious, 43
developing, 161, 179
entrepreneurial, 94, 97
monkey, 202, 211
Mindfulness, 32, 56–57, 63–65, 113, 197–222, 270–71
Mindset, 46, 57, 60, 74, 77–81, 83, 85, 87, 110–11, 195, 201–2, 208, 231
Mirror neurons, 267–68
Mission, 165, 185, 227, 248
Mistake, 28, 45, 156, 170
Motivation, 67, 70, 96, 164–65, 172, 177–78, 274

N
Nanotechnology, 73
Neurochemistry, 129–30
Neurohormones, 377
Neuromodulators, 376–77
Neuroplasticity, 49, 80, 85, 96, 102, 265, 270, 275
neuroscience, 26, 71, 73–74, 77–78, 80–83, 150–51, 160, 178, 221, 249, 256, 273–74, 276, 288, 343
Neurotransmitter, 52
Non-judgemental, 115, 199, 203
Non-verbal signals, 175–76
Nurture, 62, 169, 171, 177
Nurturing, 175, 185, 335

O
Open-mindedness, 218
optimism, 143, 218, 320
Optimum operating conditions, 128–29, 142
Optogenetics, 371
Other, 16–17, 38–39, 108–11, 114–16, 122–23, 127, 129–31, 138–42, 162–64, 167–69, 172–75, 182, 193–94, 205–8, 229–30, 240–41, 263–64, 266–68, 272–73, 344–45
Oxytocin, 52–53, 130, 140, 234, 331

P
Parallel Distributed Processing, 369
parasympathetic nervous system, 77, 79
Patience, 201, 218, 259
Perception, 20, 54, 59, 80–81, 86, 117, 169, 174, 248, 252, 270, 273–74, 360
Perfectionism, 37, 48
Performance, 61, 63, 81–83, 122, 127–28, 136, 159–61, 166–67, 171–72, 191–92, 224–25, 231, 248–49, 278–79, 298–99, 332, 335
Persistence, 65, 75, 218

Phrenology, 354–55
Physiology, 131, 278–79, 286, 298, 343, 347, 350, 379
Place, 123, 125, 145, 182, 184–85, 190, 192–94, 232–34, 246–47,
    298, 300, 321, 323
Play, 39–40, 98, 133, 144, 154, 161, 175, 267, 273, 311–15, 317–39
Pre-frontal cortex, 33
Problem-solving, 41, 110, 238–39
processes
 analytical, 97
 cognitive, 94, 166
 emergent, 230
 emotional, 166–67
 fundamental, 230
 ideal, 157
 interpersonal, 269
 linear, 92
 mental, 71, 269
 neurobiological, 175
 physiological, 346, 377
 relational, 64
 self-organizing, 174
 sensory, 352
Procrastination, 37, 48
Purpose, 10–11, 70, 74, 77, 90–91, 93, 107, 109, 226–27, 239, 241,
    248, 319, 321, 367

R
Recruiting, 165
Regulators, 40–41
Relationships, 14, 16, 36, 39, 79–80, 111–12, 140–41, 161, 163,
    170–79, 228–30, 242, 269, 271, 293
Relaxing, 198, 217, 272
Renaissance, 343, 348, 350
Resilience, 55, 70–71, 74, 77, 81–86, 102, 120, 123, 211, 226, 311–40
 treasure chest, 320
Reskilling, 77
Respect, 114, 123, 127, 239, 245, 276, 351
Reticular activating system, 42

S
safety, psychological, 53, 60, 226
Self, 15–17, 31–32, 36–37, 44–47, 60, 62, 64–65, 98–99, 108, 110–11,
    115–16, 137, 141–42, 174, 201, 205–7, 210–11, 214–17,
    222–59, 263–73
Senses, 41, 130, 198, 202, 207, 267, 296, 344, 353
Serotonin, 234, 331
Sleep, 33, 53, 209, 218–20, 300, 308, 330, 345
Social intelligence, 218
Standard operating procedures, 156
Strategy, 28, 109, 136, 151, 157–58, 161, 248, 290, 296, 308

Stress, 33, 36, 47–50, 53, 56–57, 63–65, 71–86, 204, 212–13, 219–22, 265, 314–15, 318, 330–31, 337–38
Support, 53, 58, 60, 81, 84, 137, 140, 144–45, 190–91, 236, 243–44, 247–48, 300, 315–19, 323
Survival, 33–34, 39, 41–42, 45, 47, 49–50, 75–76, 128, 162–63, 167, 171, 174–75, 224–25, 318–19
synapse, 265, 363, 371

T
Teams, 64, 70–72, 124–27, 129–31, 136, 145–46, 149, 151, 180–81, 183–95, 323, 327–28, 332–33
Testosterone, 39
Theatre, 327
Thinking system, 12, 16, 30
Threat, 33, 53, 57, 75, 117, 128–31, 141, 145–46, 167, 169, 263–65, 269, 272
Thrive, 10, 22, 73, 78, 148, 158, 225–26, 228, 247–48, 313, 318
Transformation, 73, 87, 111–12, 120, 213, 220, 335
Trauma, 19, 206, 337
treasure chest, 320
Tribe, 53
Trust, 20, 23, 52, 55, 66–67, 107–9, 112, 121–51, 167, 169–70, 175–77, 269, 291, 293, 327–28

U
Uncertainty, 72, 74–75, 85, 122, 189–90, 194

V
Values, 48, 53, 55, 70, 74, 111, 115, 164–65, 234–35, 272, 274, 292–93, 296
Verbal signals, 175–76
Vision, 109, 113, 165, 170, 248, 356
VUCA, 242

W
Watts, 33
Wellness, 70
Wetware, 370, 378
Wholehearted, 148
Wholeness, 227, 235, 257
Wholesomeness, 206
WISER, 154, 242, 248, 259
Women on Boards, 40

Y
Yoga, 200–202, 221

www.ingramcontent.com/pod-product-compliance
Lightning Source LLC
Chambersburg PA
CBHW071730020426
42333CB00017B/2458